JOSEPHINE

By

Kevin Sacco

Distributed by
SLG Publishing
44 Race Street
San Jose, CA 95126

www.slgpubs.com

isbn
978-1-59362-286-2

Printed in Canada

To Noah,
My favourite
storyteller.

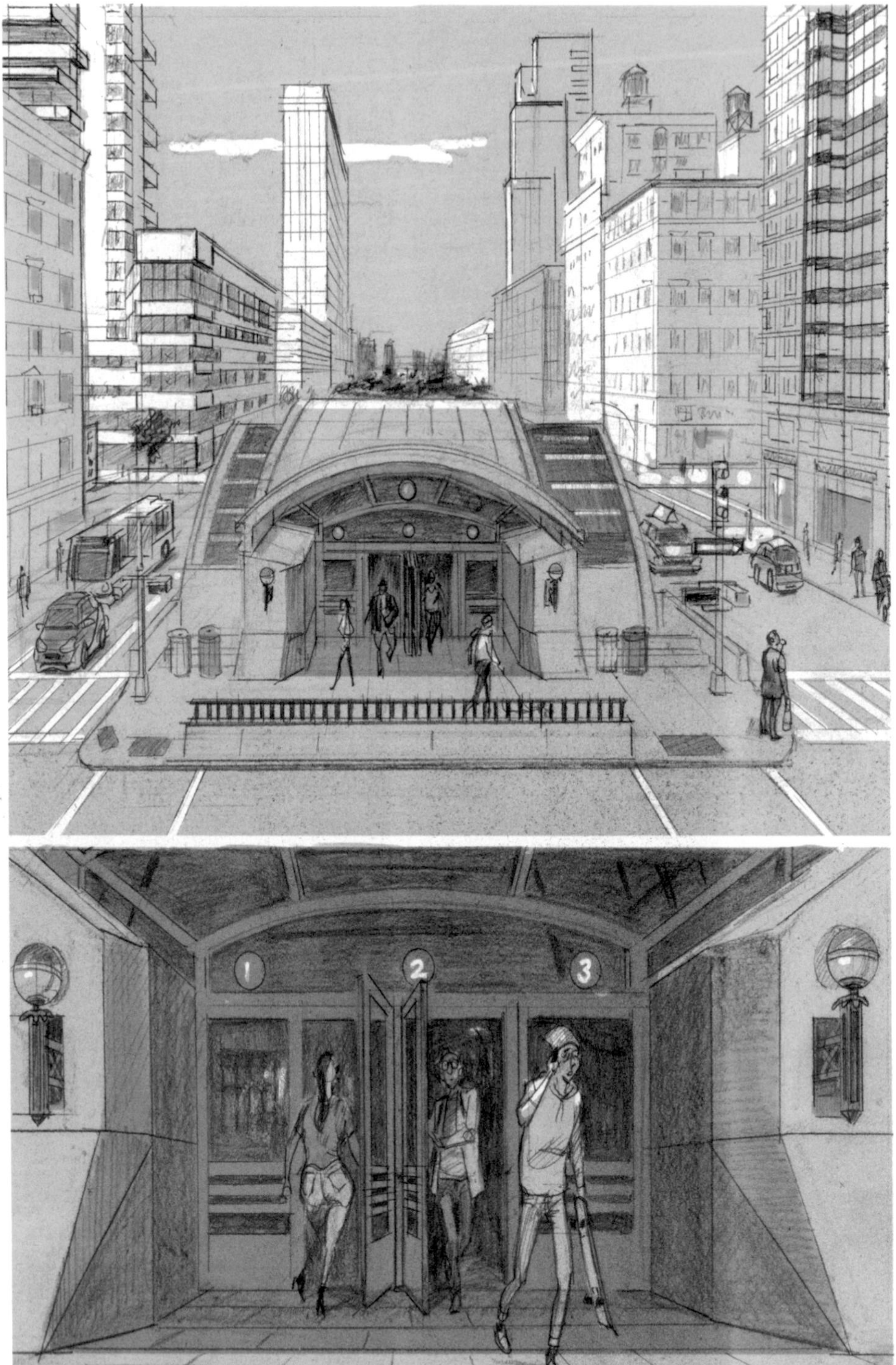
1
2
3

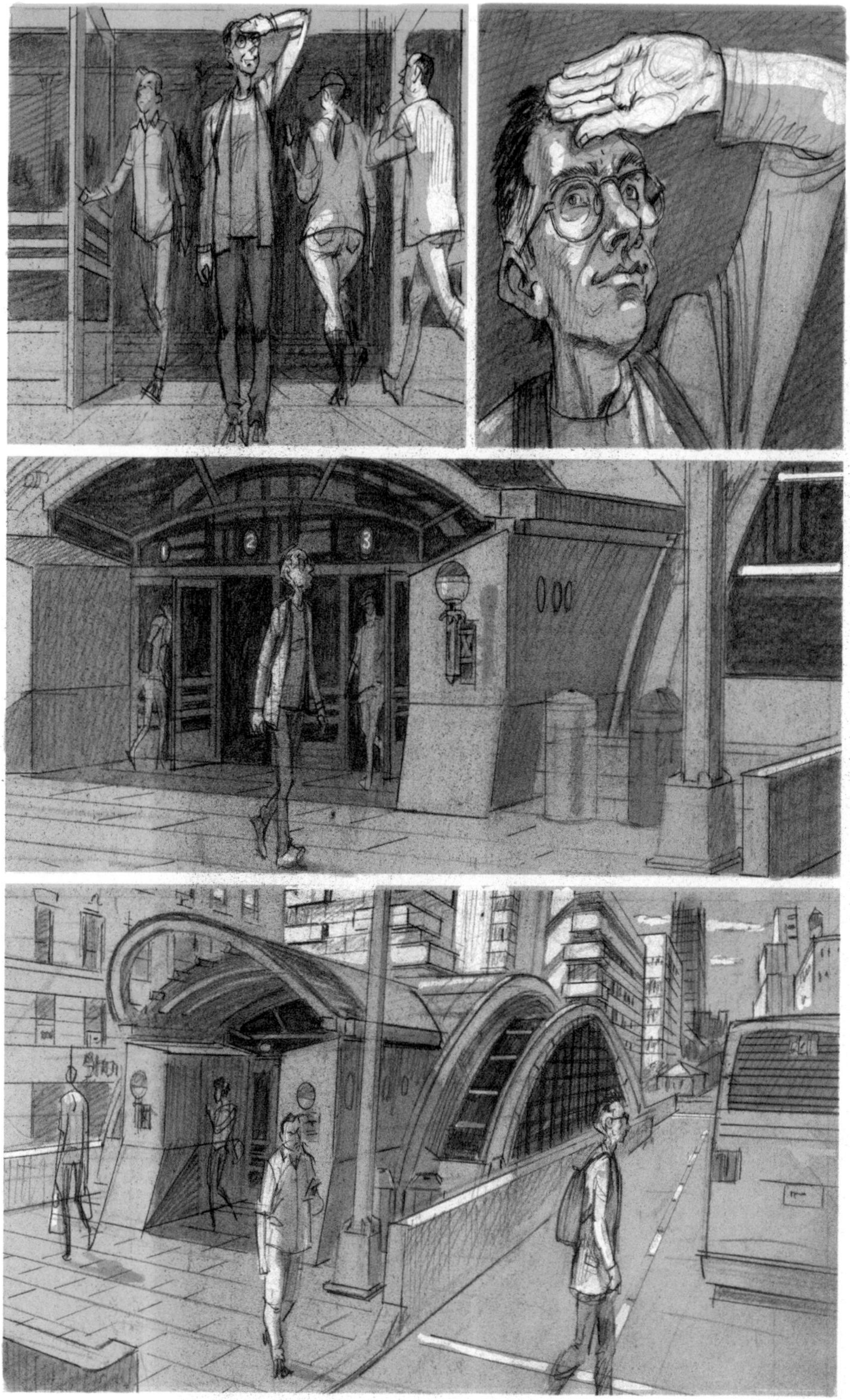
1
2
3

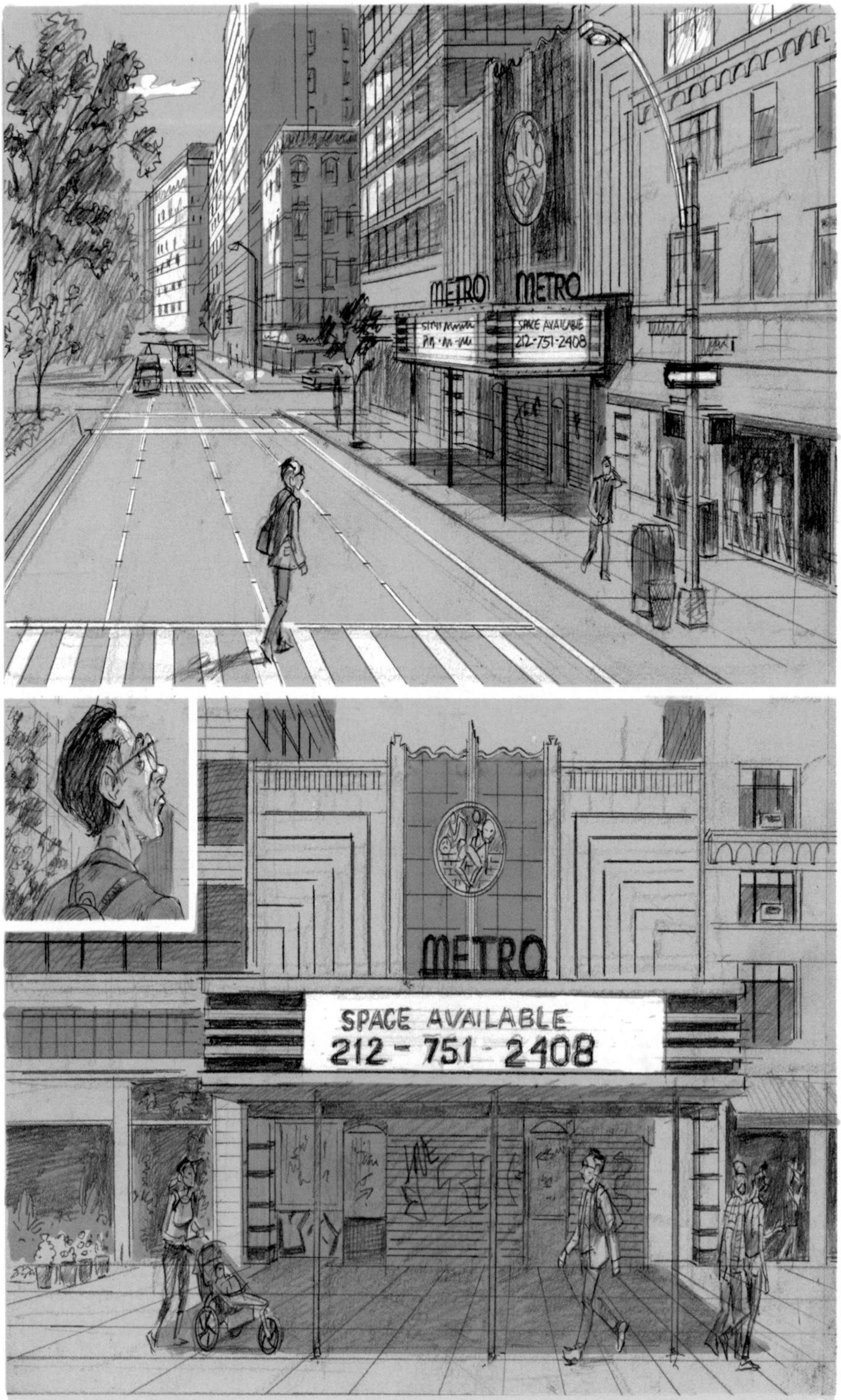
METRO
METRO
SPACE AVAILABLE
212-751-2408
METRO
SPACE AVAILABLE
212 - 751 - 2408

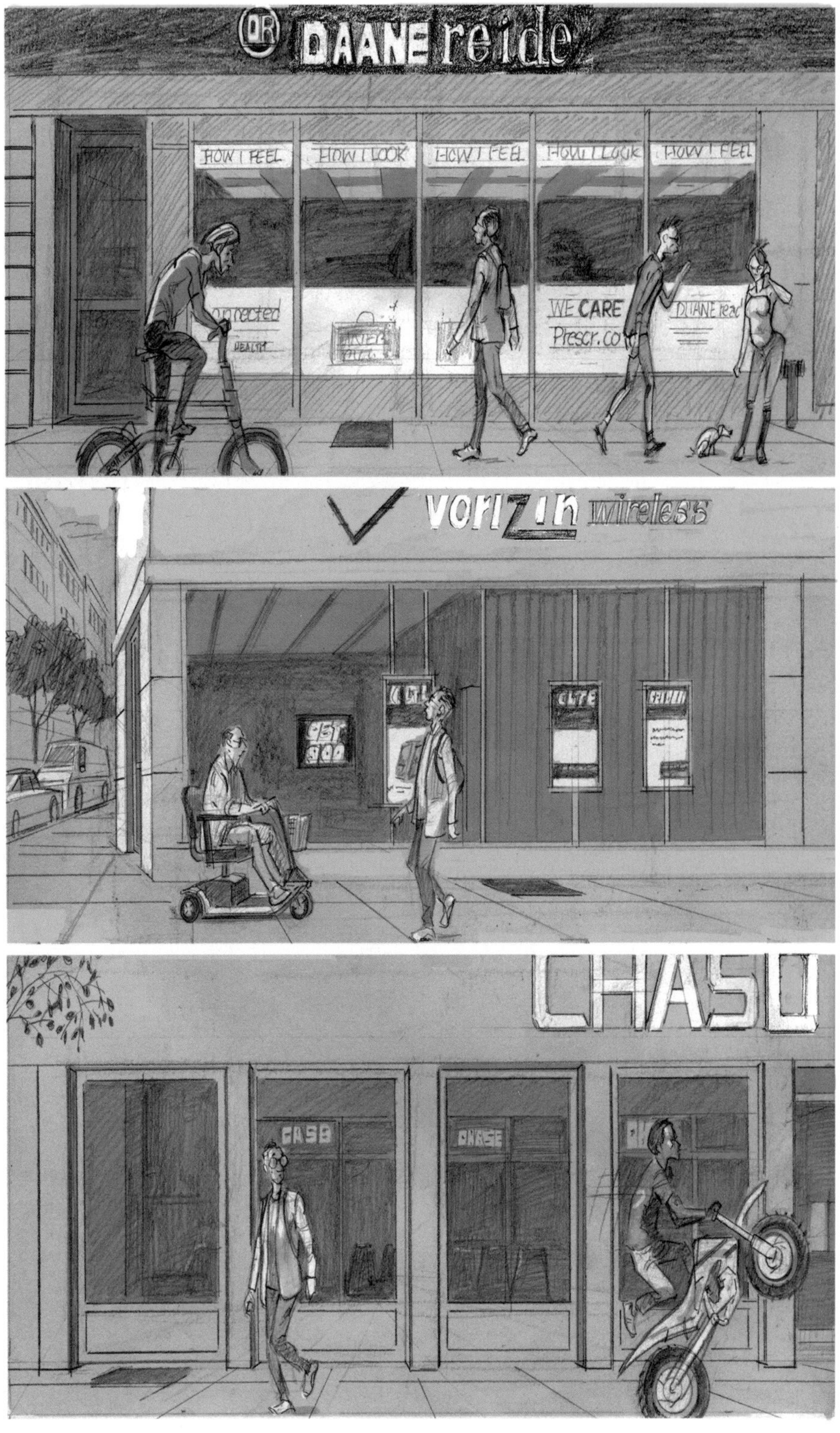
DR
DAANE reide
HOW I FEEL
HOW I LOOK
HOW I FEEL
HOW I LOOK
HOW I FEEL
WE CARE
Prescr.co
vorizin wireless
CHASO

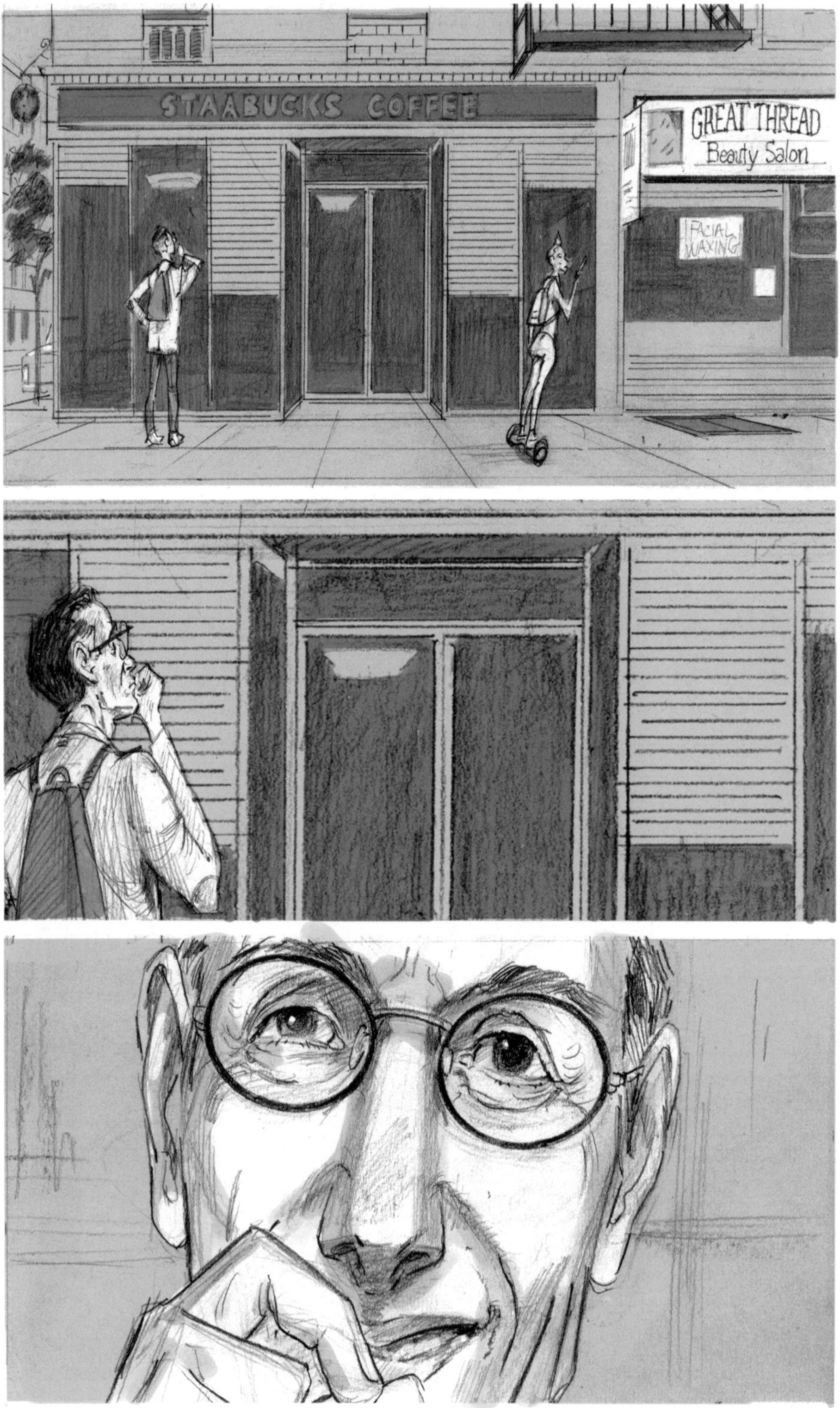
STAABUCKS COFFEE
GREAT THREAD
Beauty Salon
FACIAL WAXING

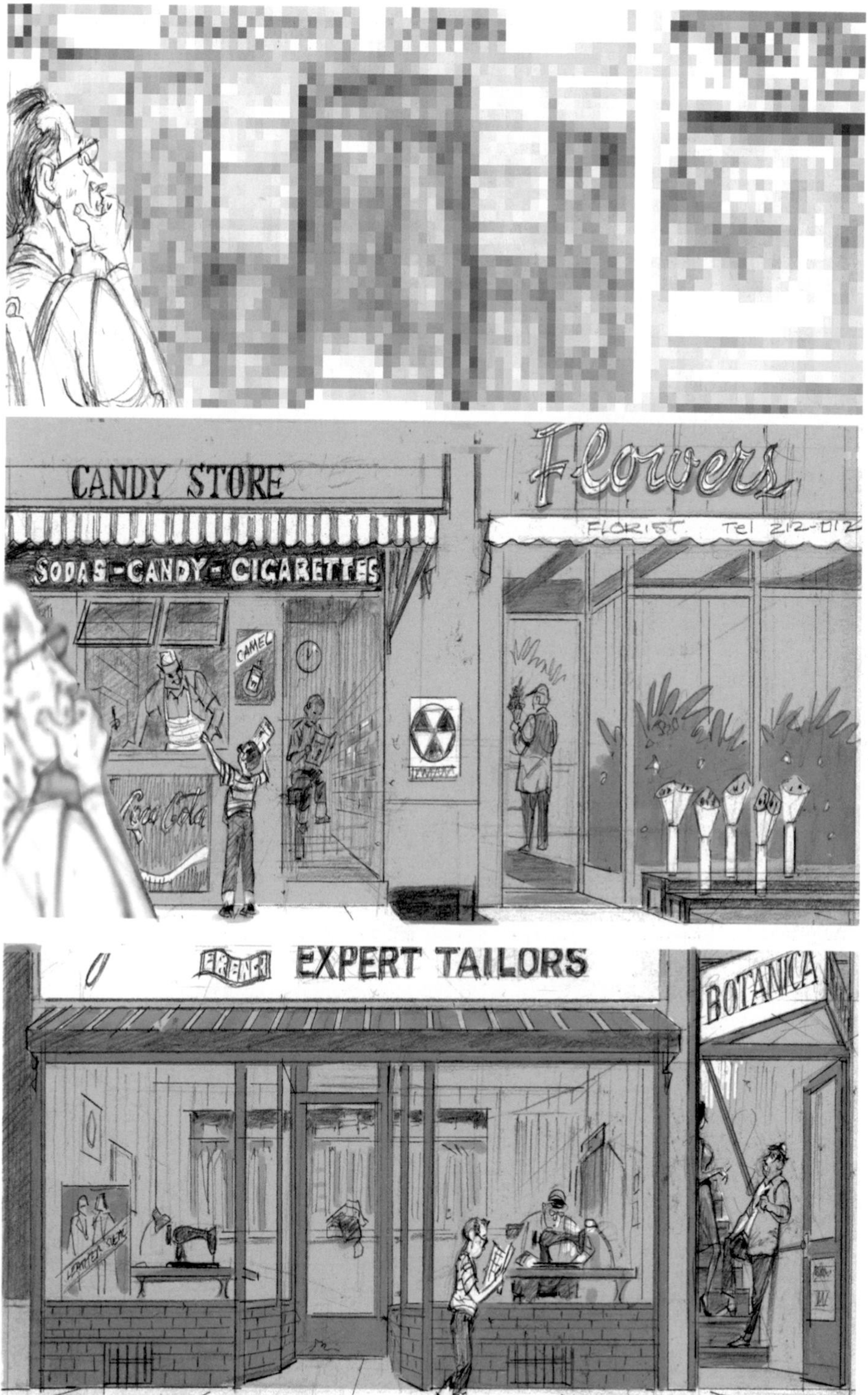
CANDY STORE
SODAS - CANDY - CIGARETTES
CAMEL
Coca-Cola
Flowers
FLORIST
EXPERT TAILORS
BOTANICA

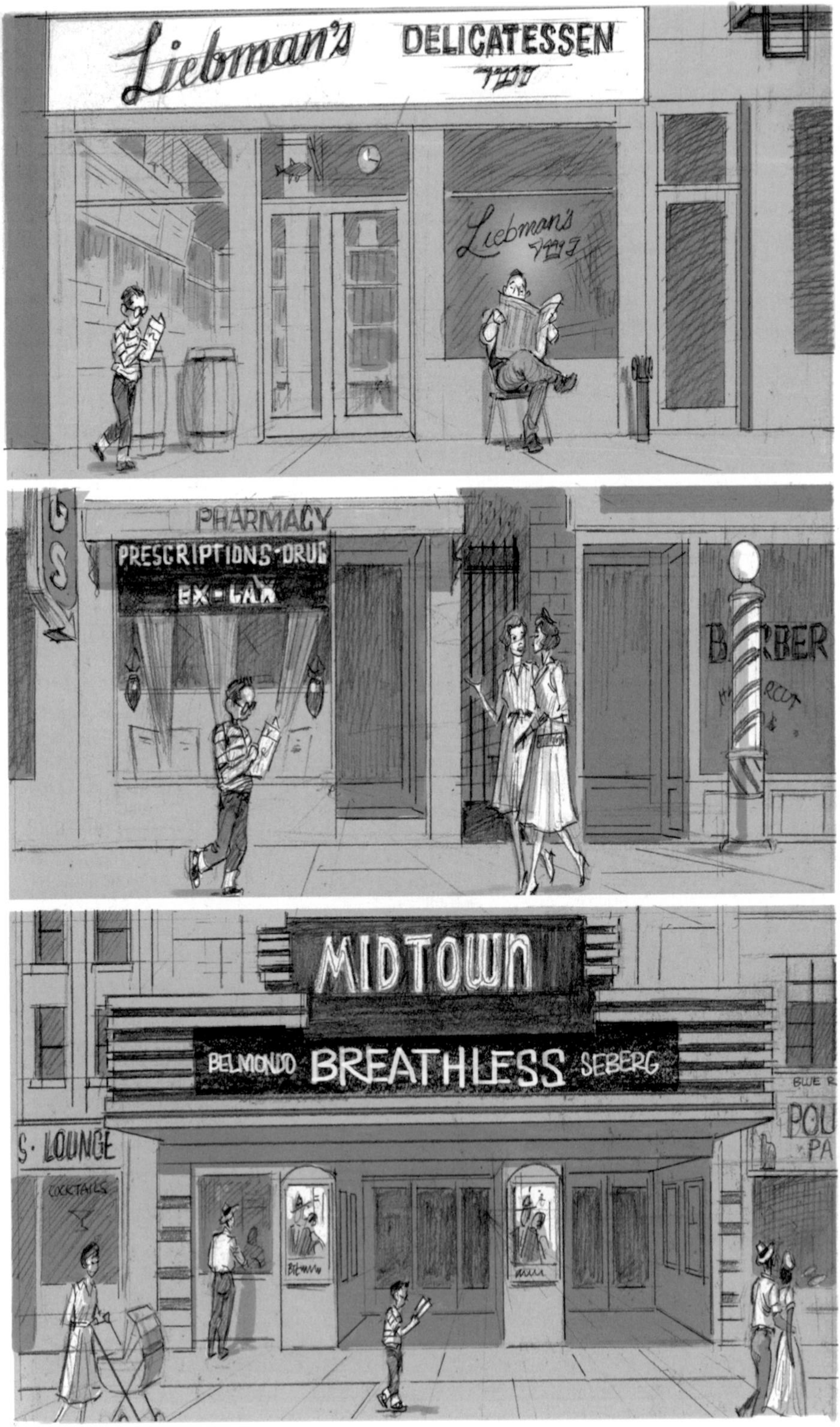
Liebman's
DELICATESSEN
Liebman's
PHARMACY
PRESCRIPTIONS-DRUG
EX-LAX
MIDTOWN
BELMONDO
BREATHLESS
SEBERG
S · LOUNGE
COCKTAILS

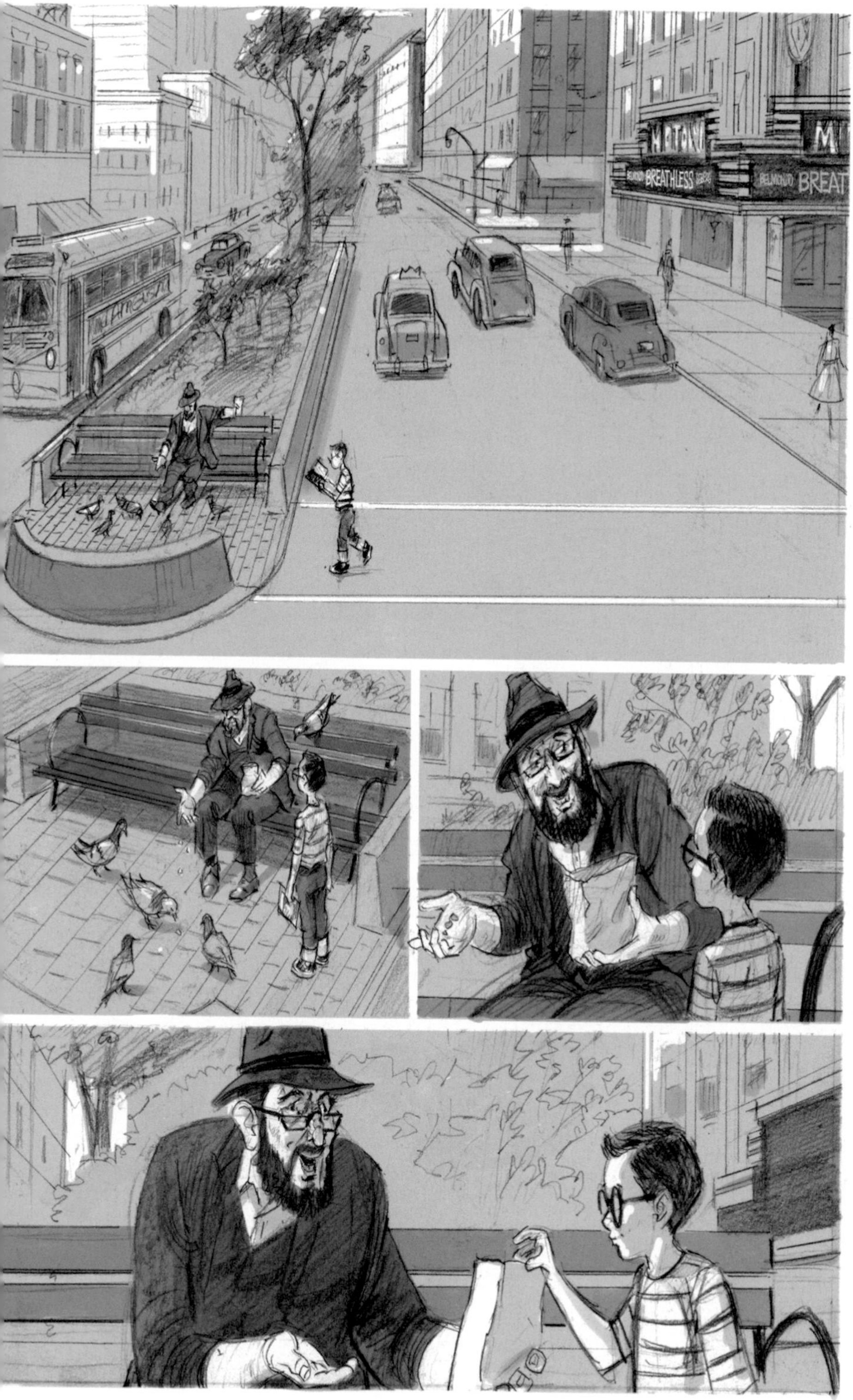
BELMONDO BREATHLESS SEBERG
BELMONDO BREAT

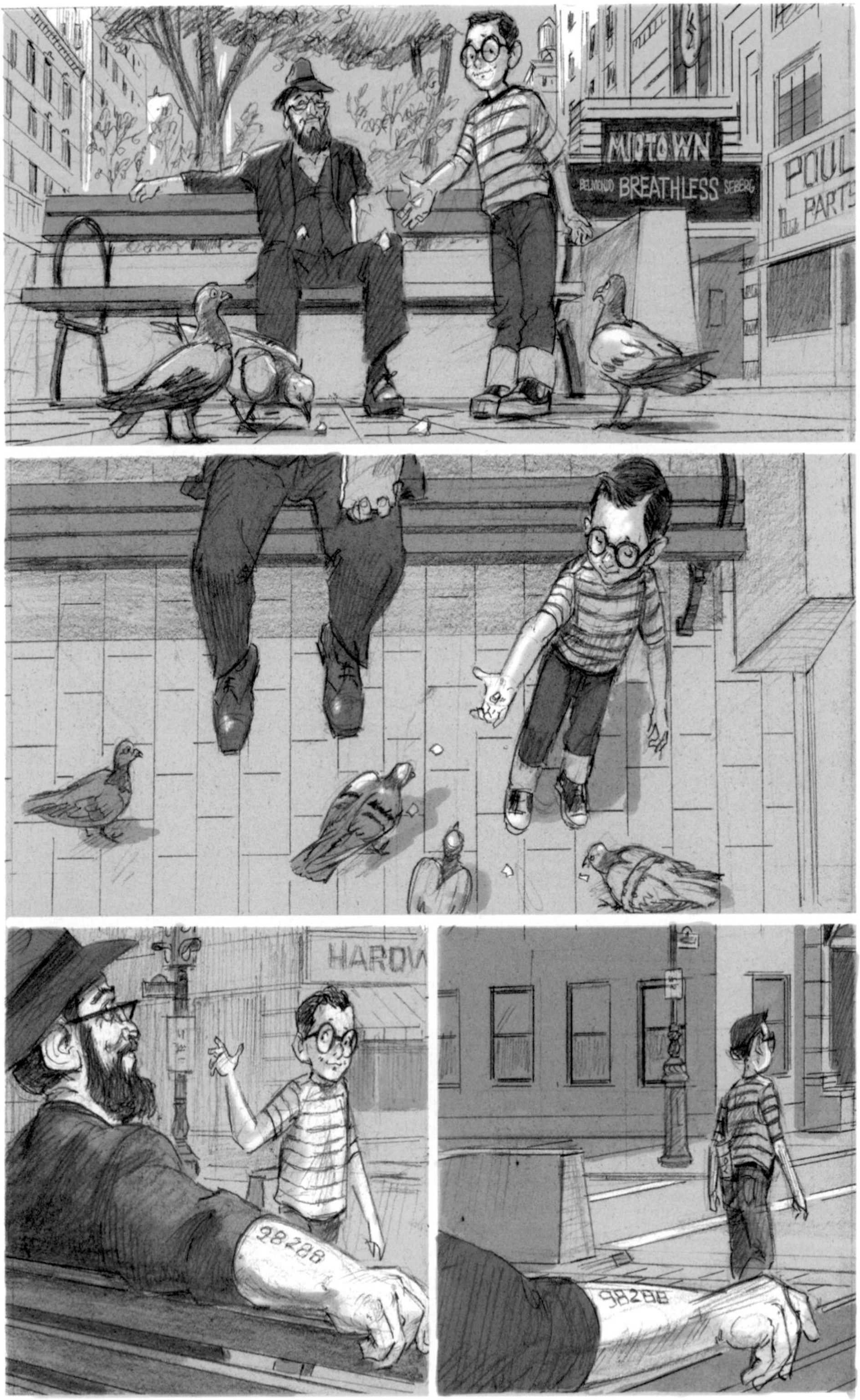
MIDTOWN
BELMONDO BREATHLESS SEBERG
POUL
PARTS
HAROW
98288
98288

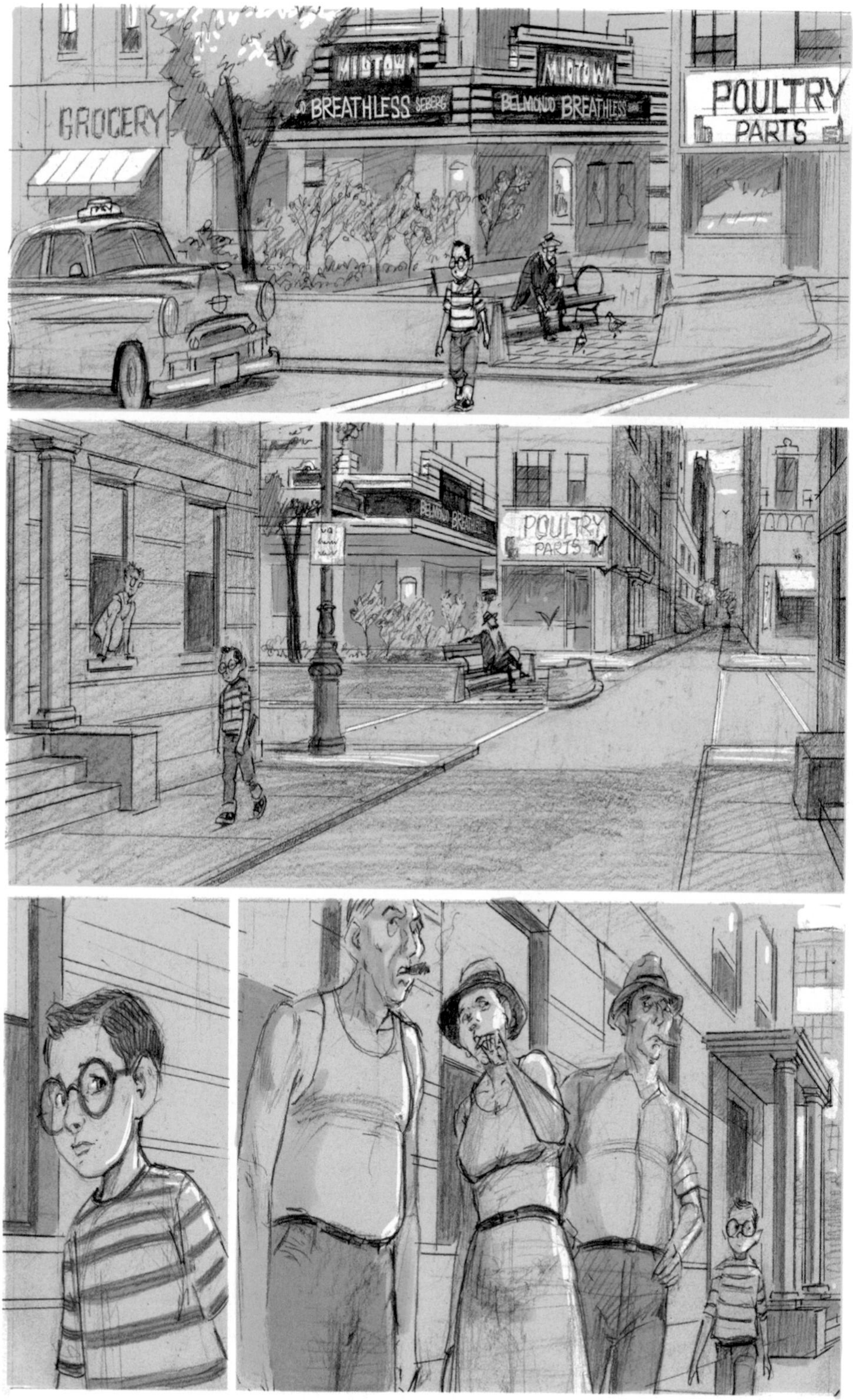
GROCERY
BREATHLESS SEBERG
BELMONDO BREATHLESS
POULTRY
PARTS
BELMONDO BREATHLESS
POULTRY
PARTS

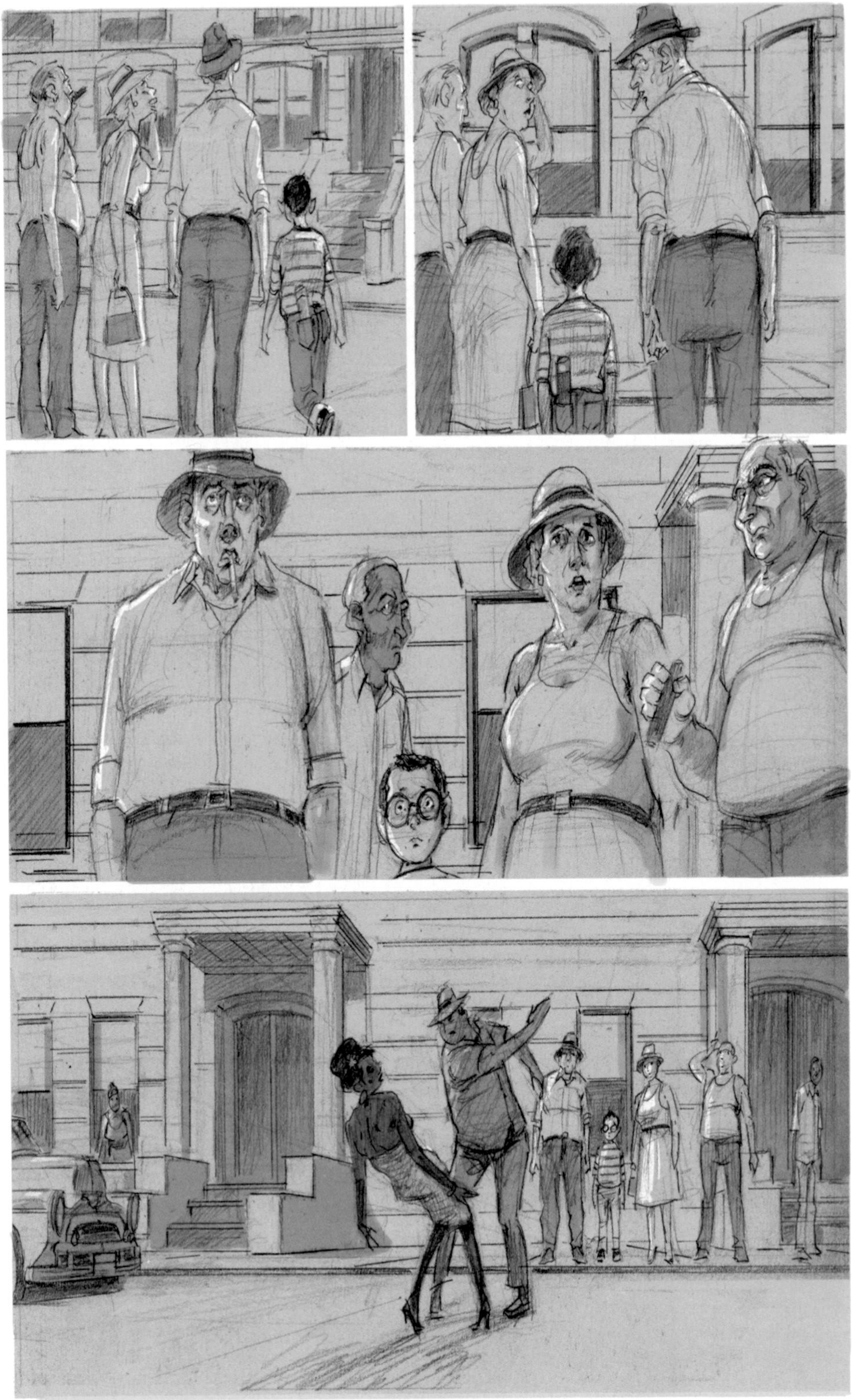

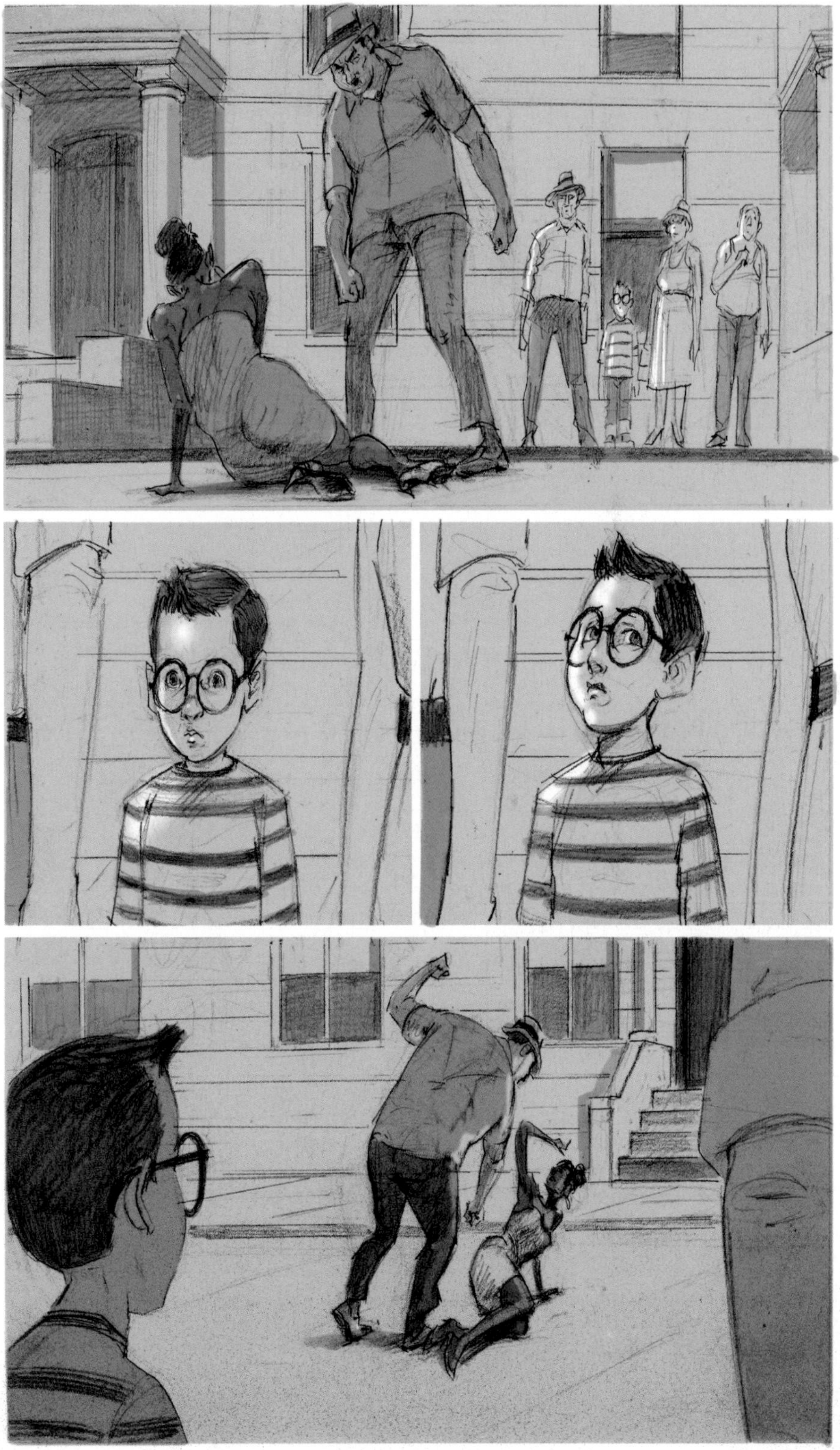

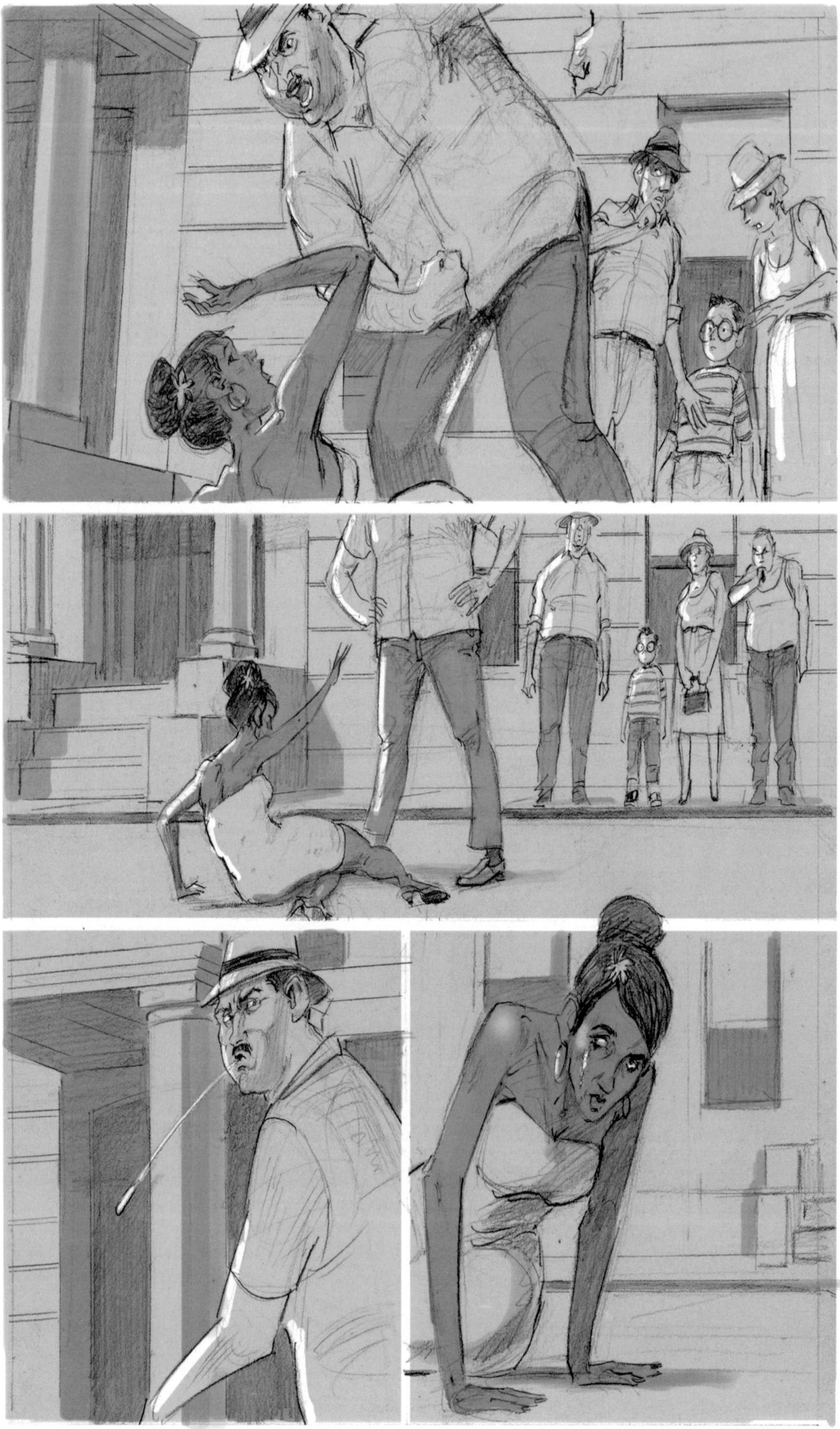

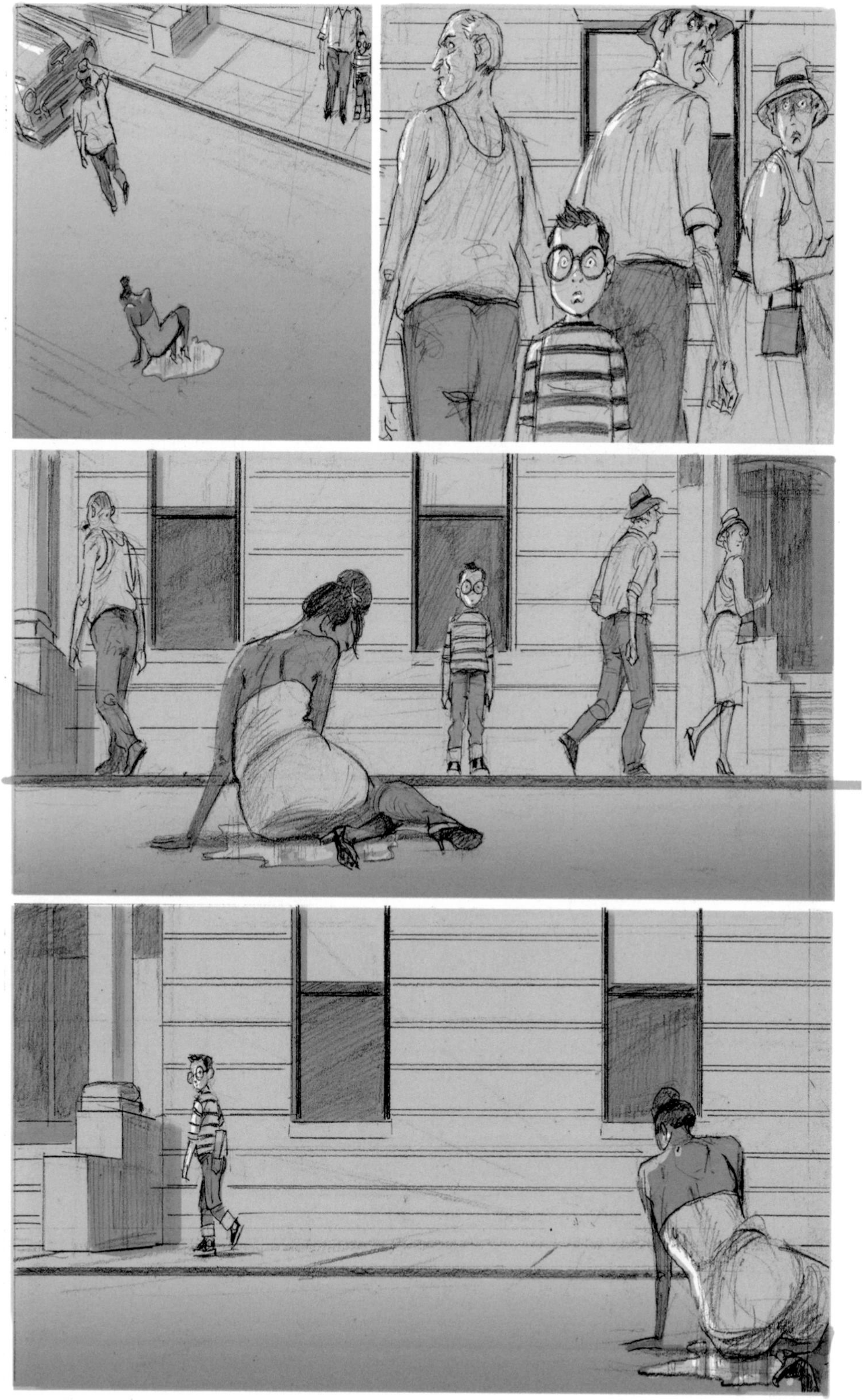

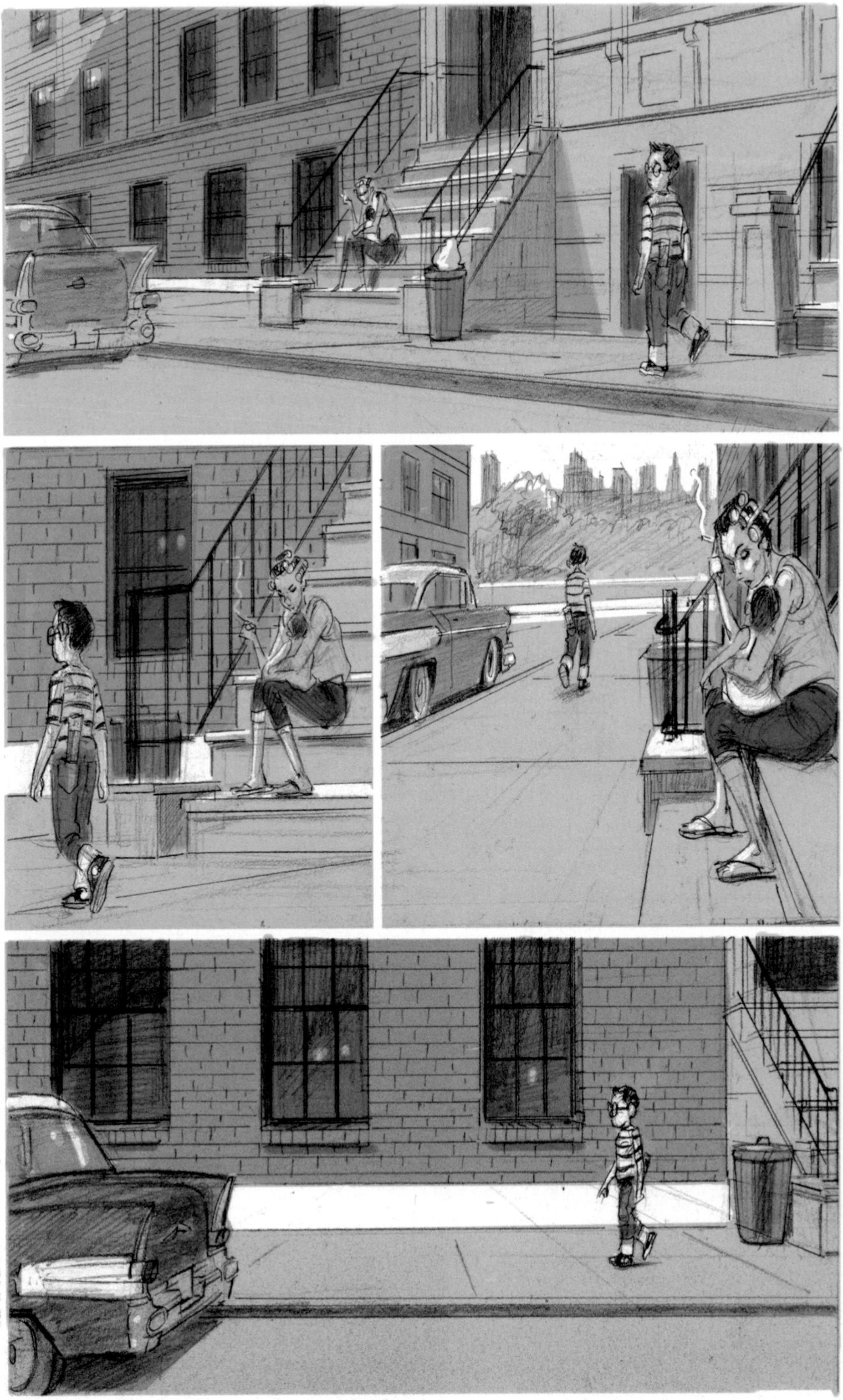

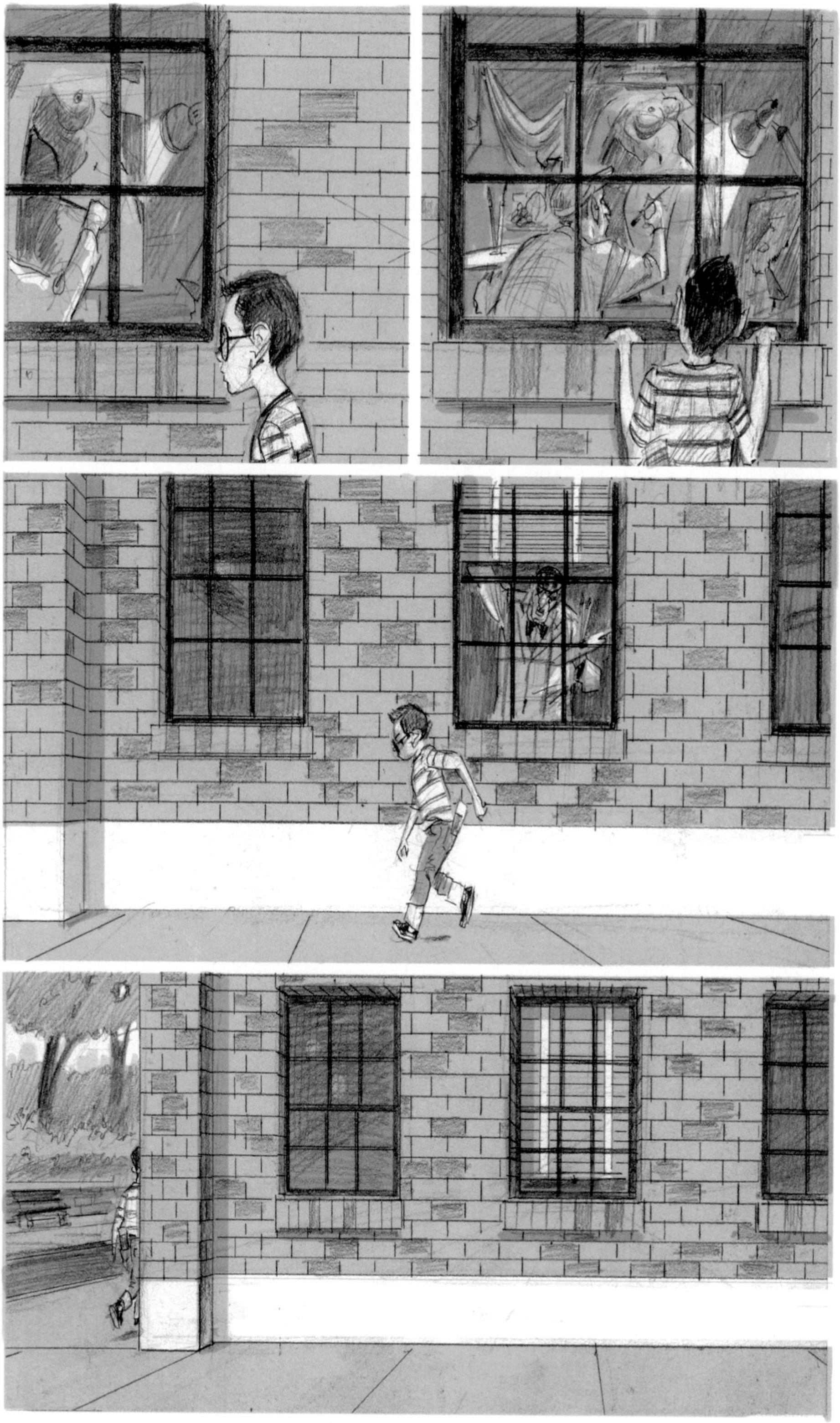

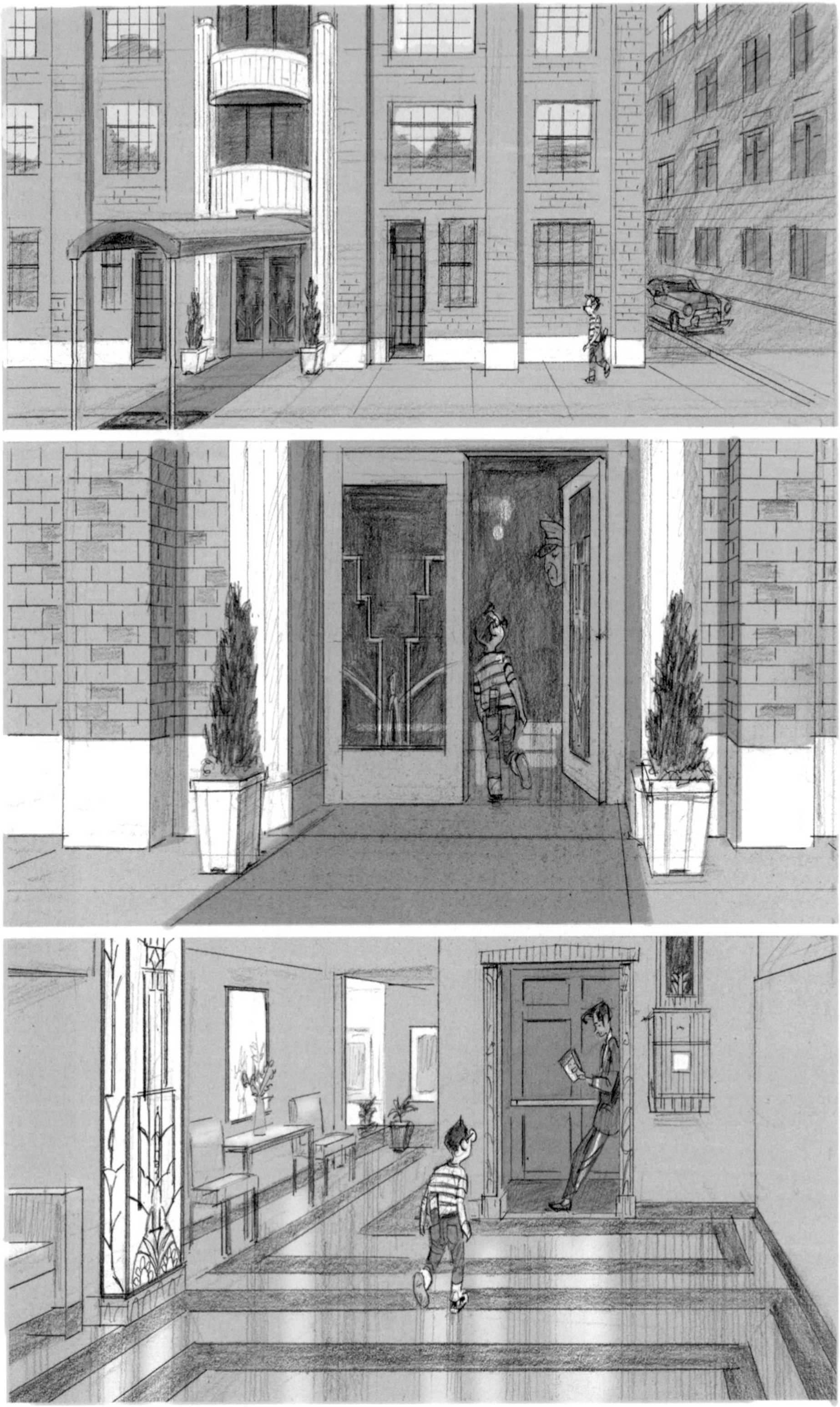

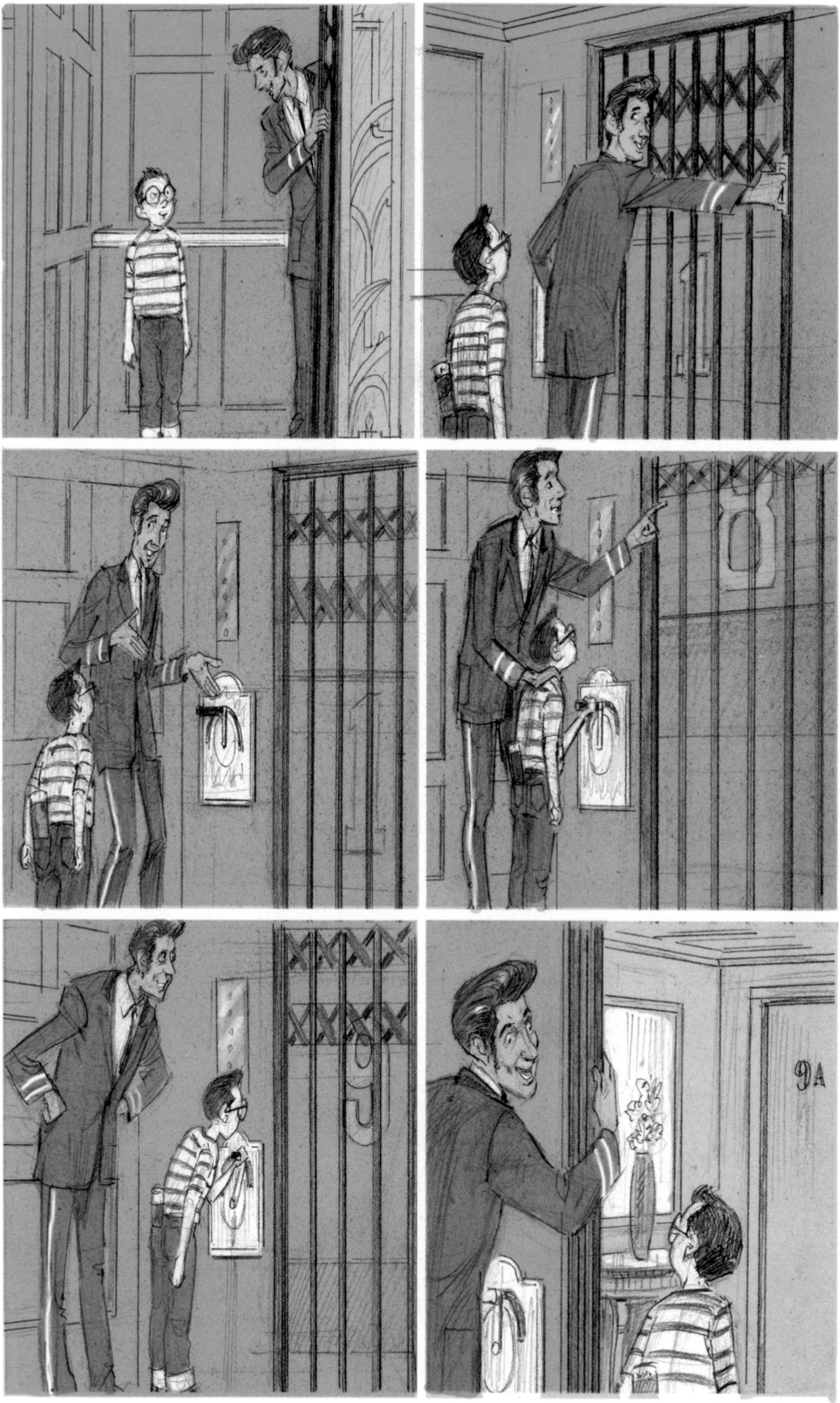
9A

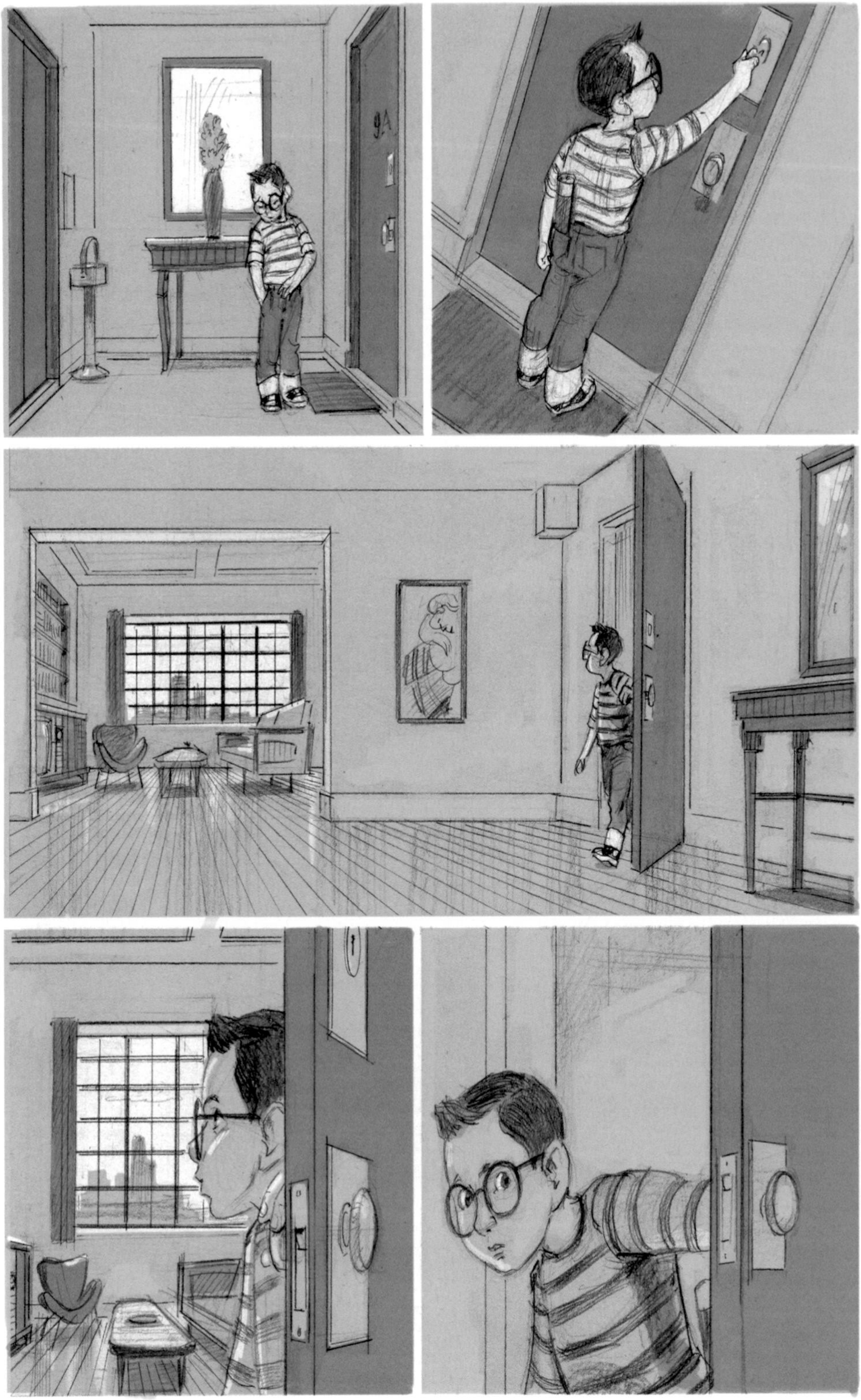
9A

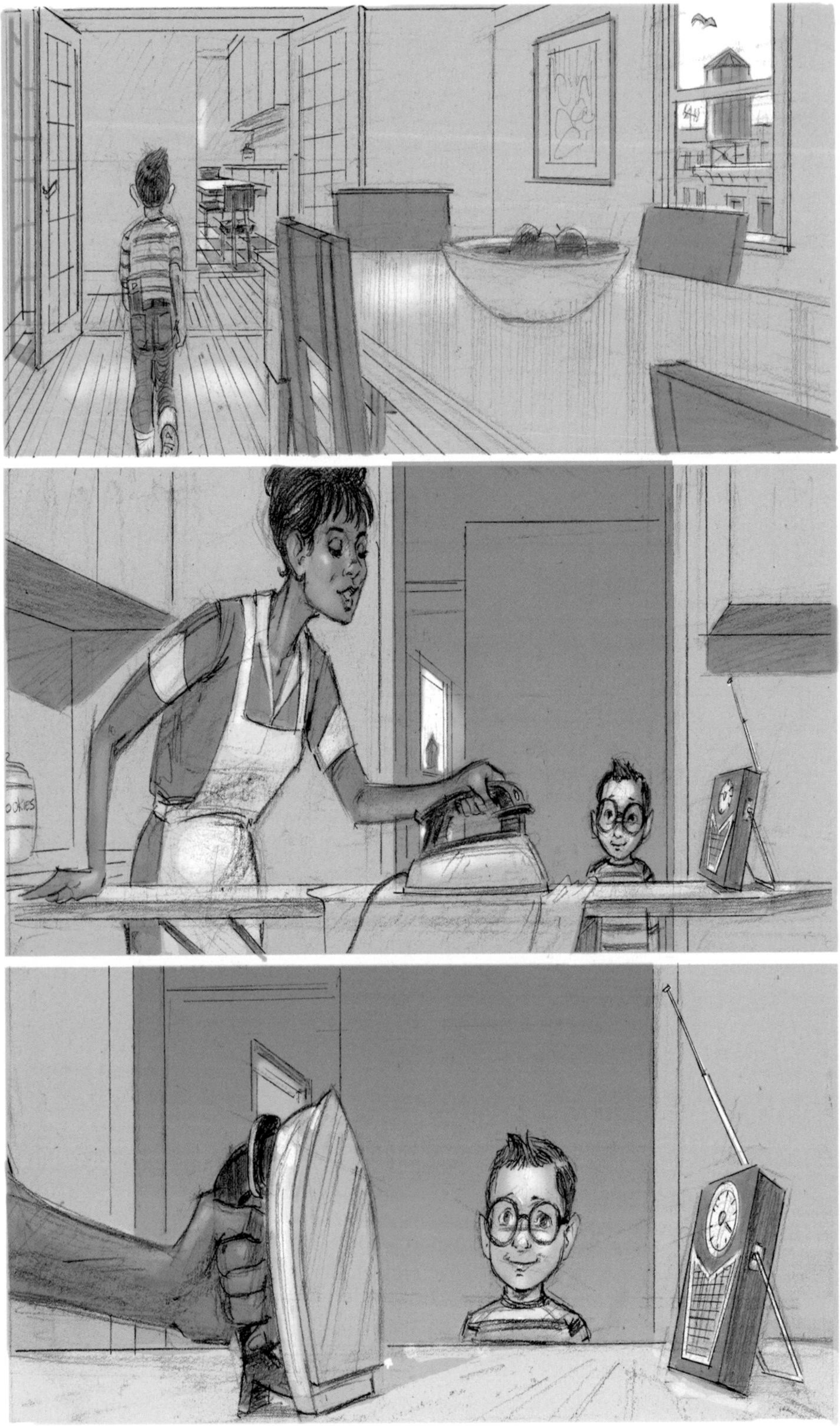

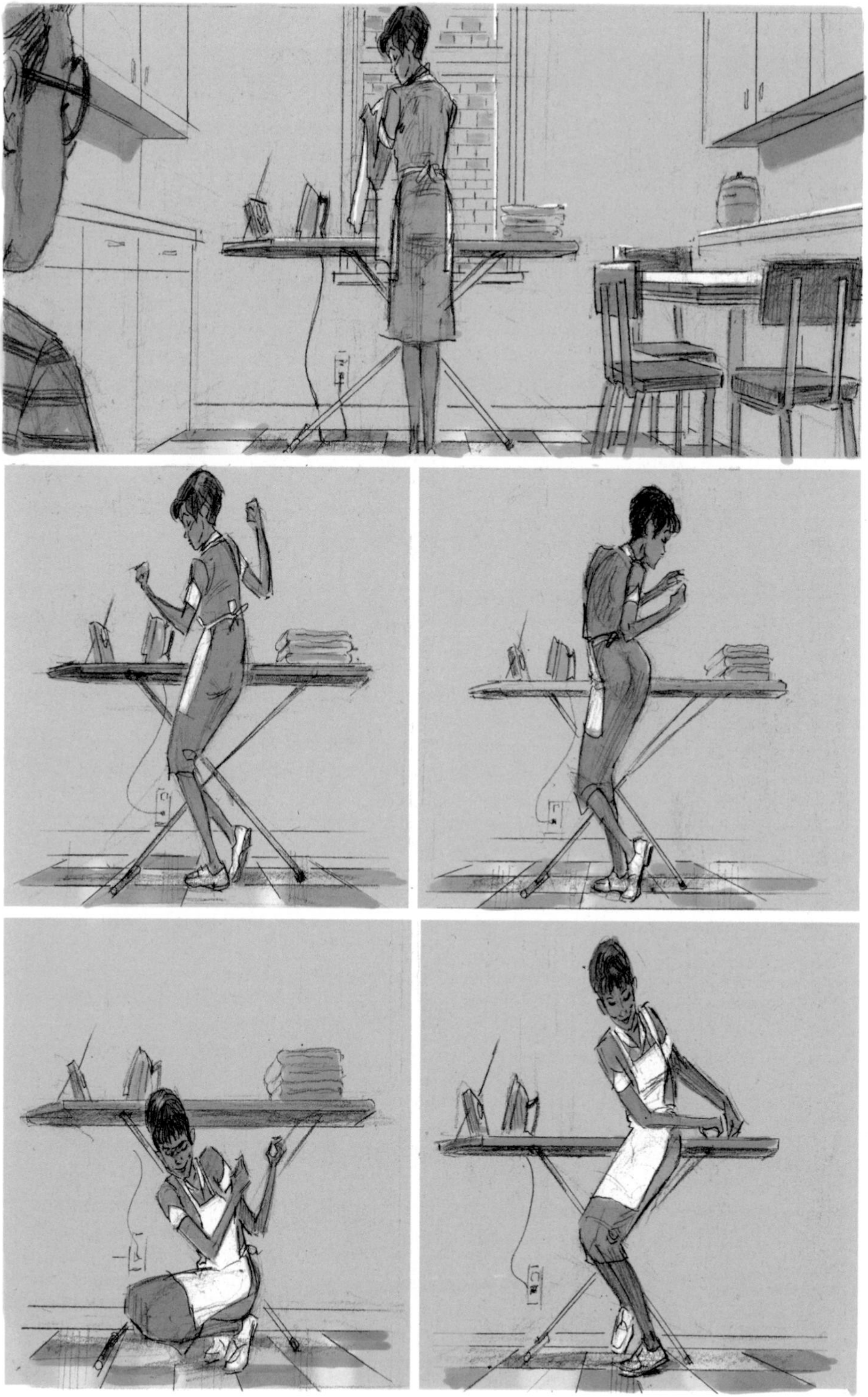

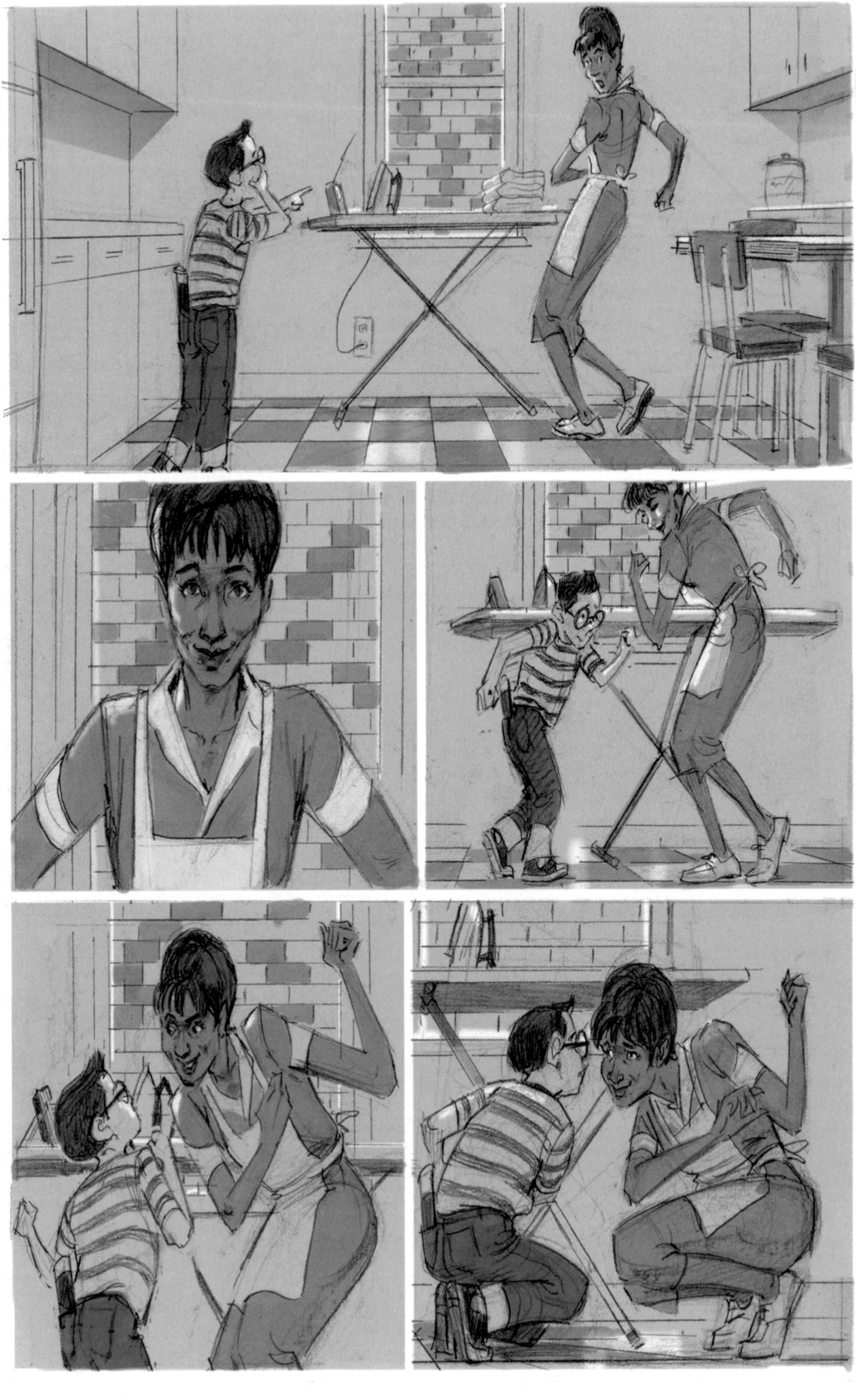

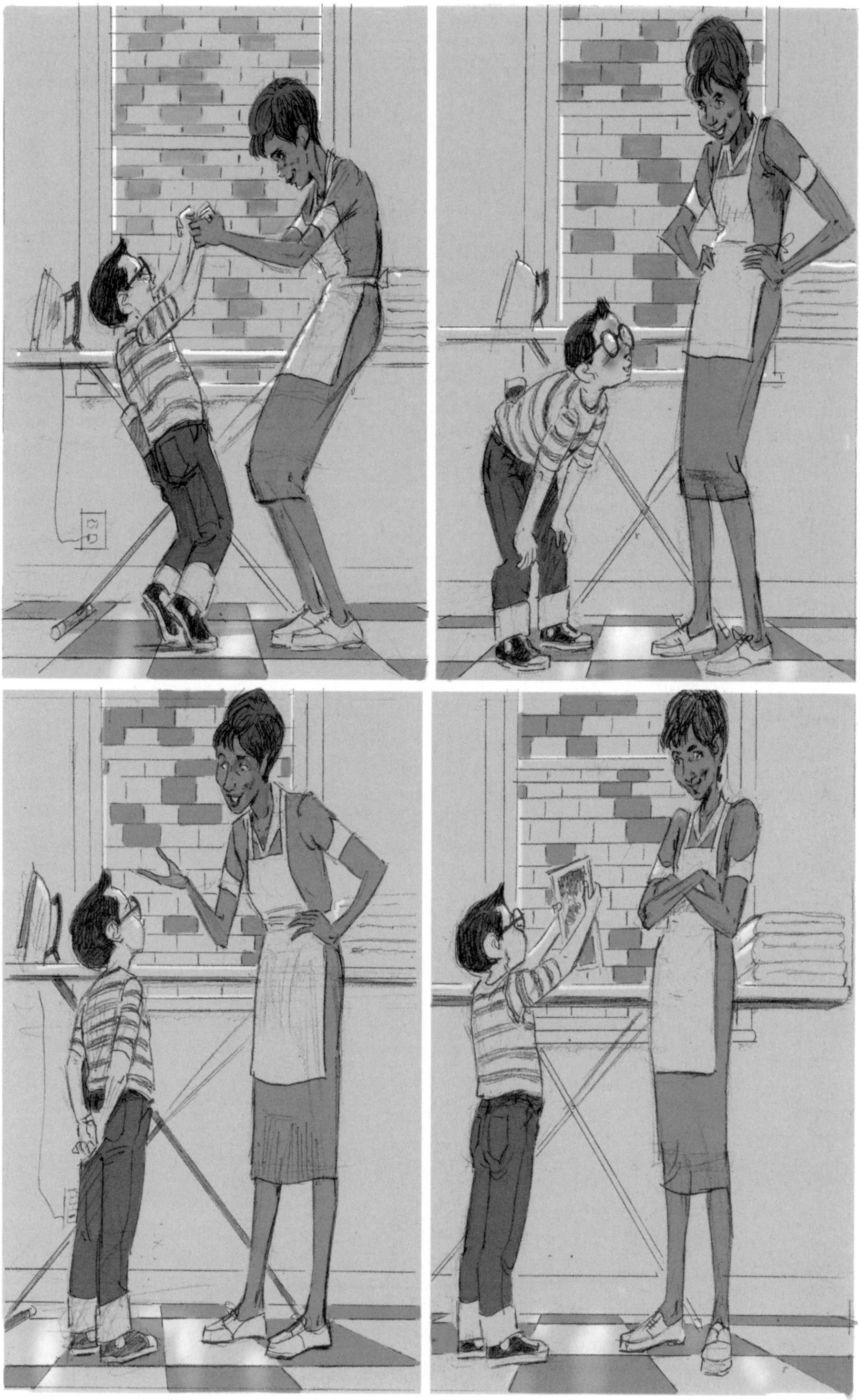

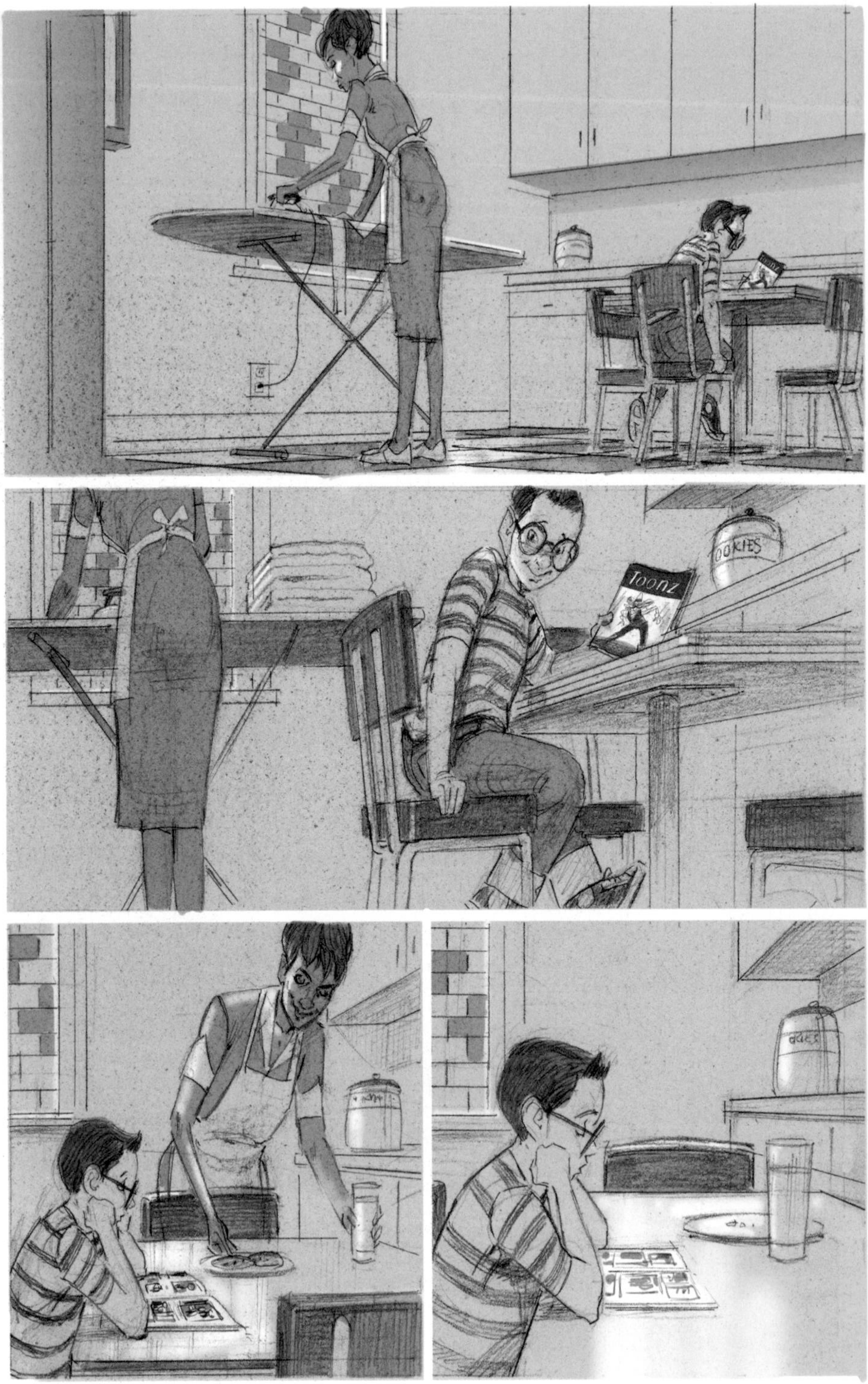
TOONZ
OOKIES

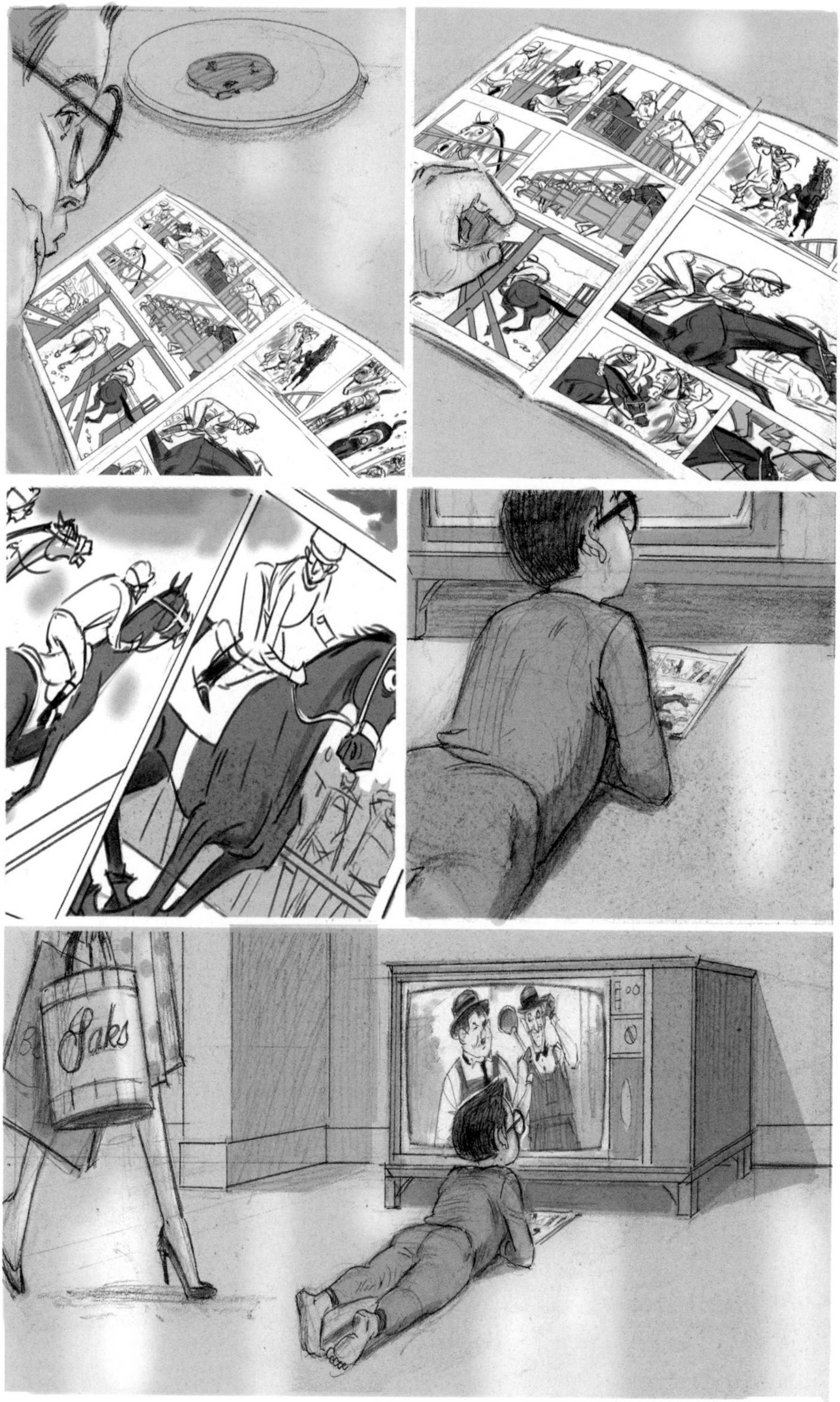
Saks

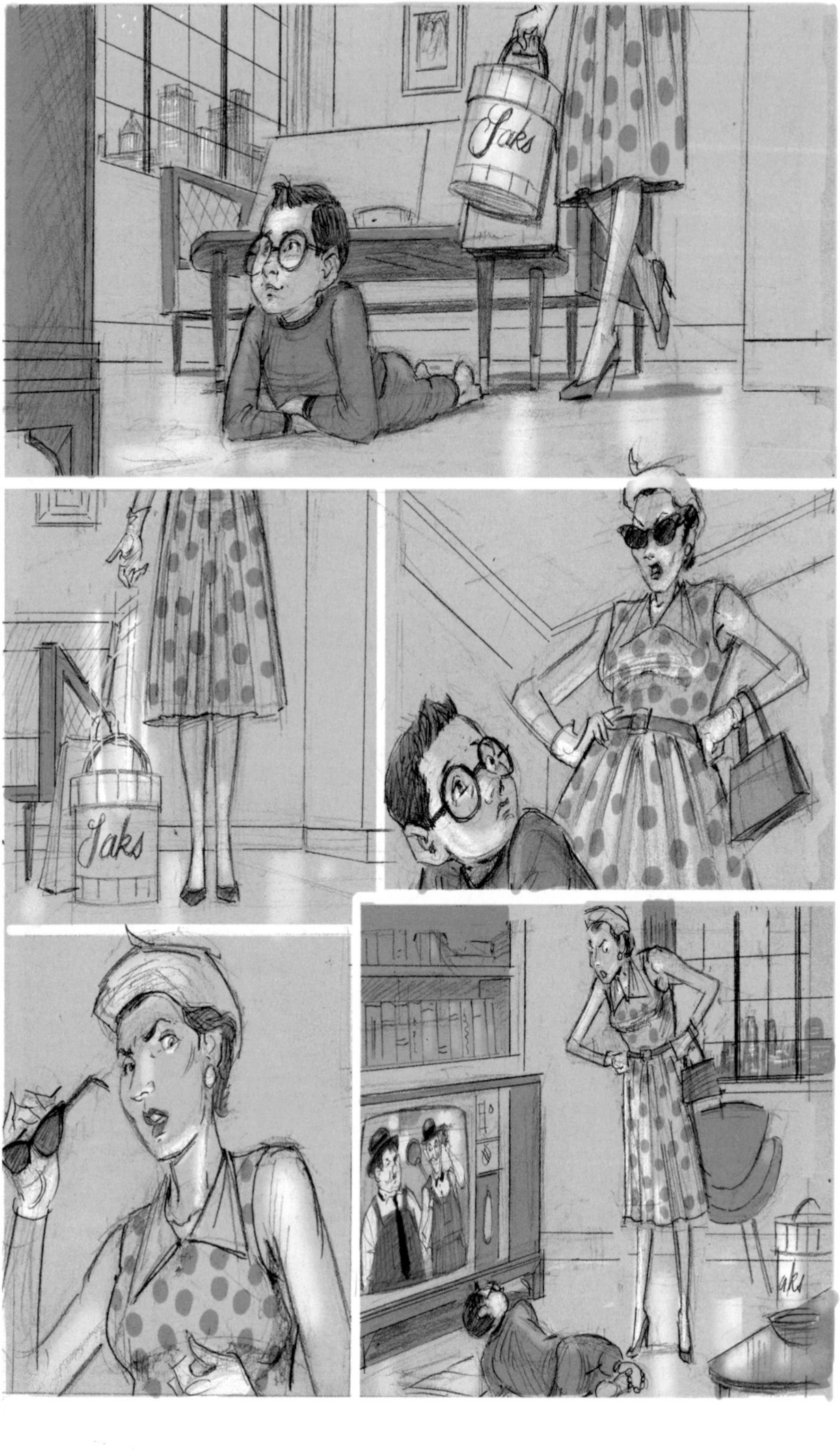
Saks
Saks

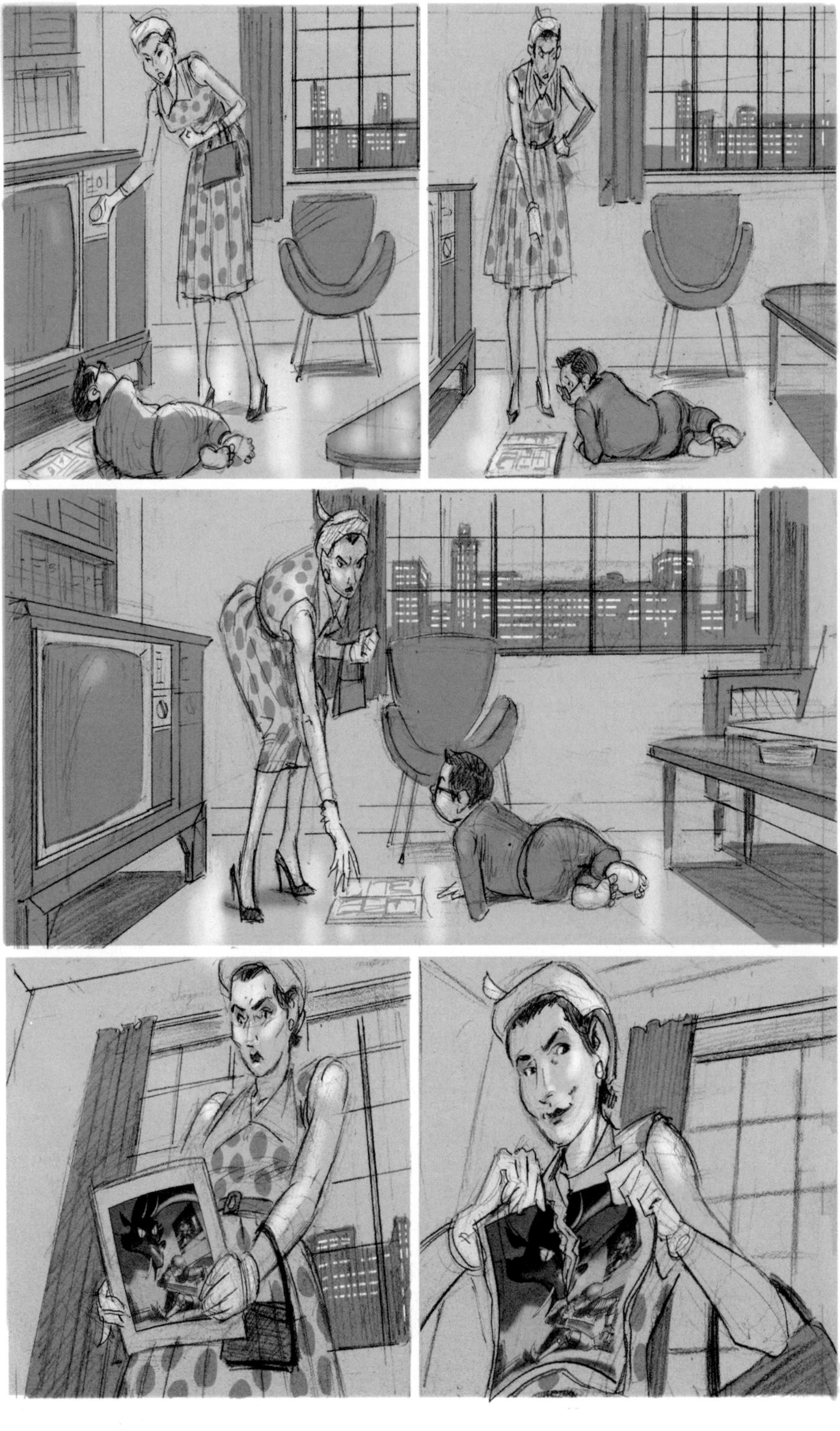

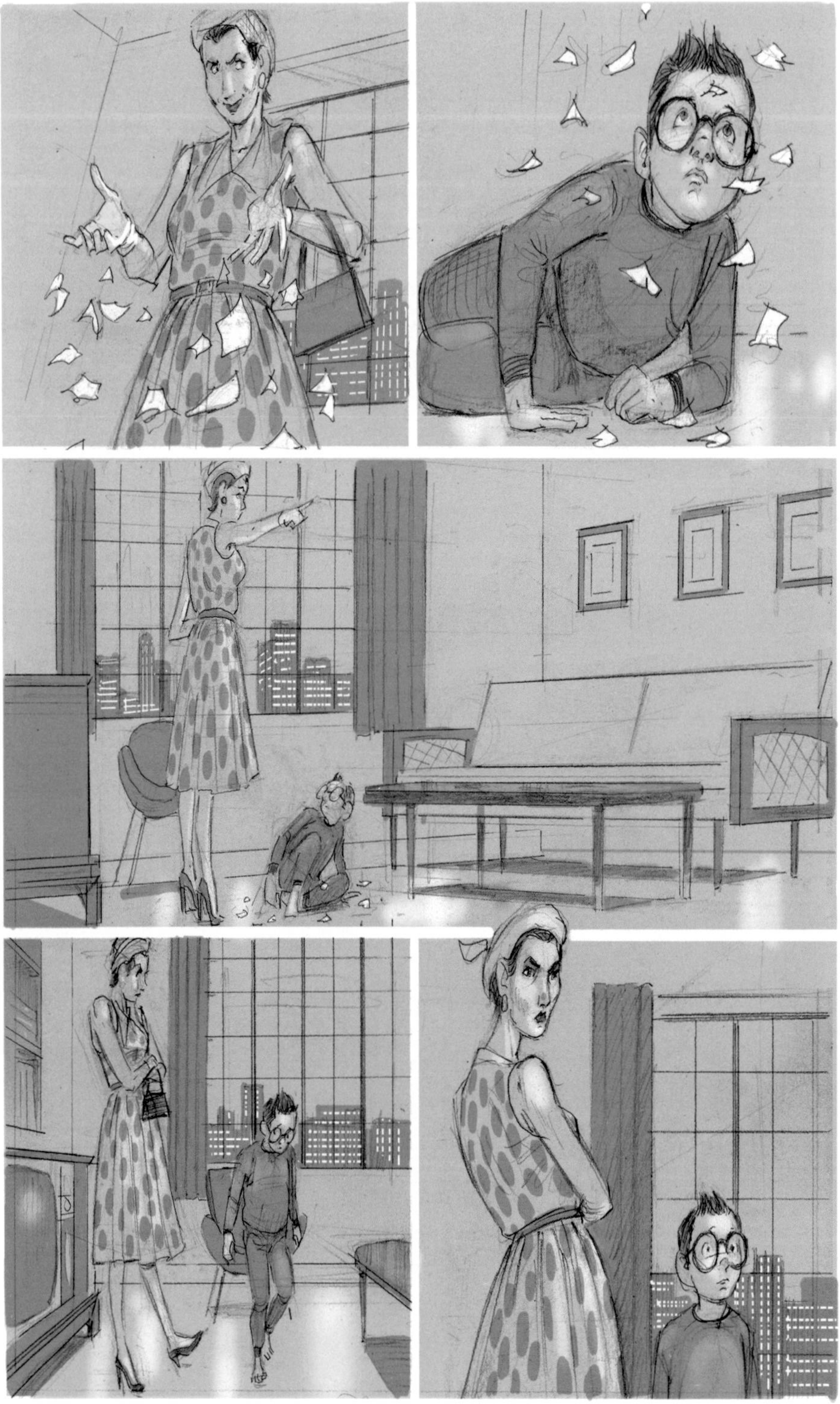

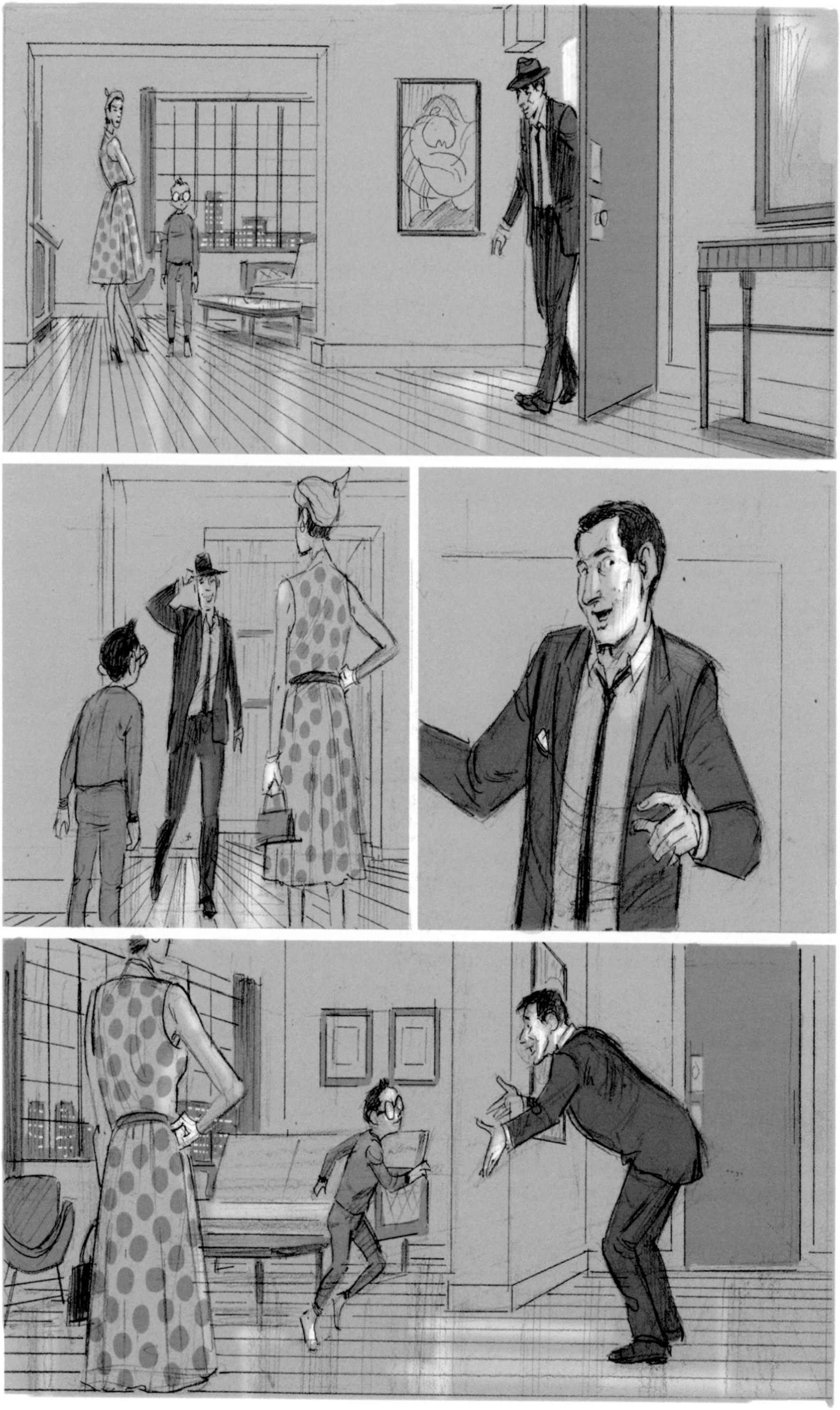

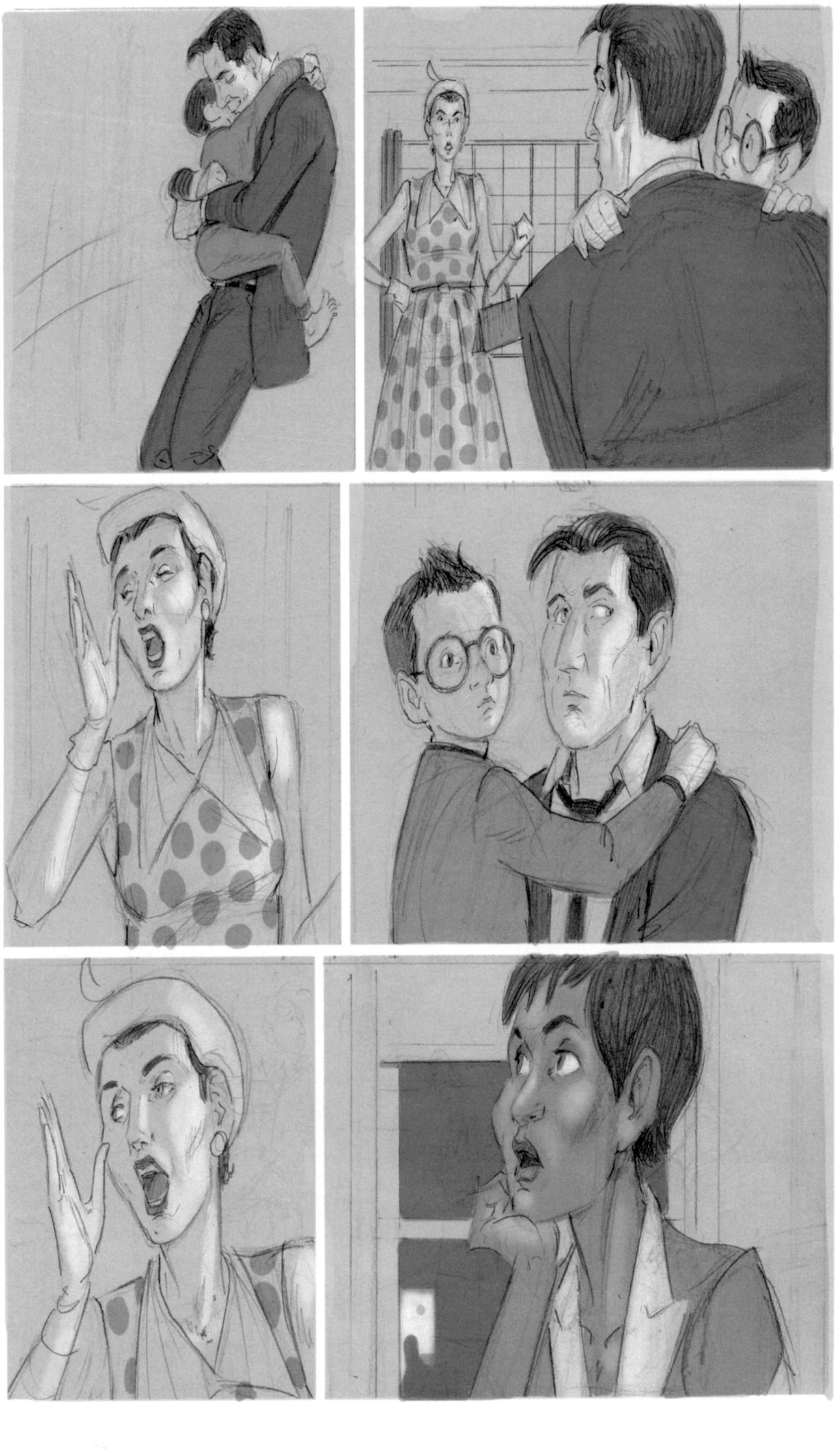

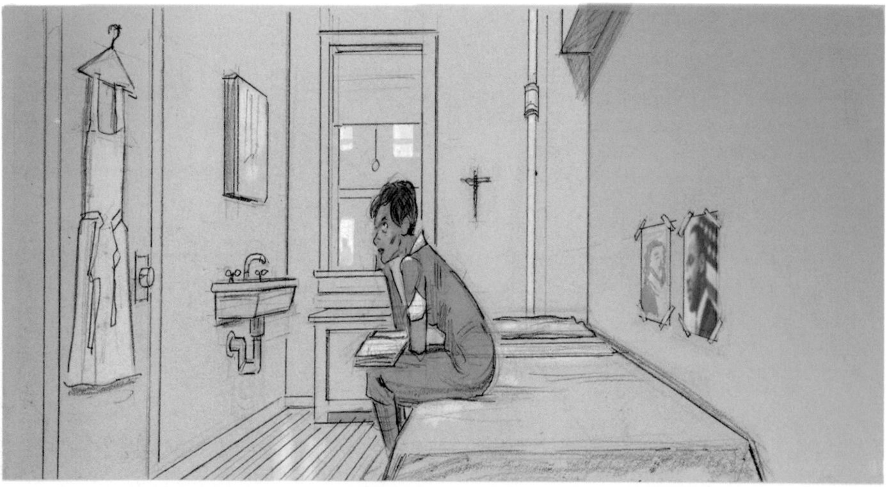
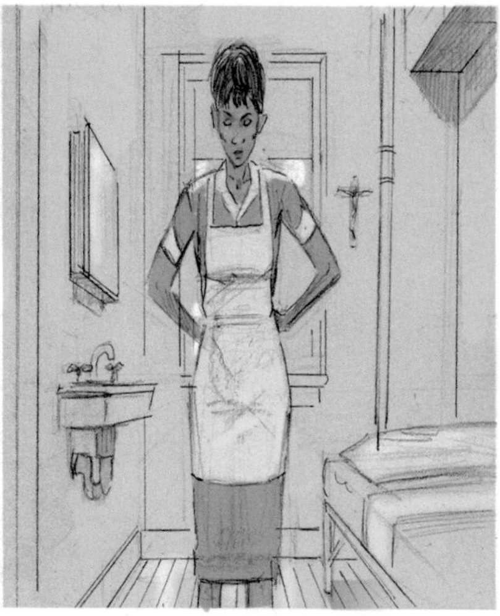
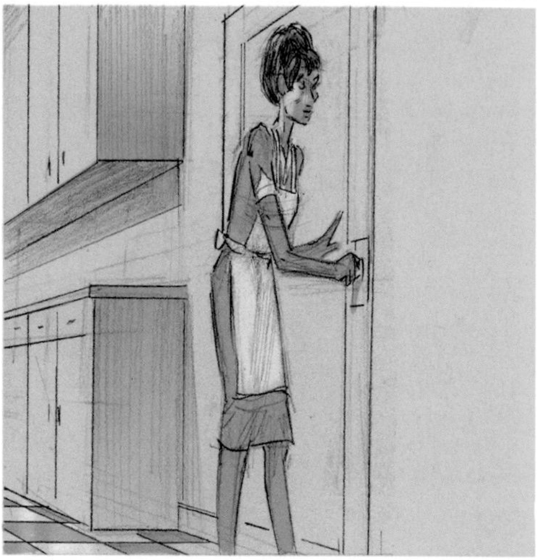
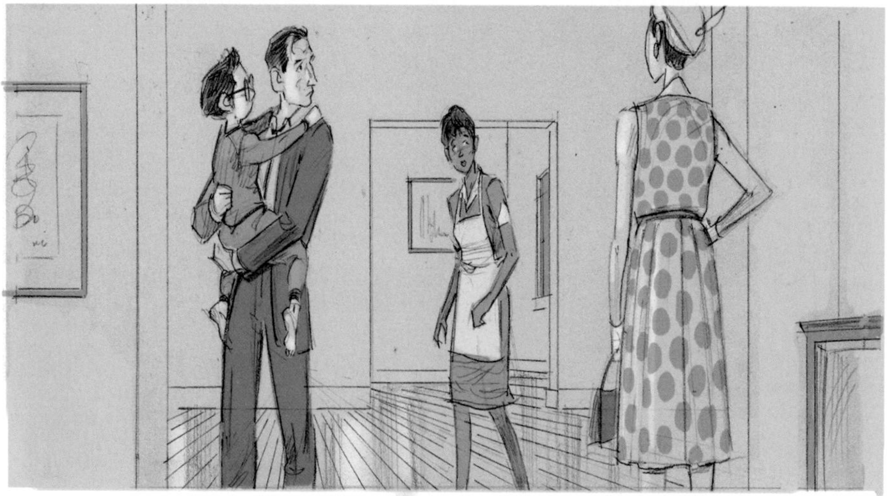

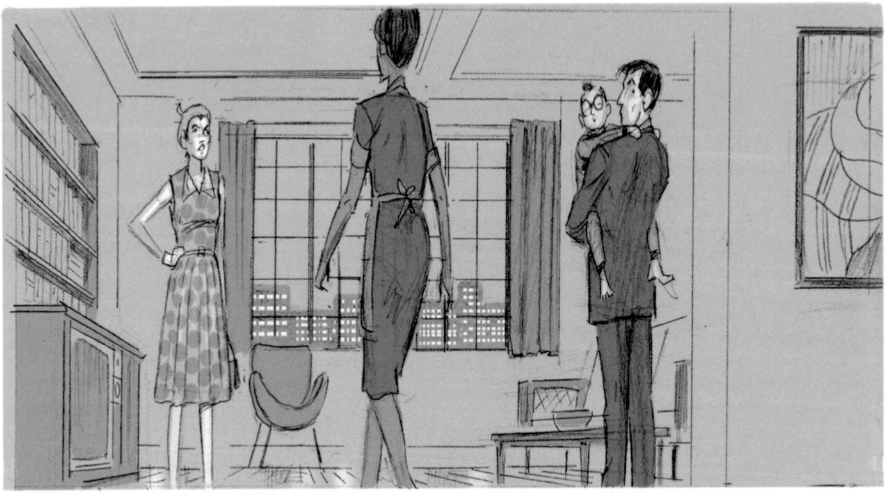
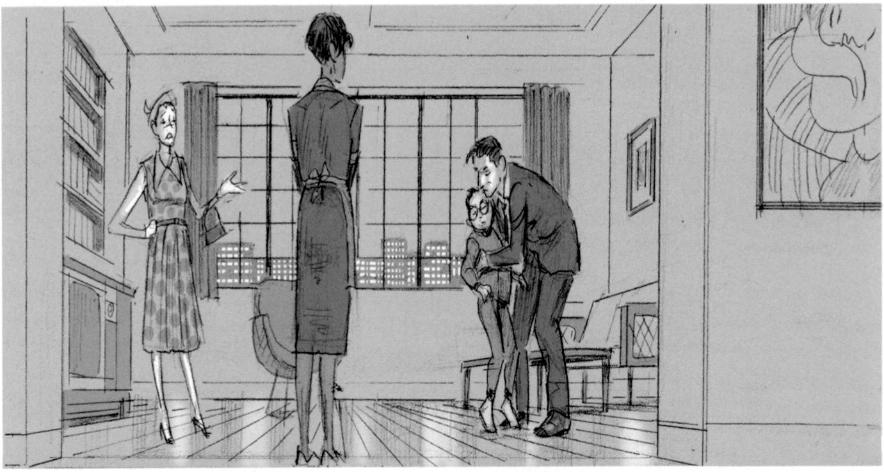
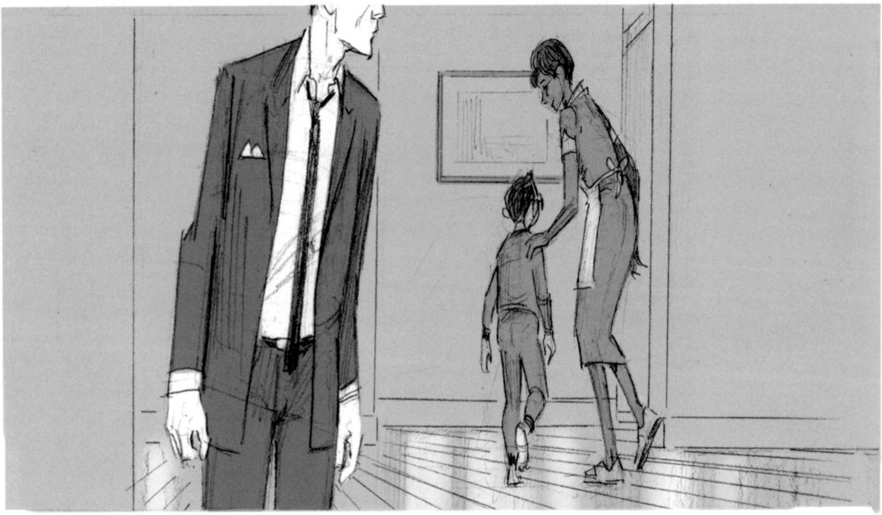

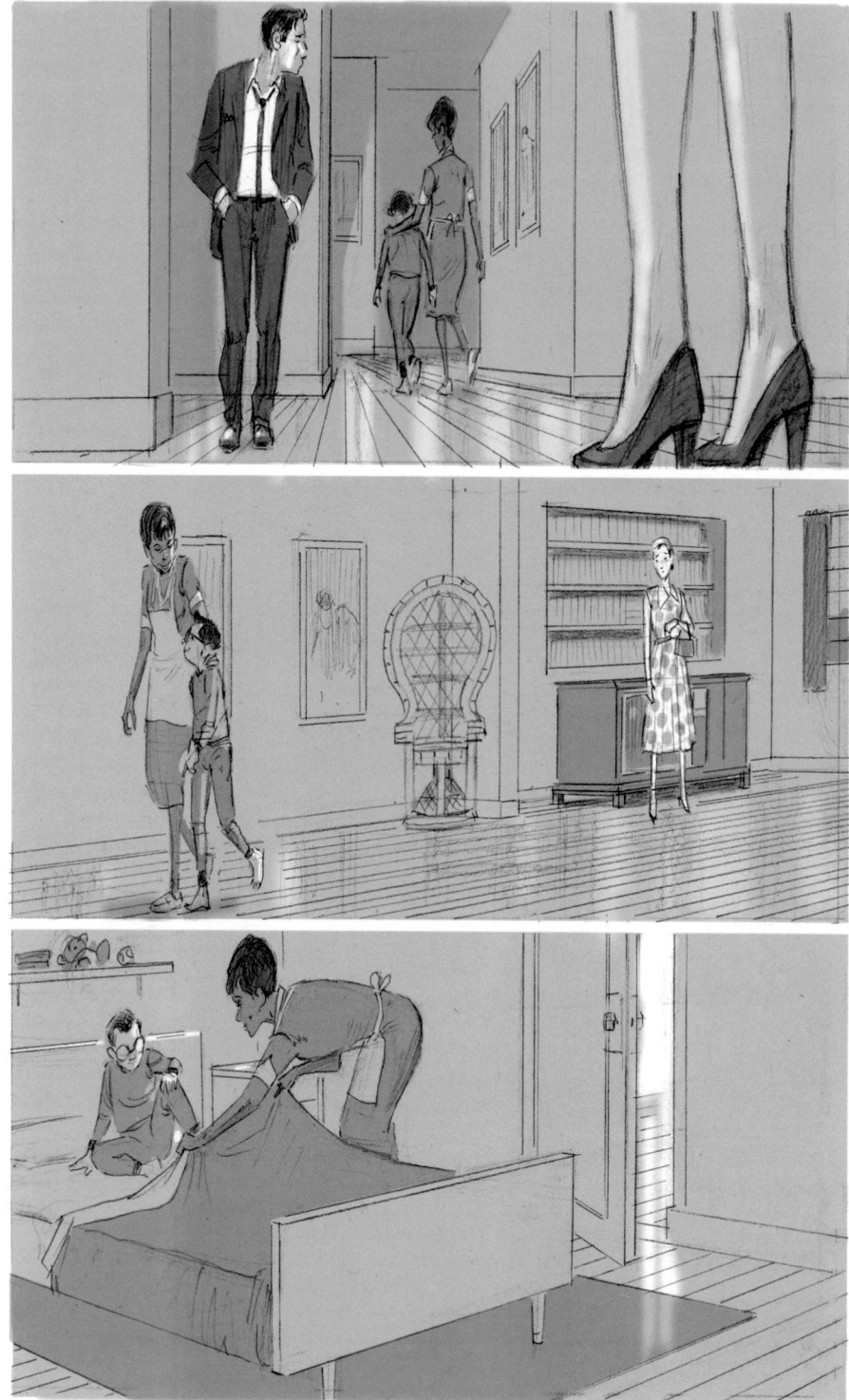

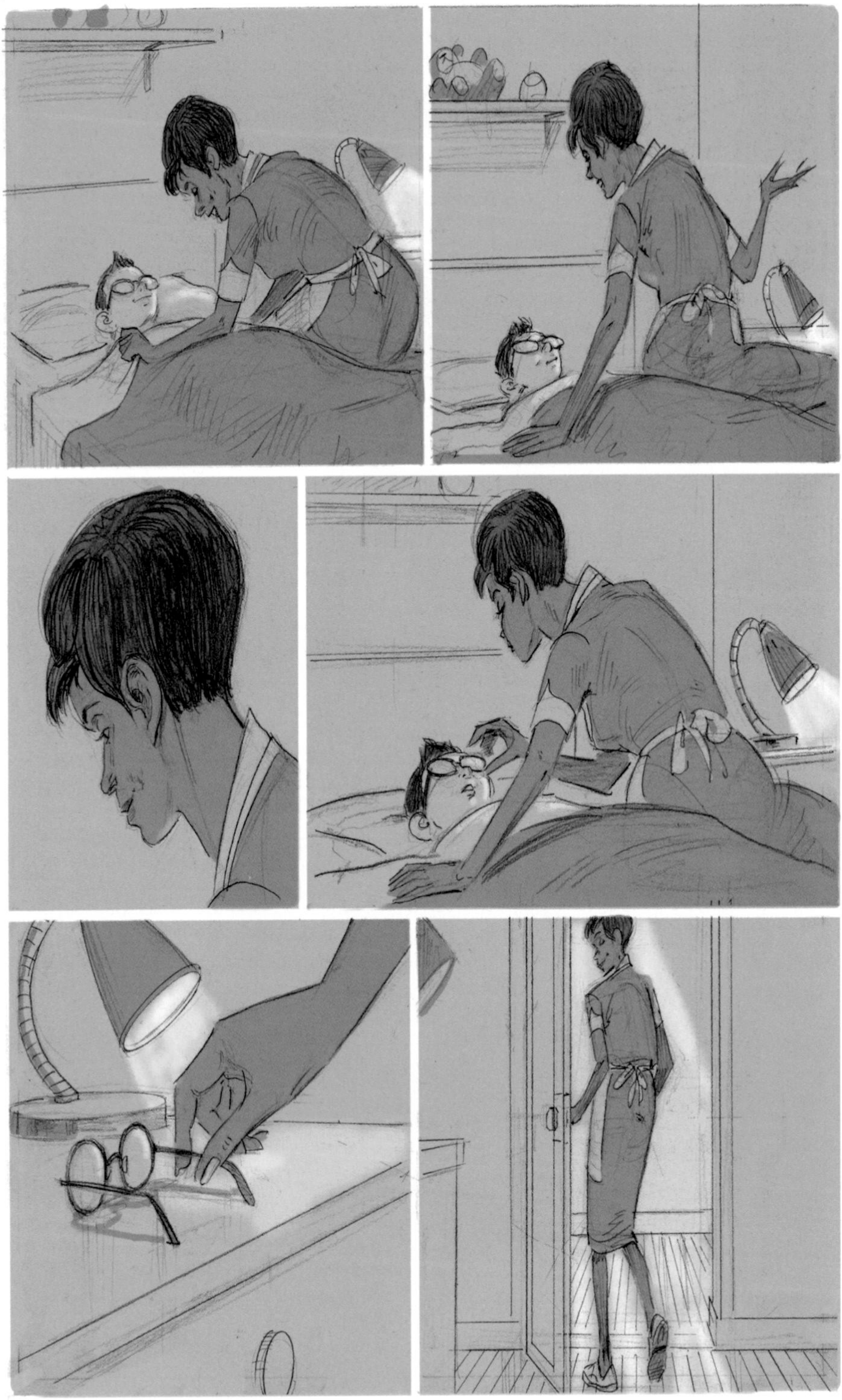

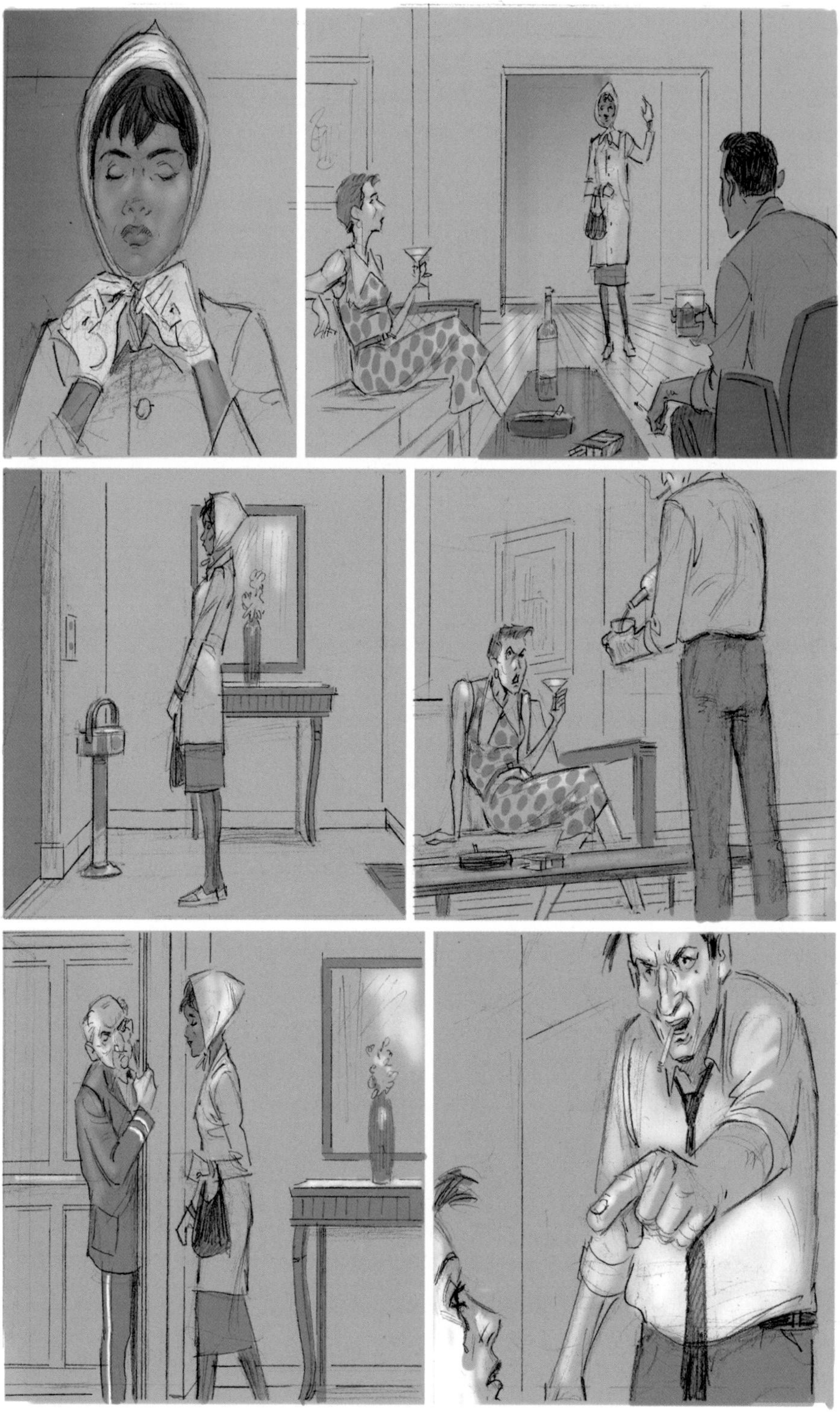

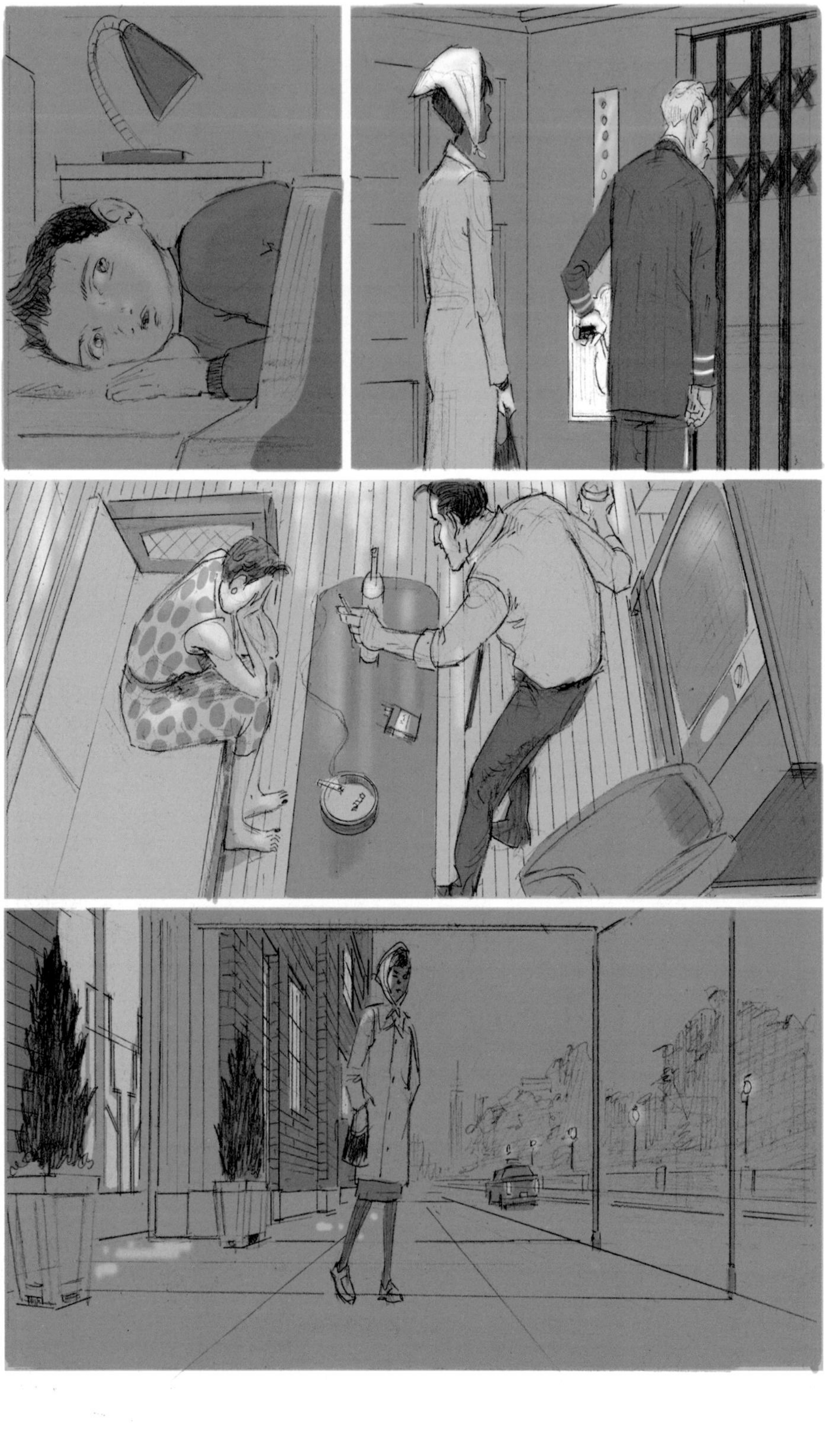

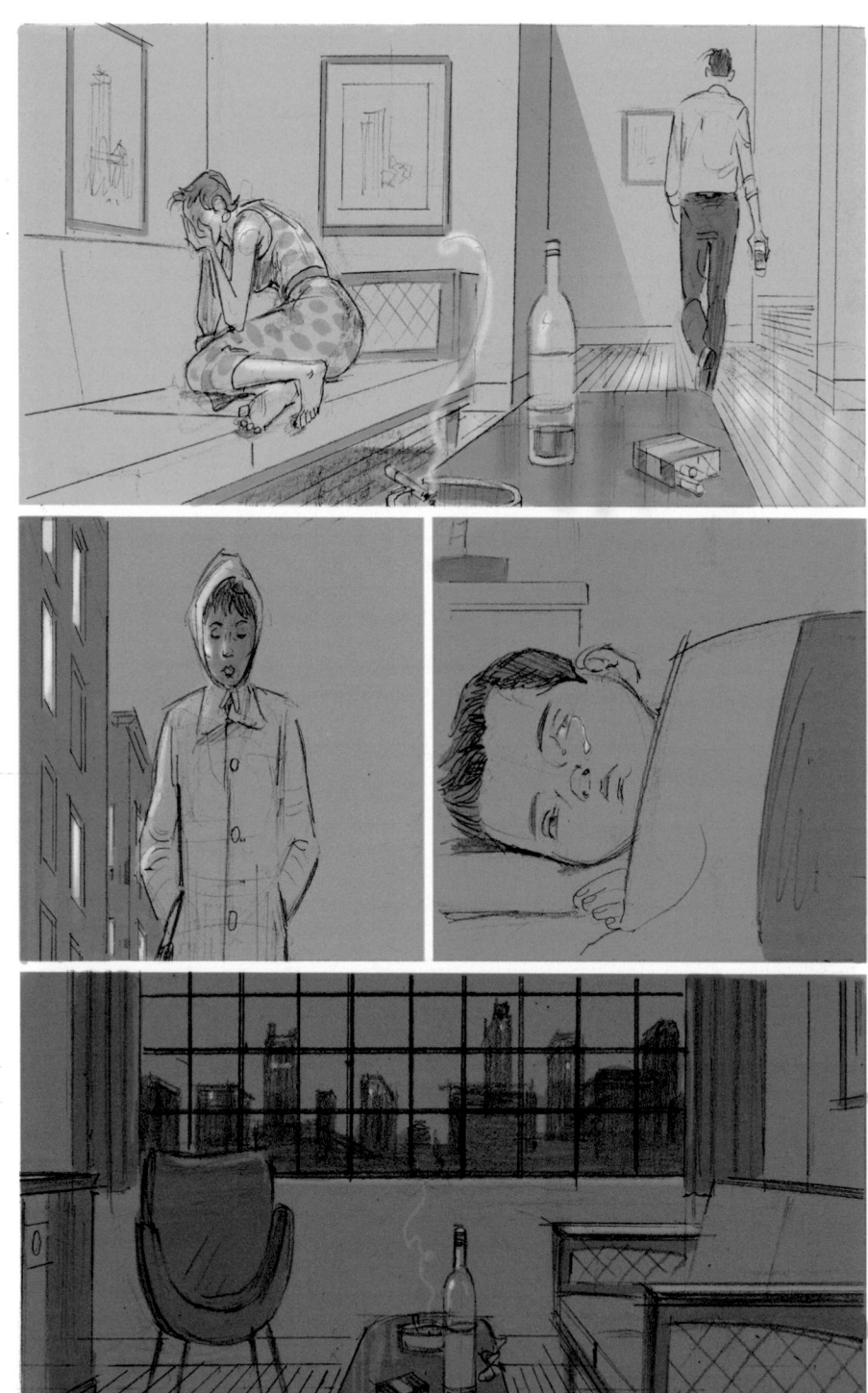

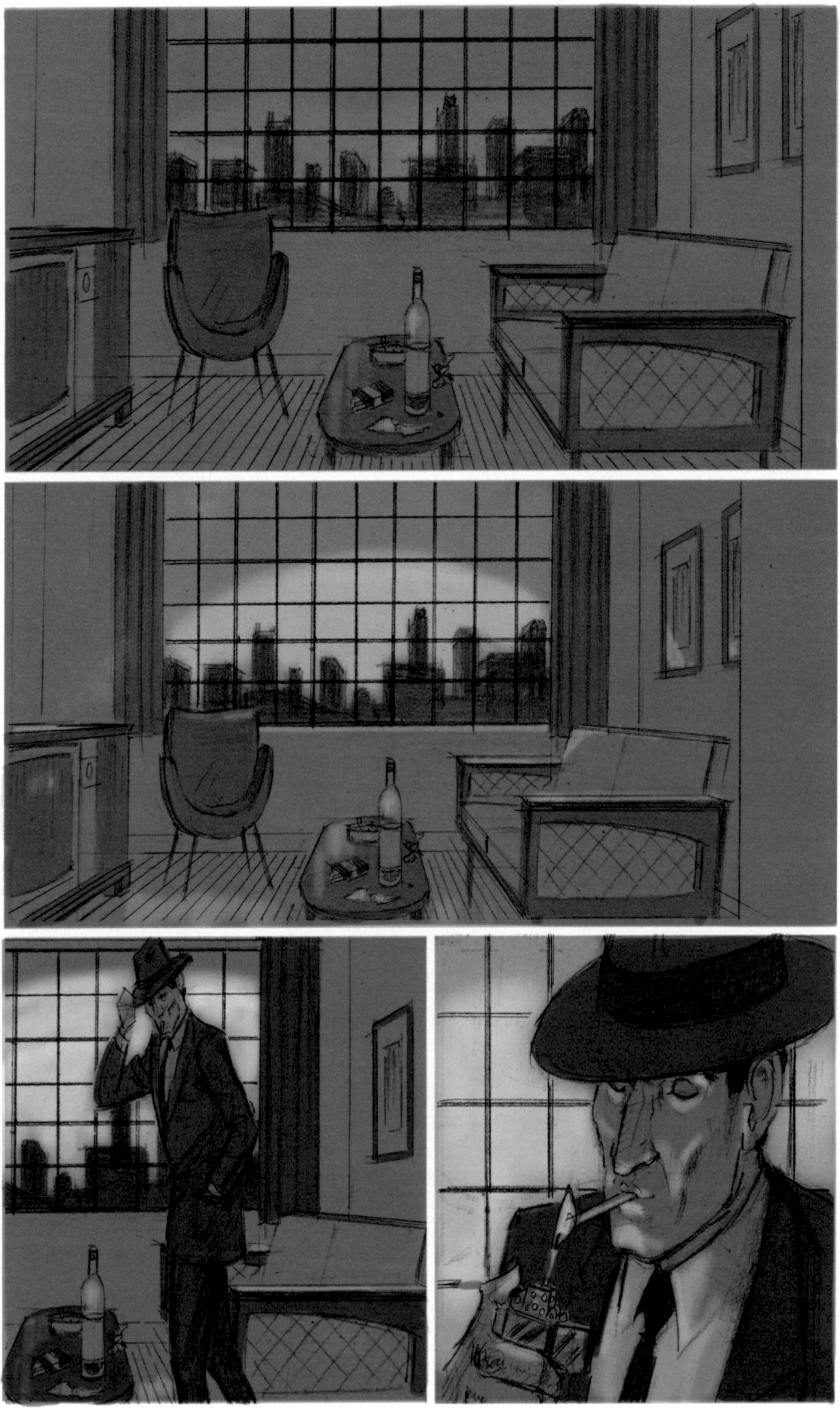

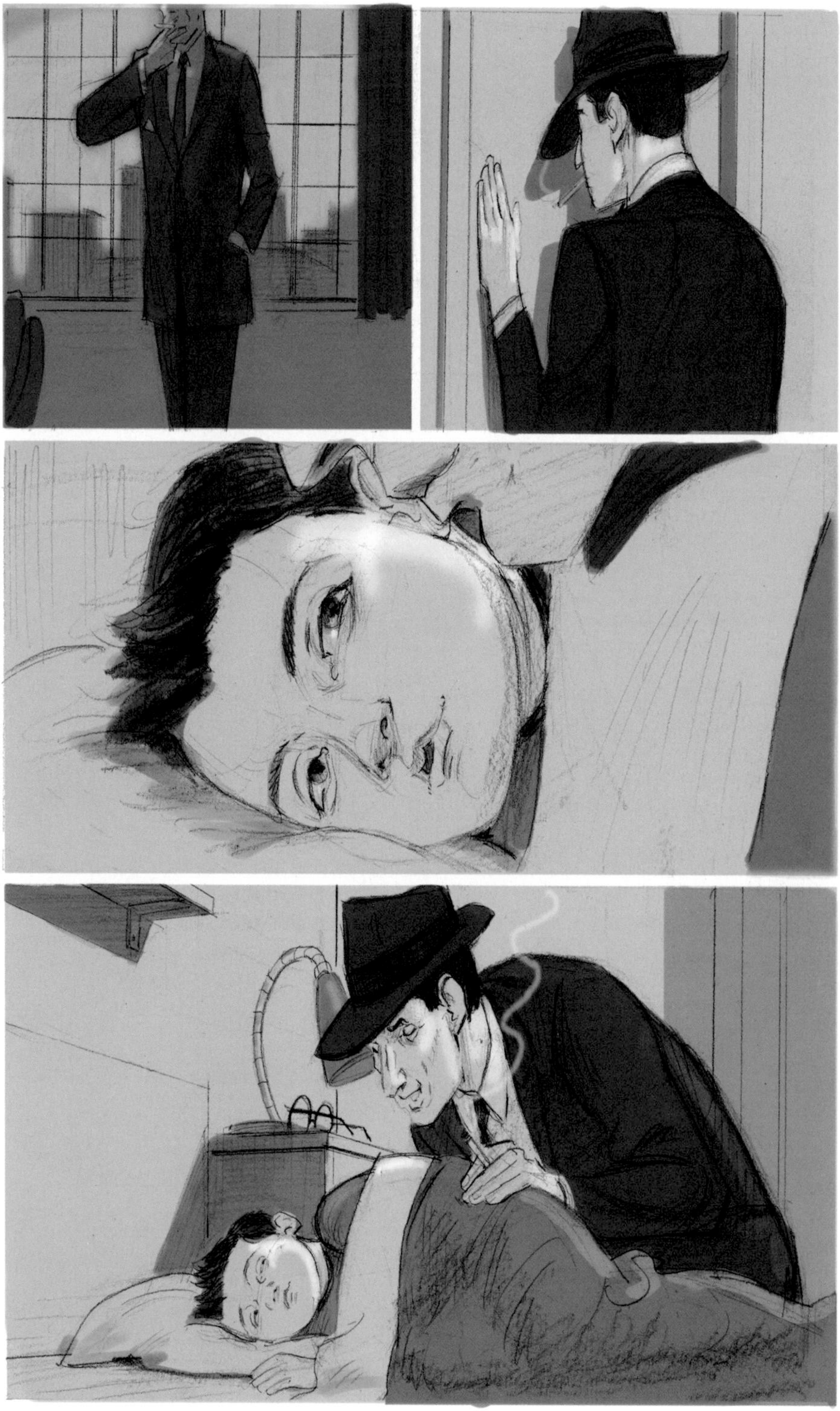

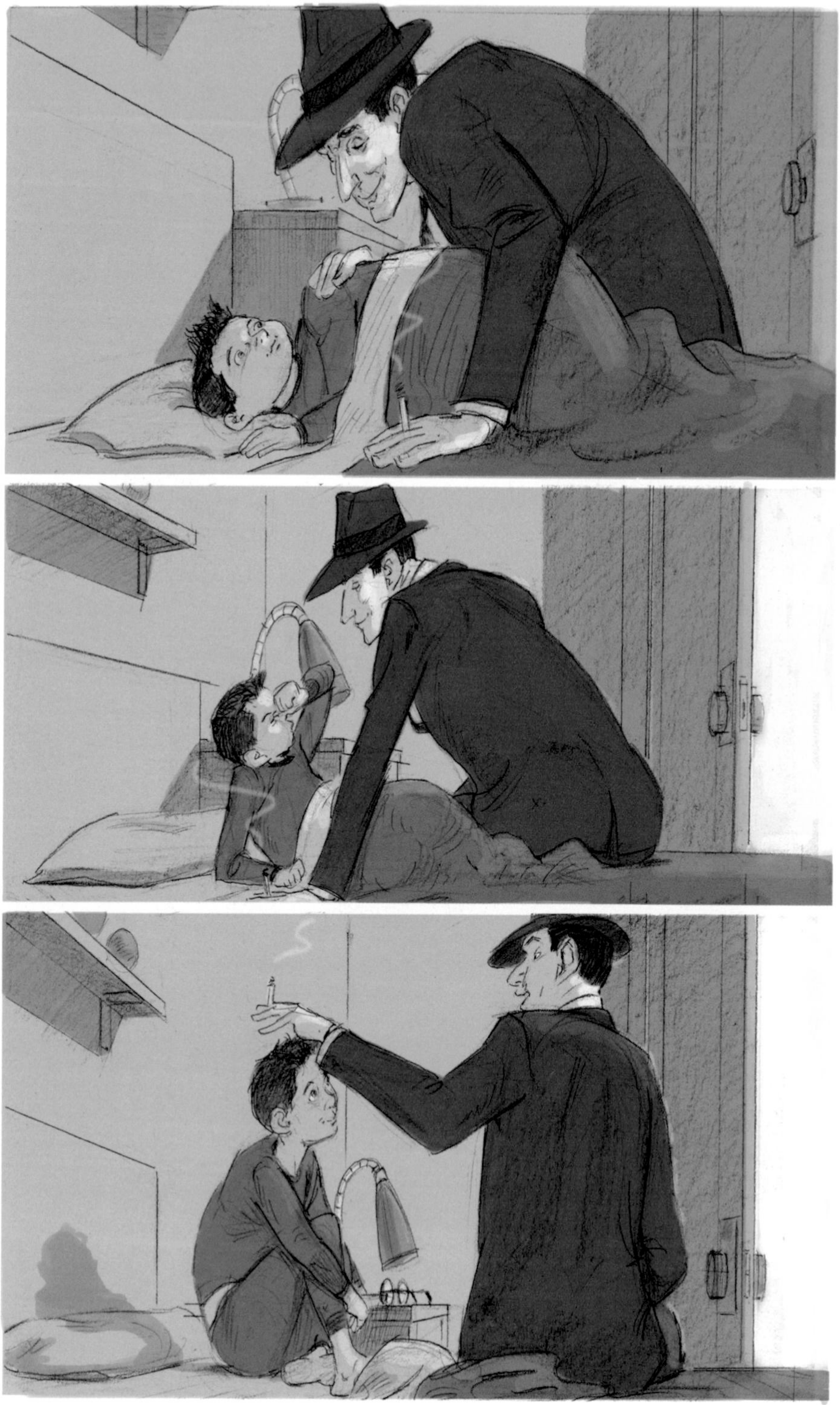

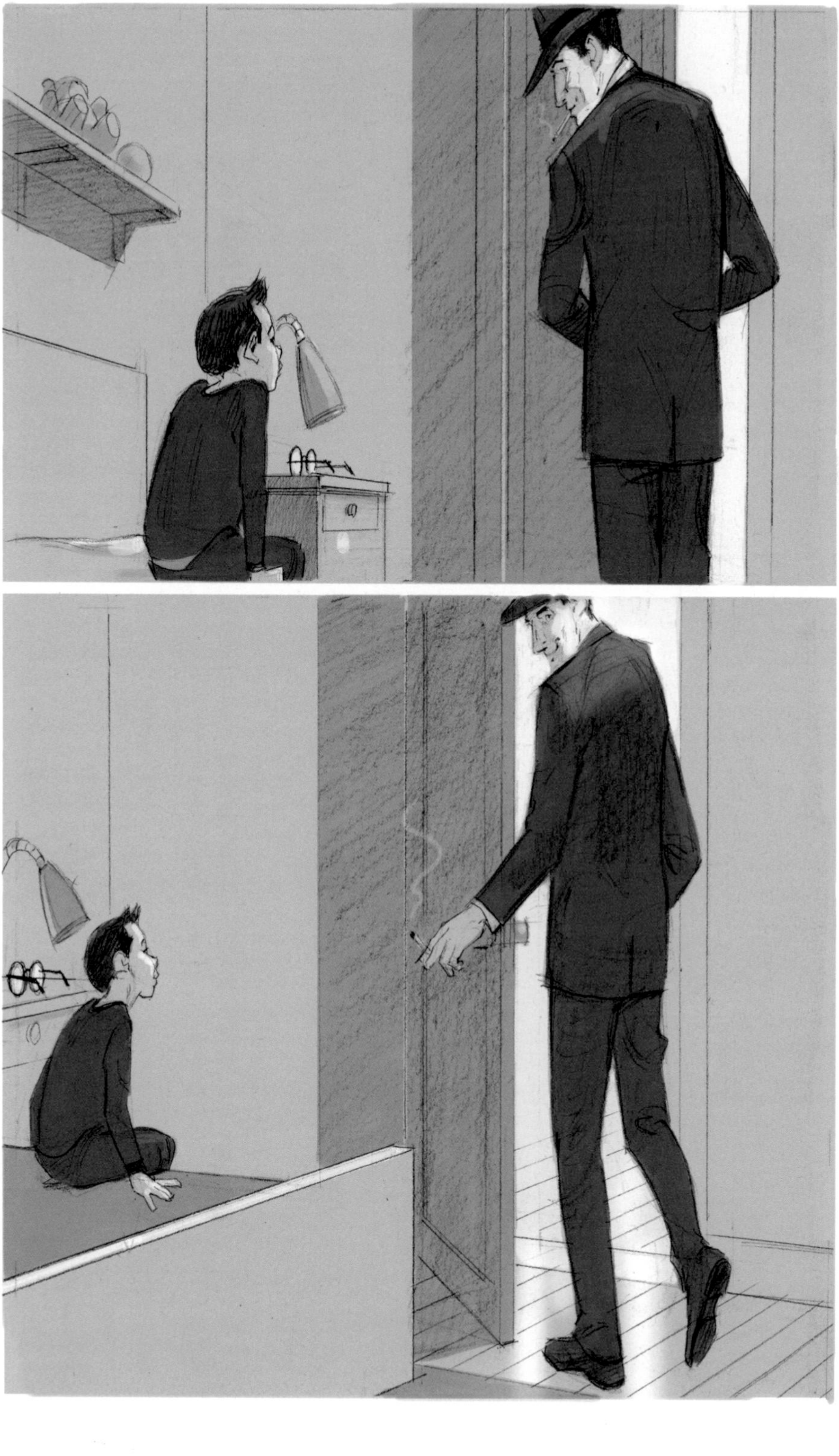

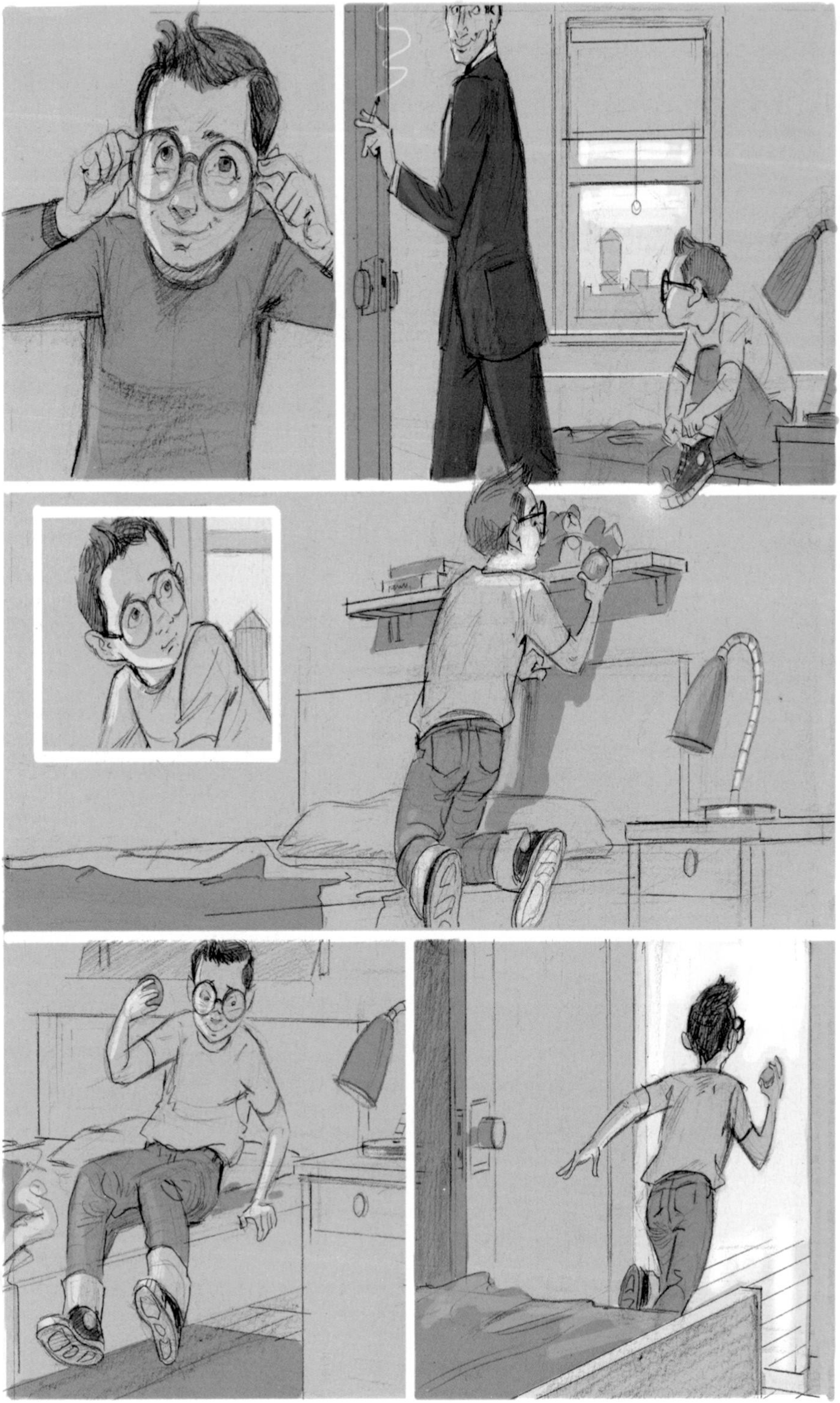

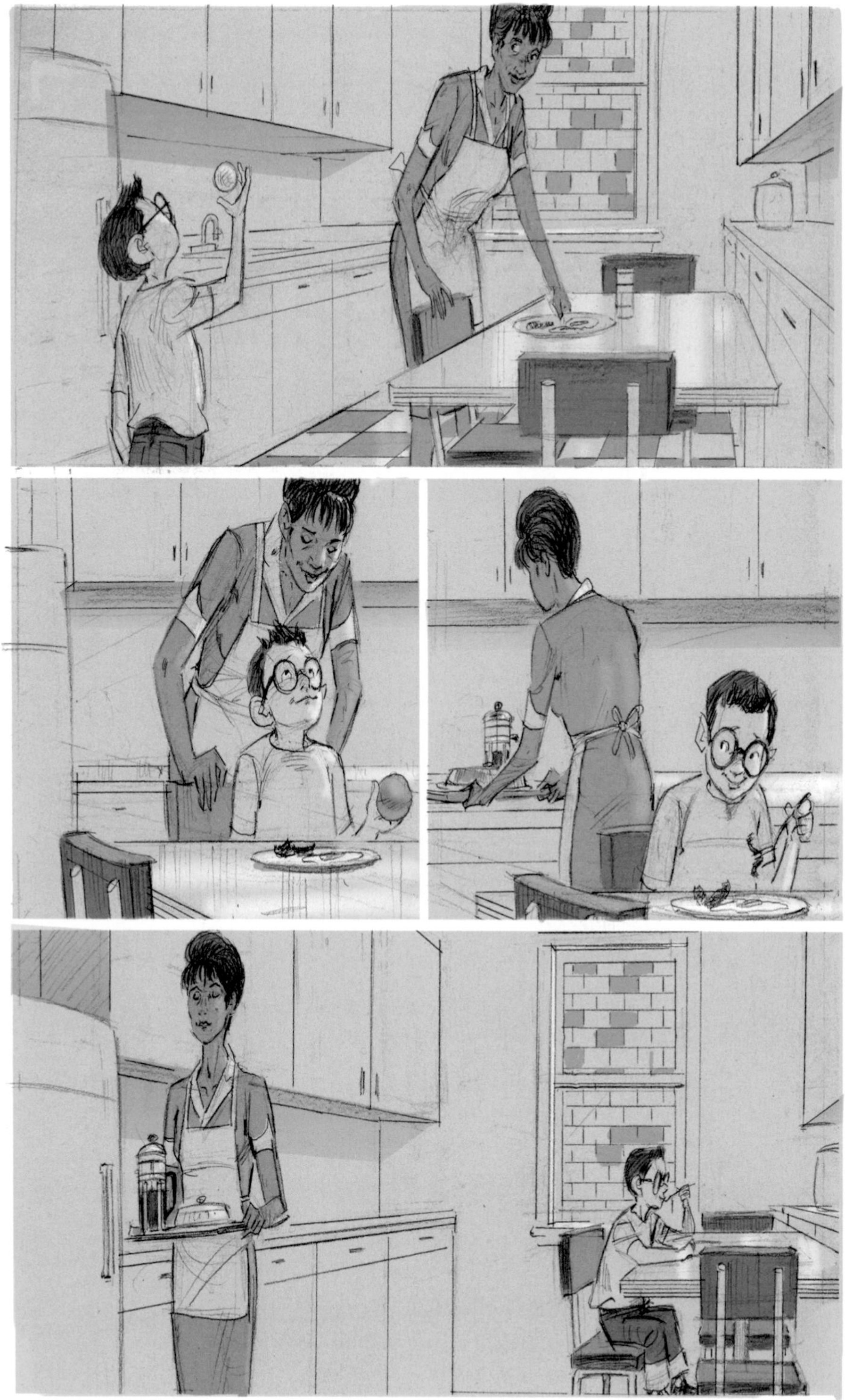

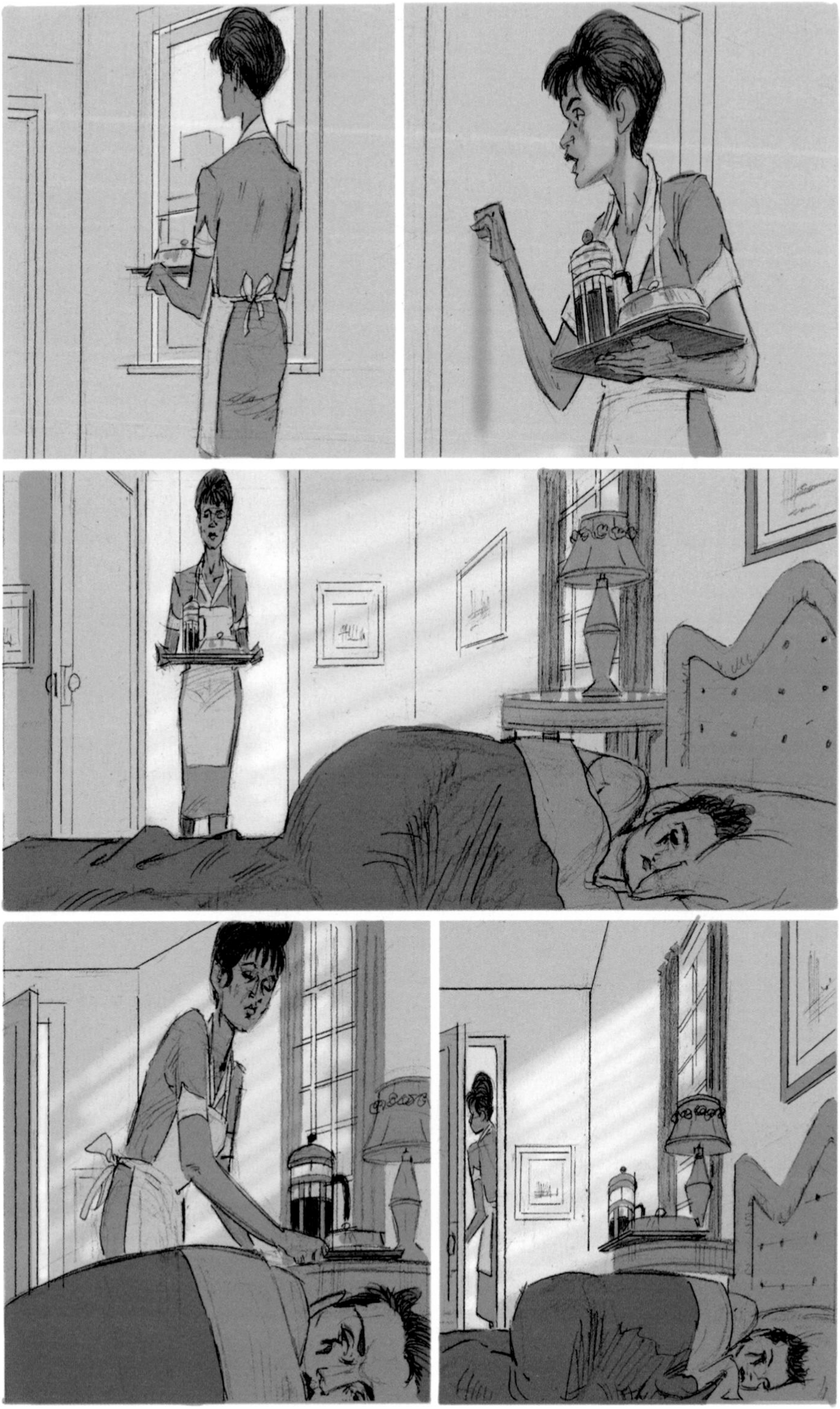

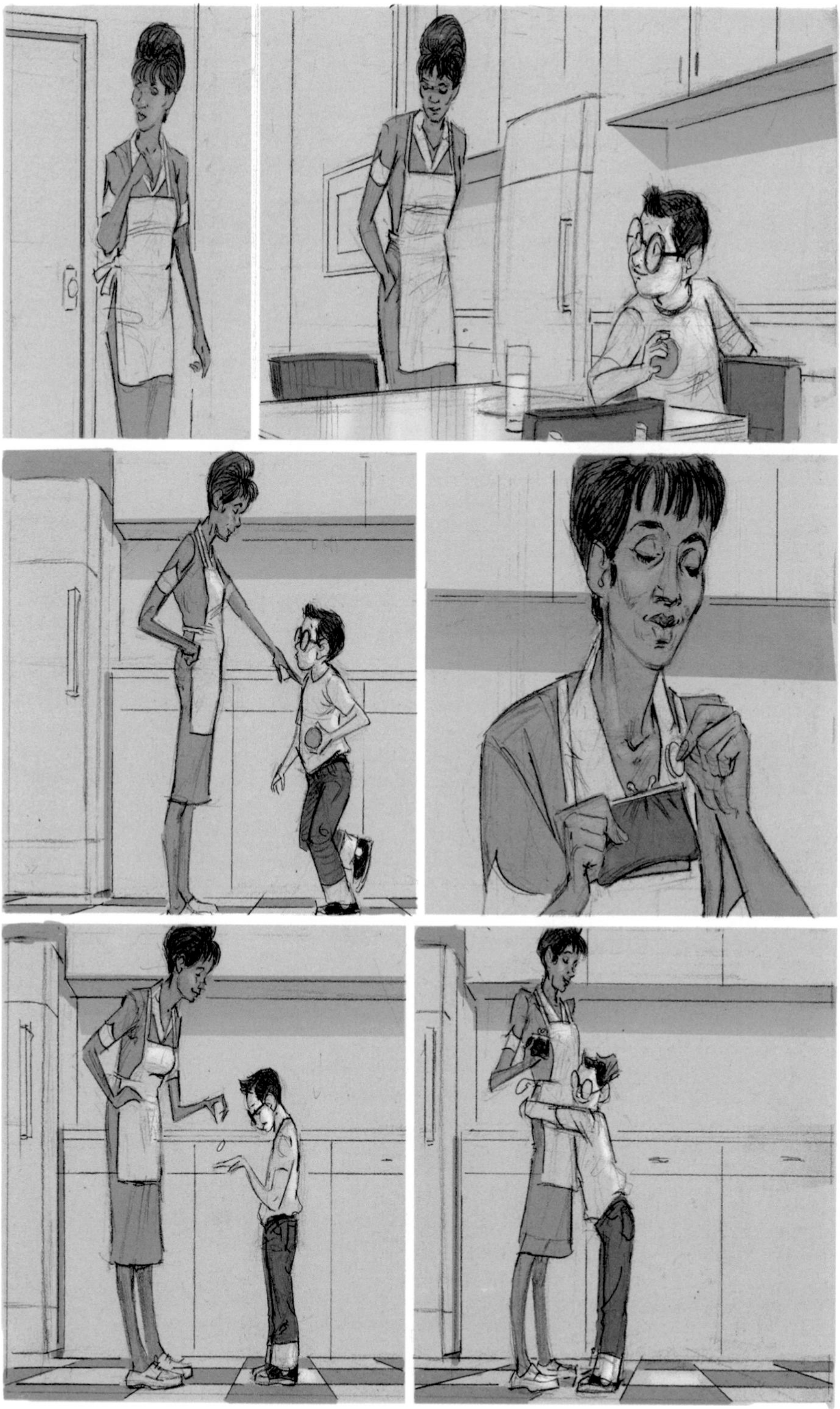

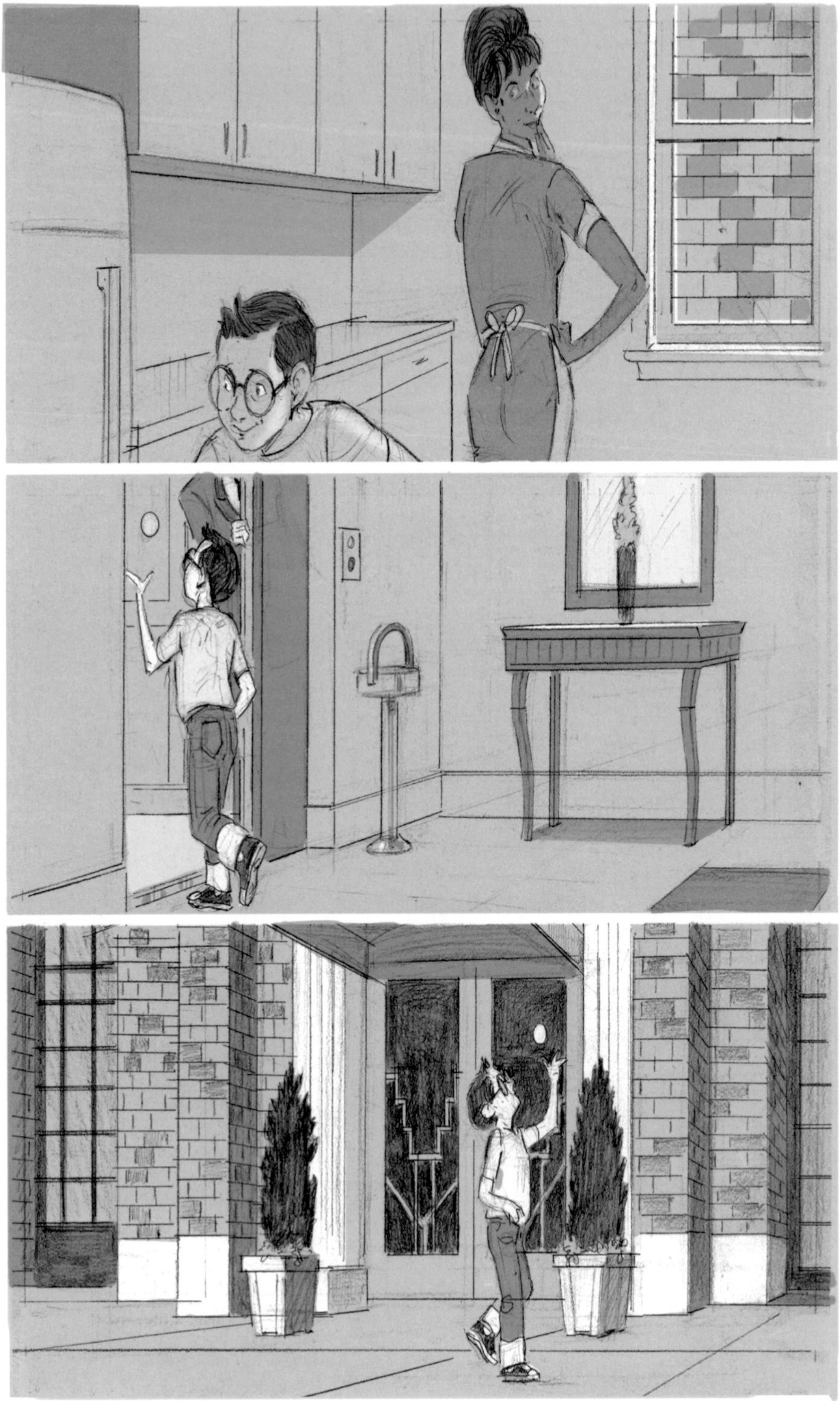

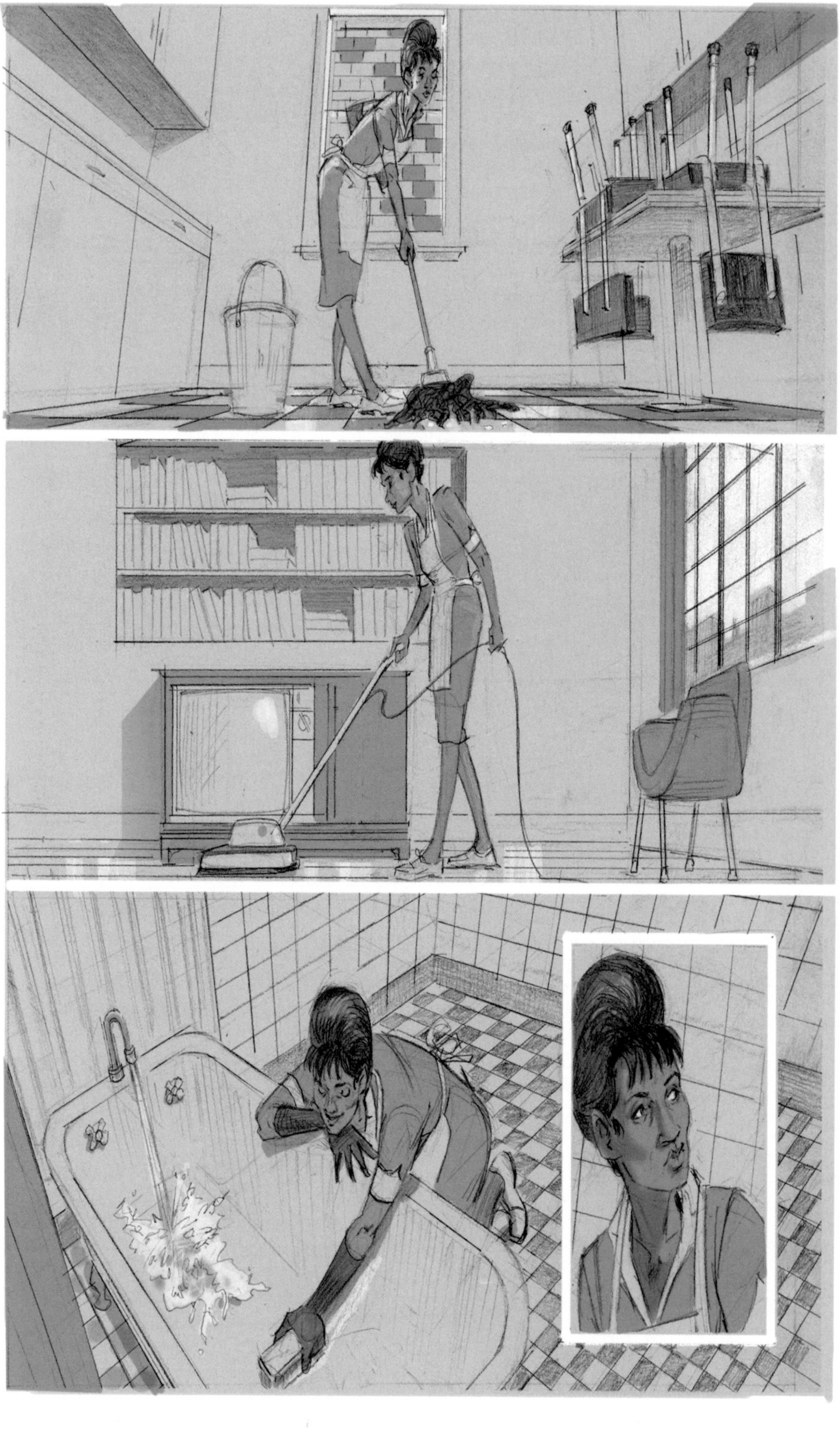

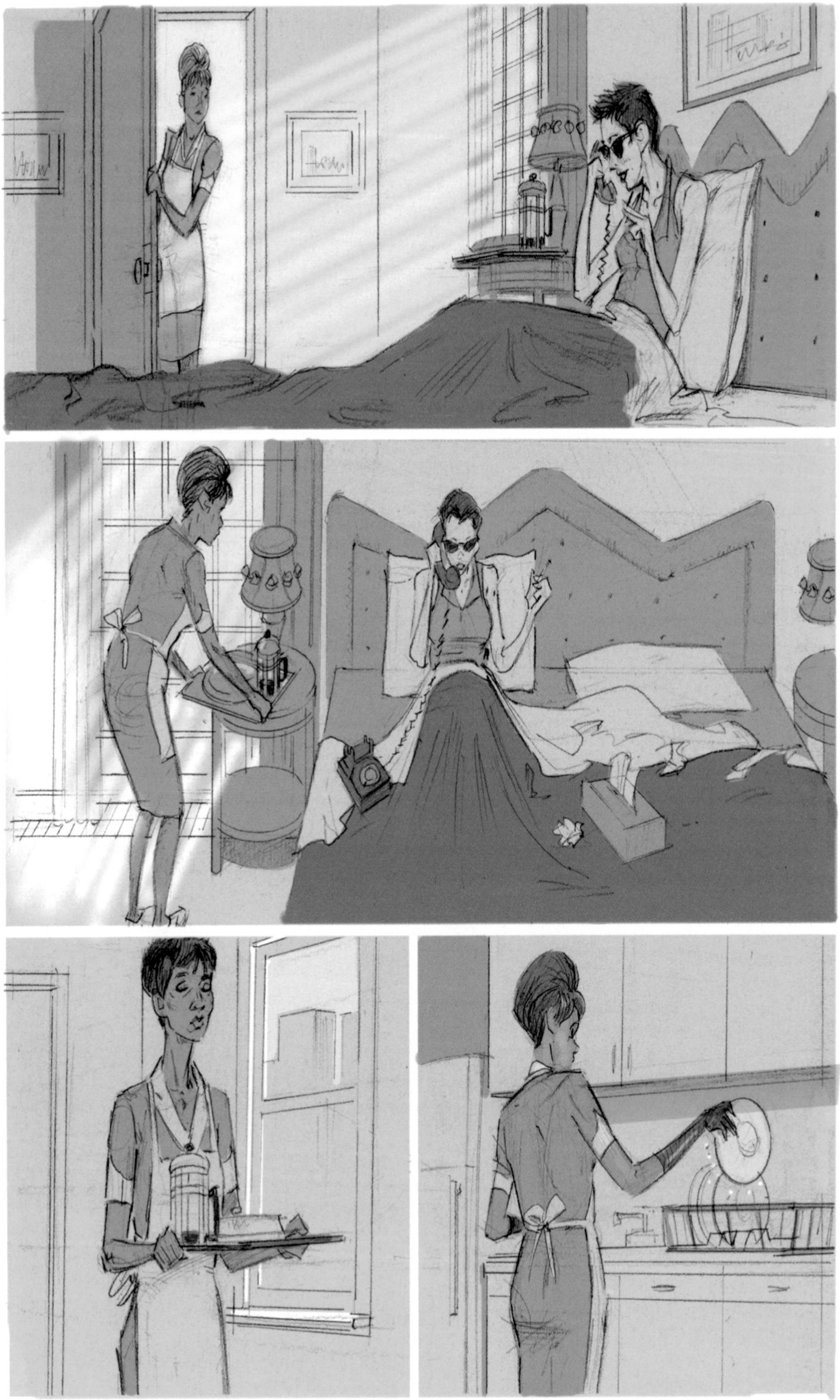

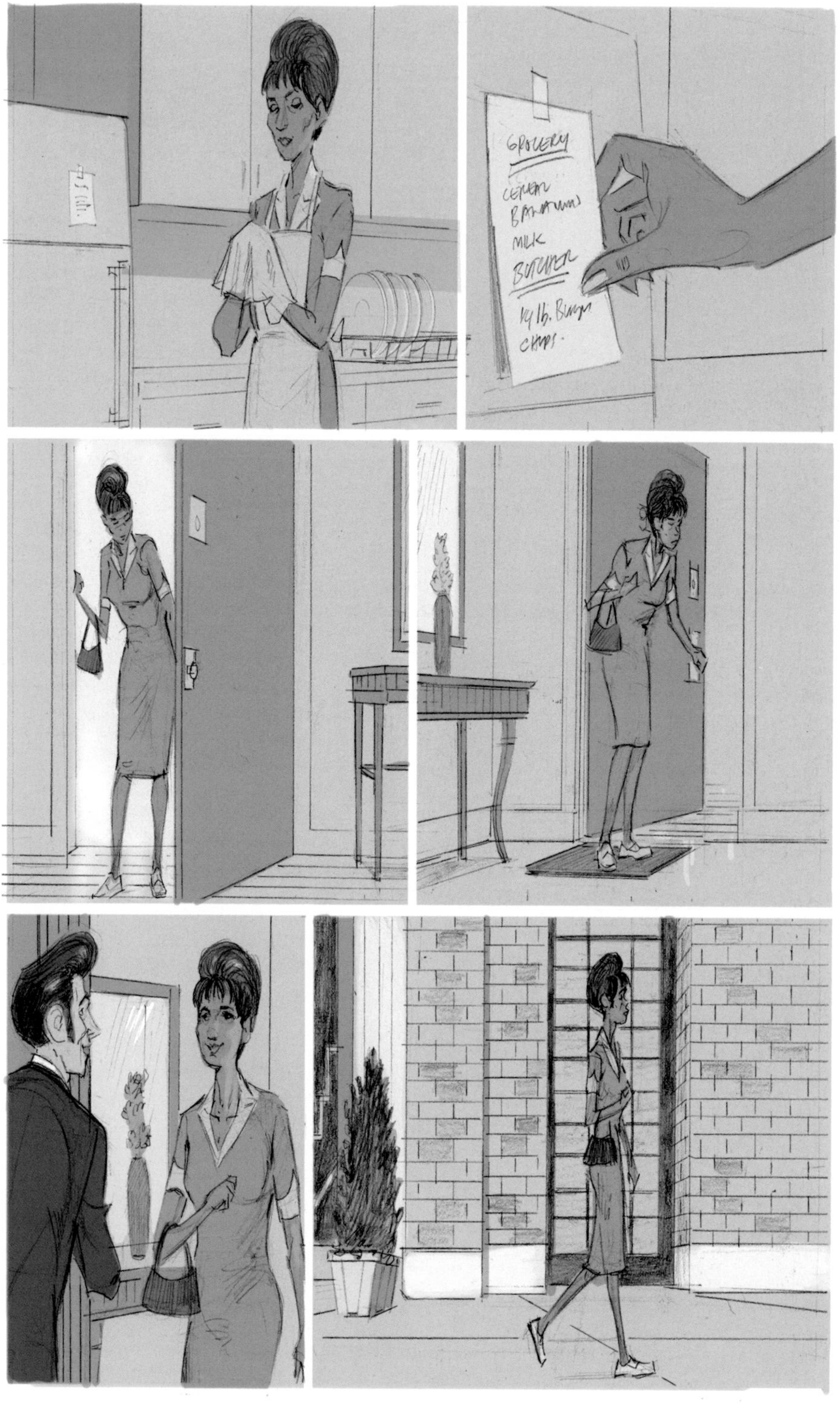
GROCERY
CEREAL
MILK
BUTCHER
CHOPS

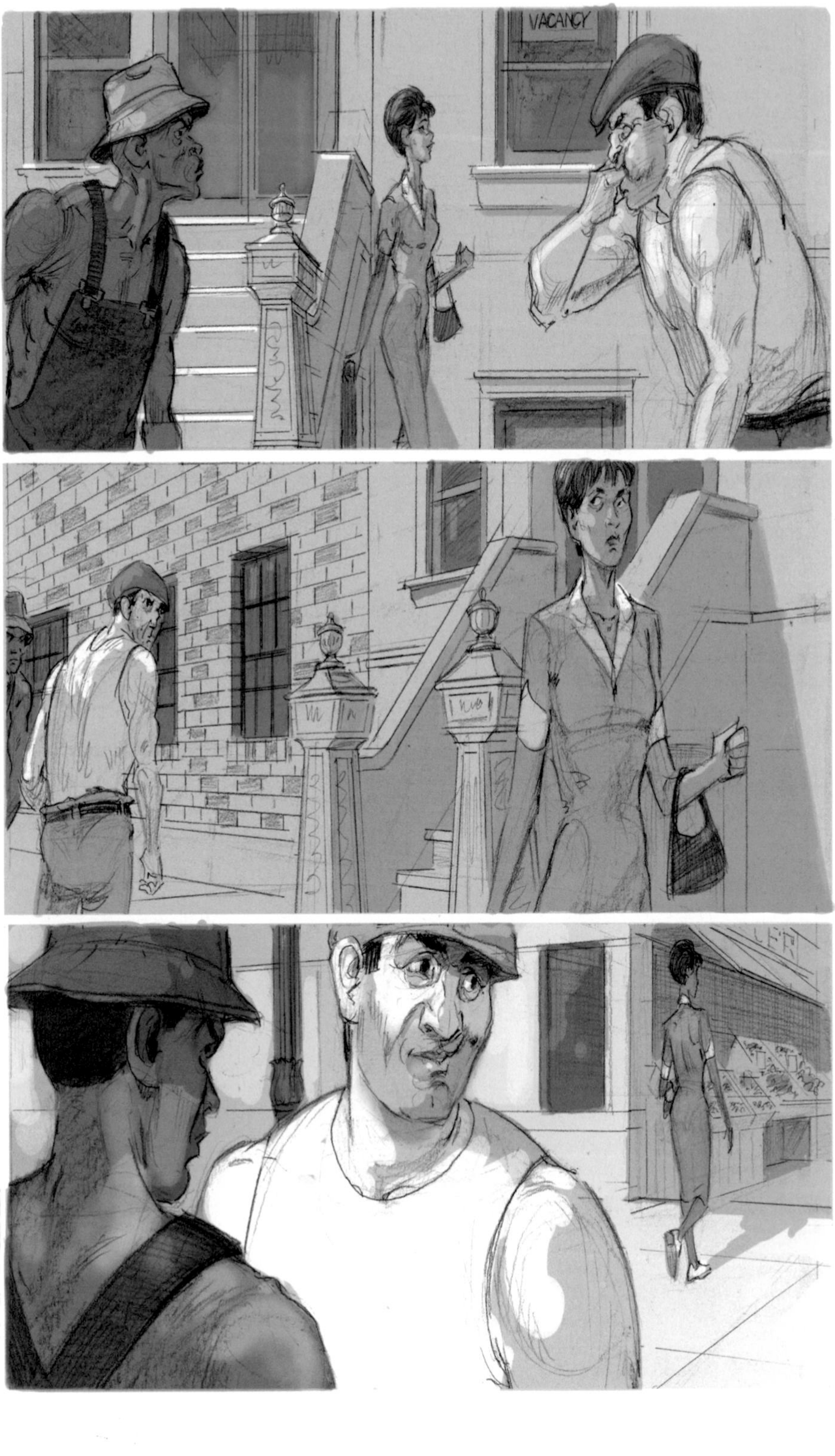
VACANCY

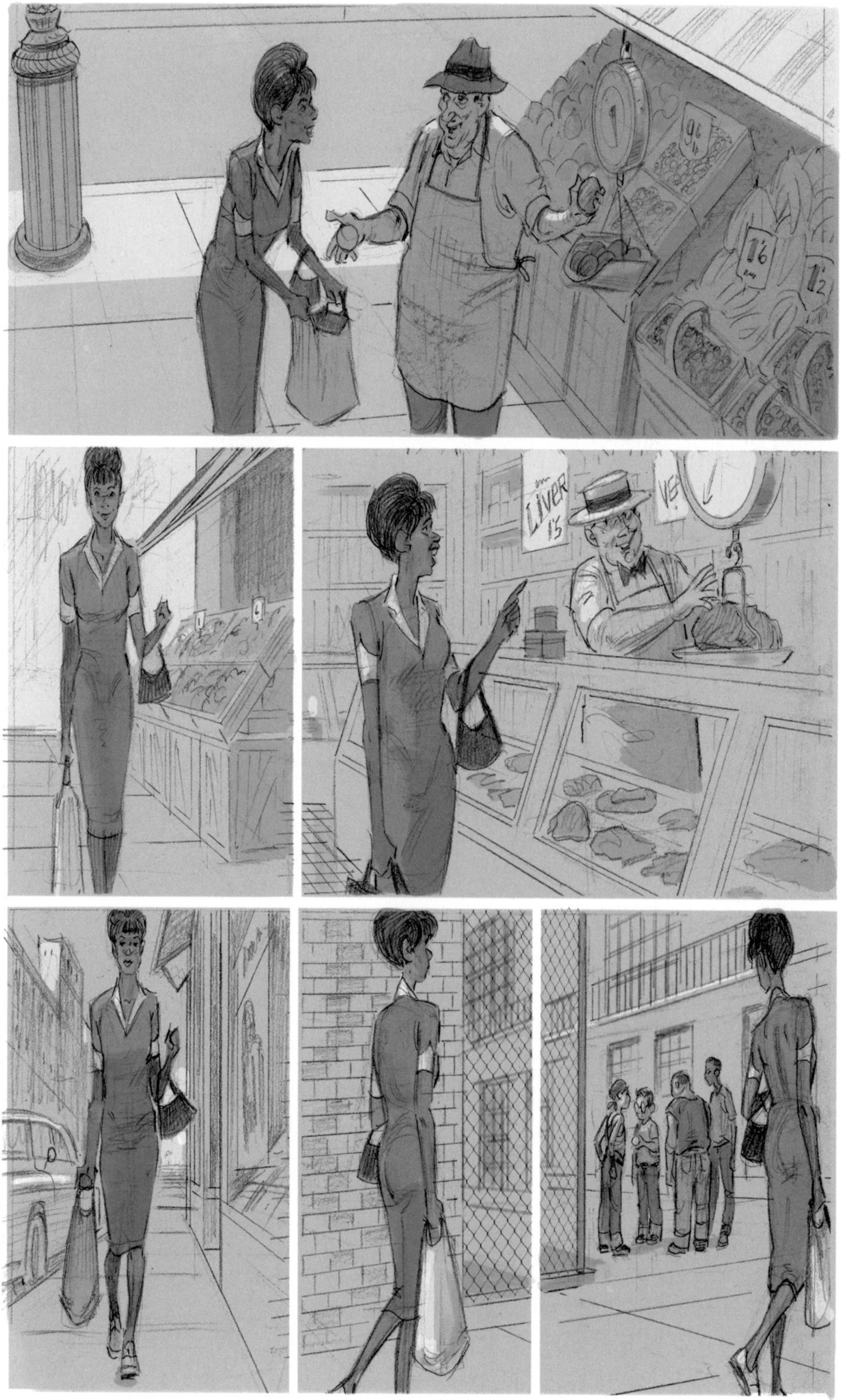
LIVER

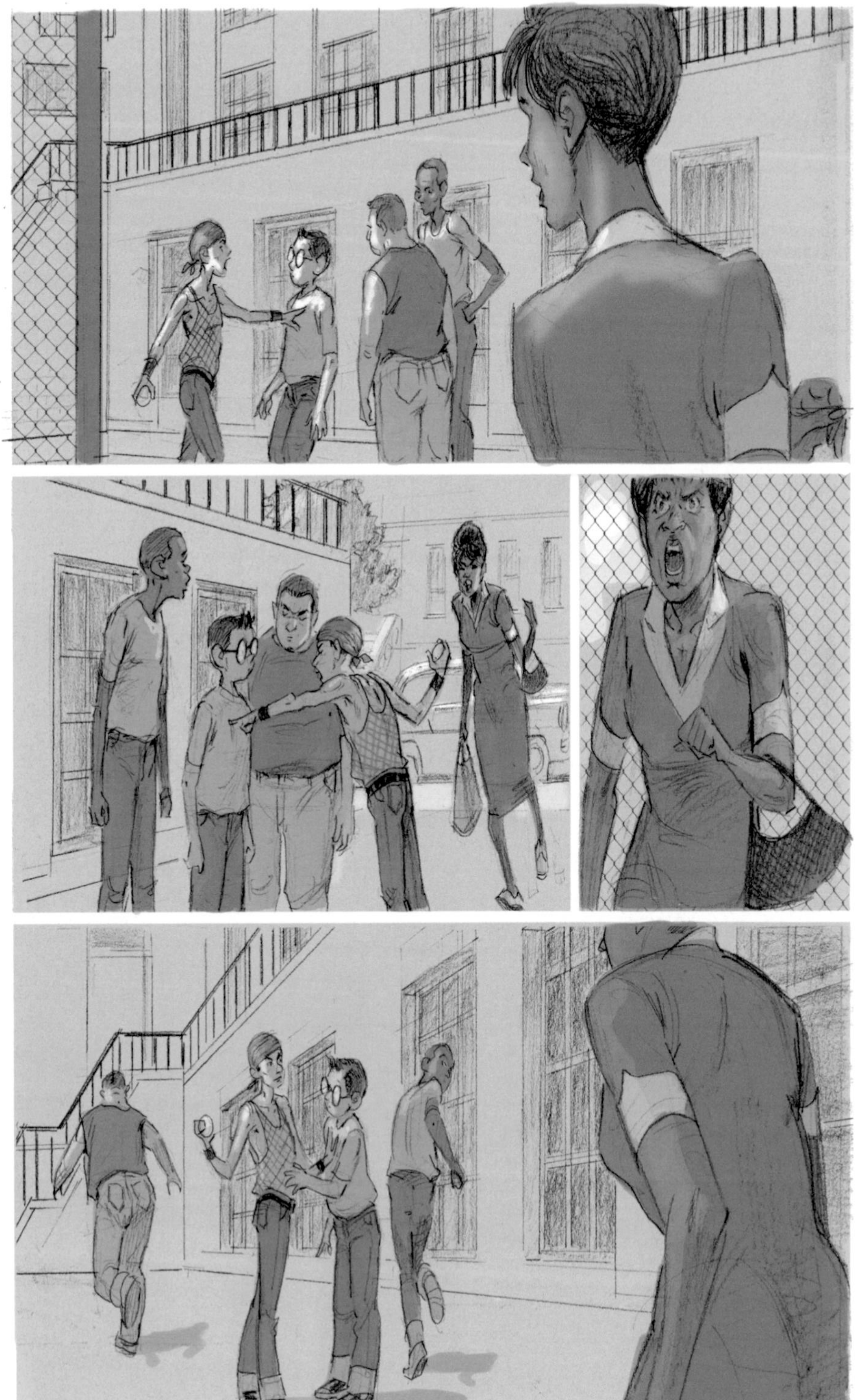

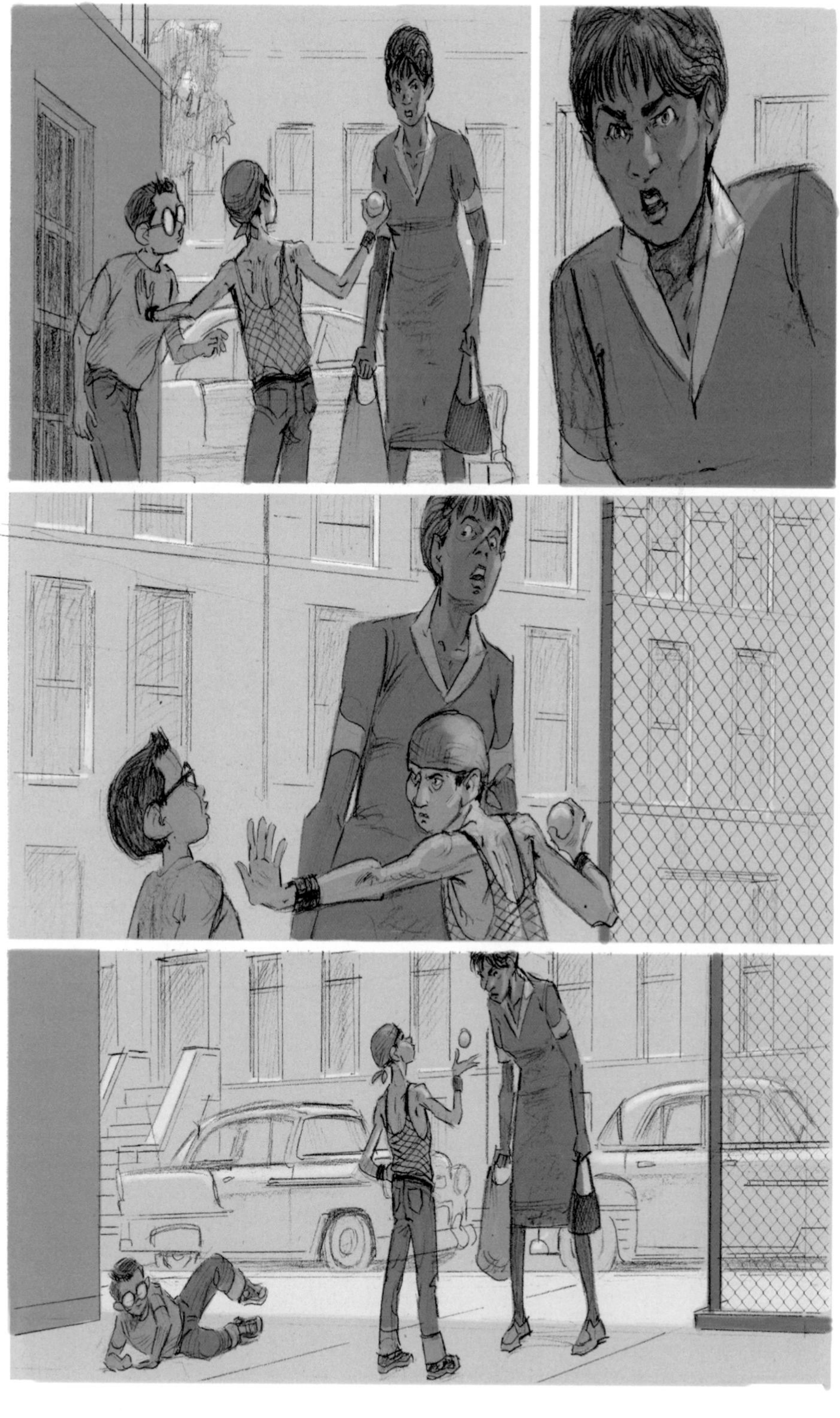

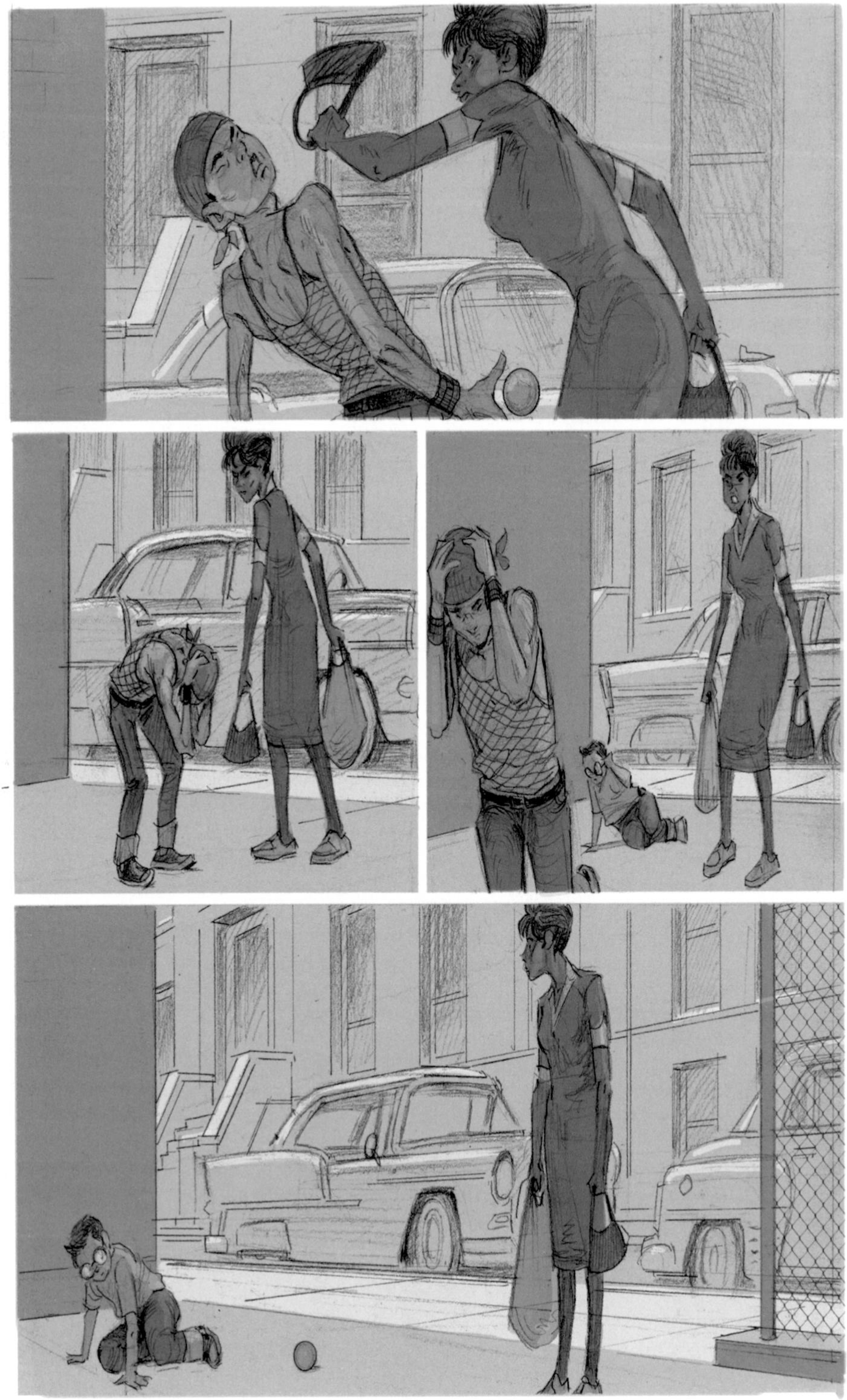

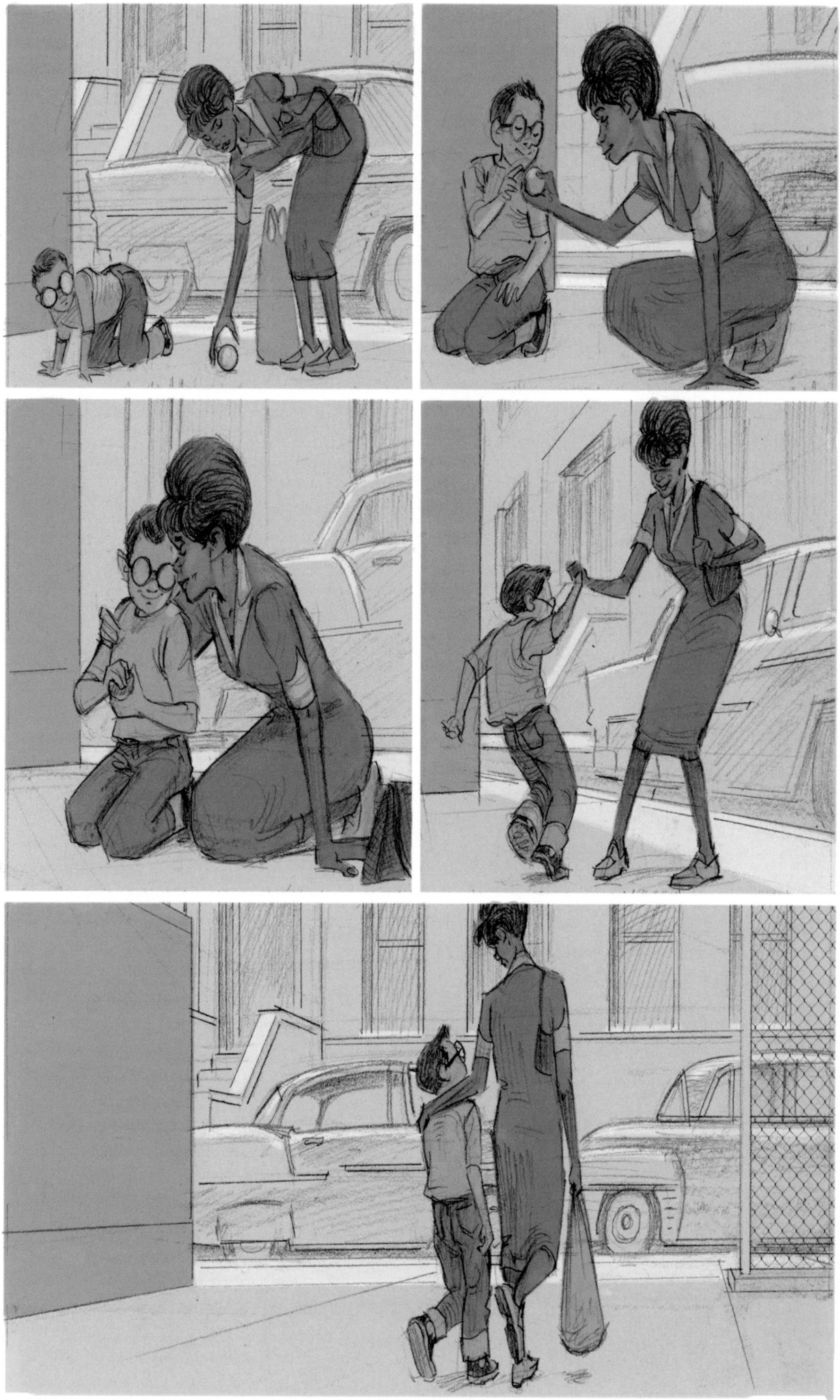

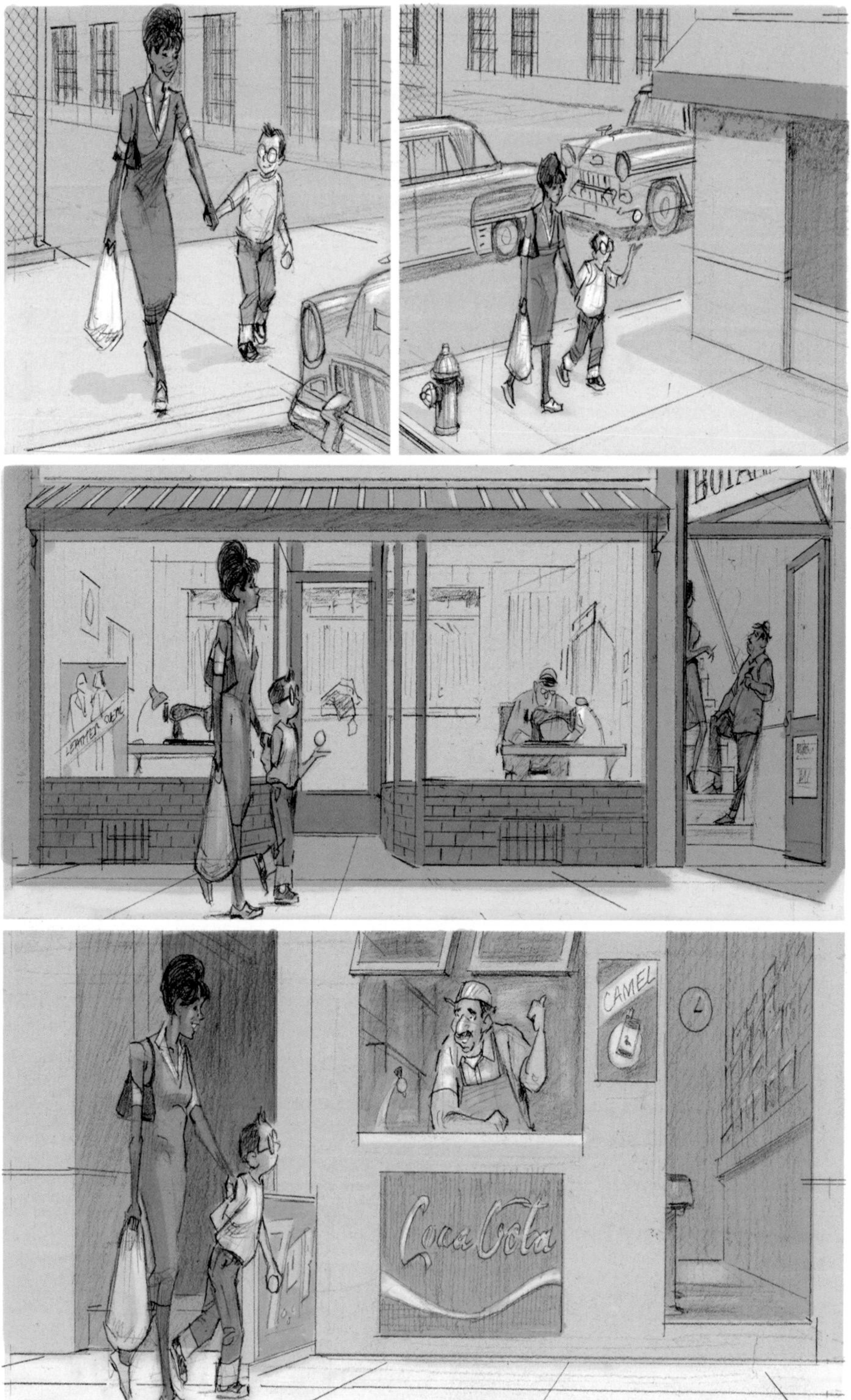
CAMEL
Coca-Cola

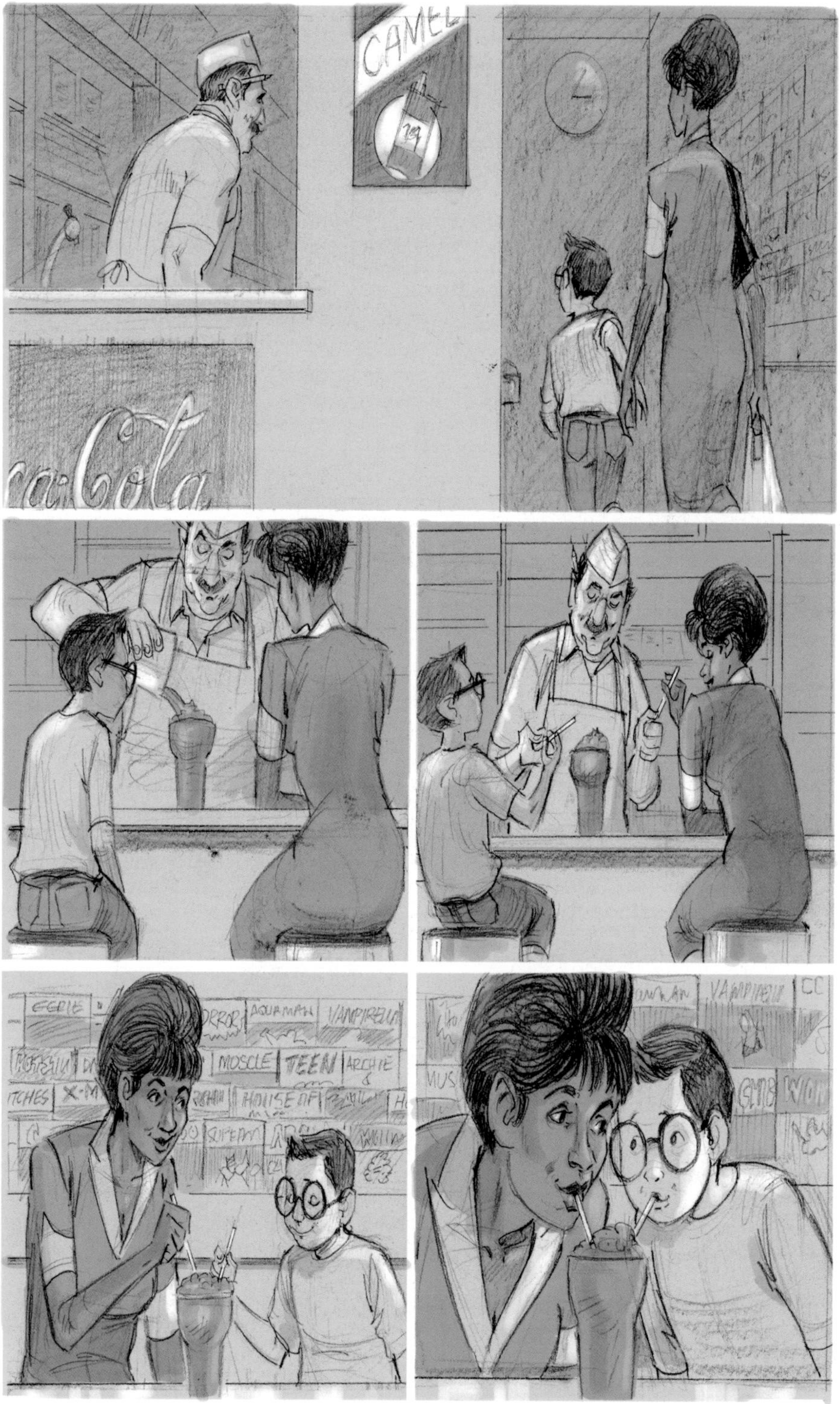
CAMEL
EERIE
AQUAMAN
MUSCLE
TEEN
ARCHIE

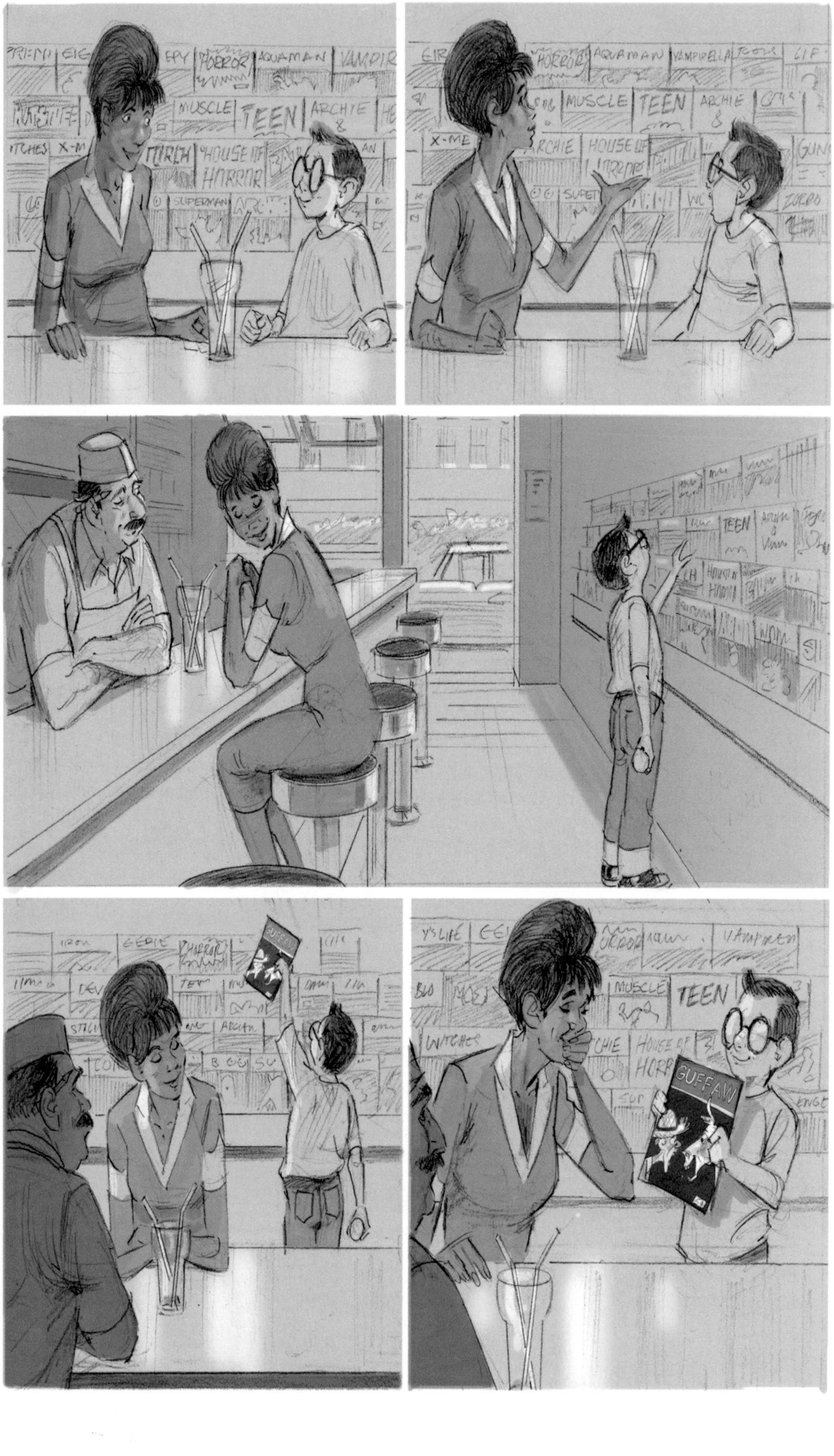

AQUAMAN
HORROR
MUSCLE
TEEN
ARCHIE
HOUSE OF HORROR
SUPERMAN
VAMPIRELLA
ZORRO
GUFFAW

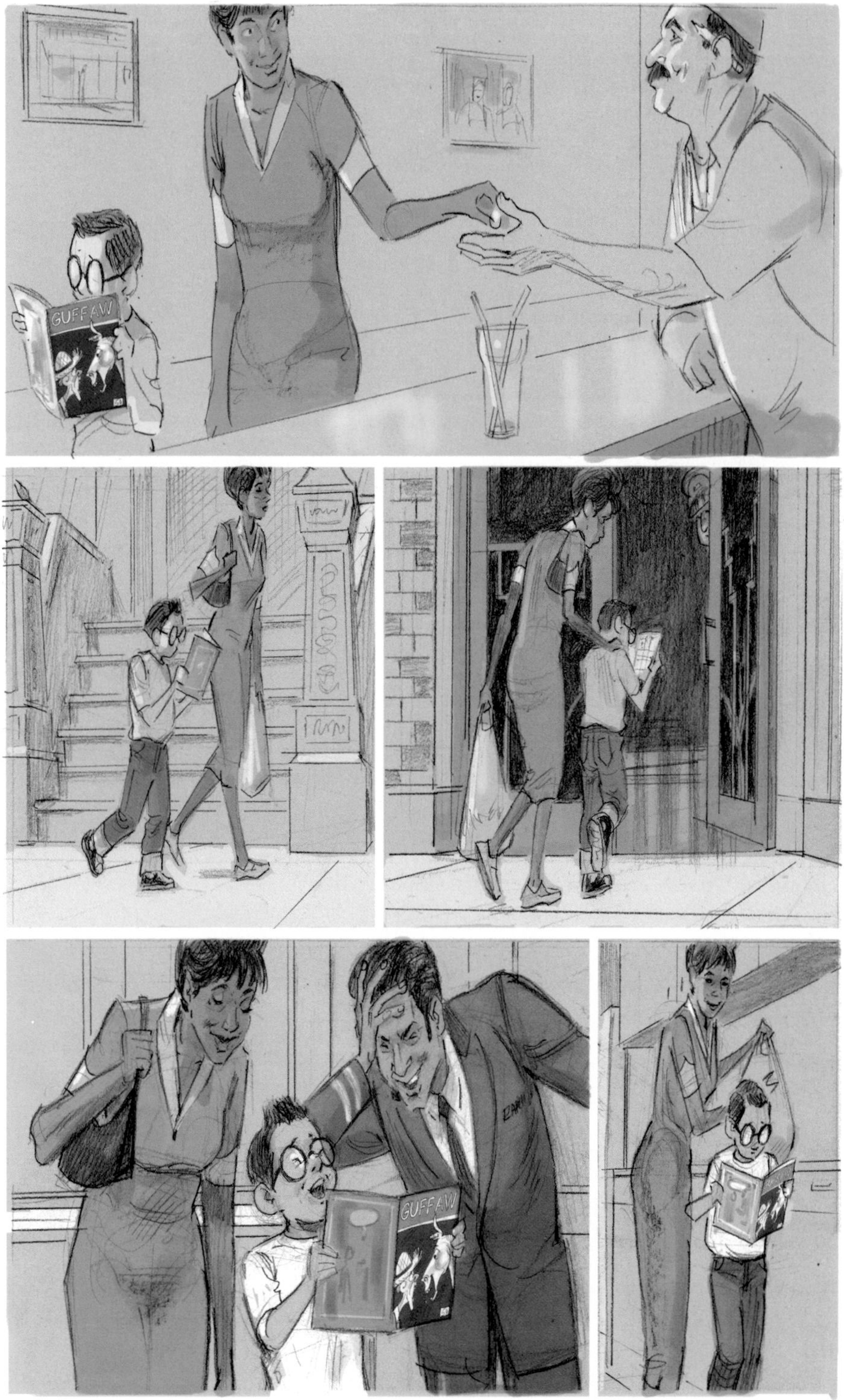
GUFFAW
GUFFAW

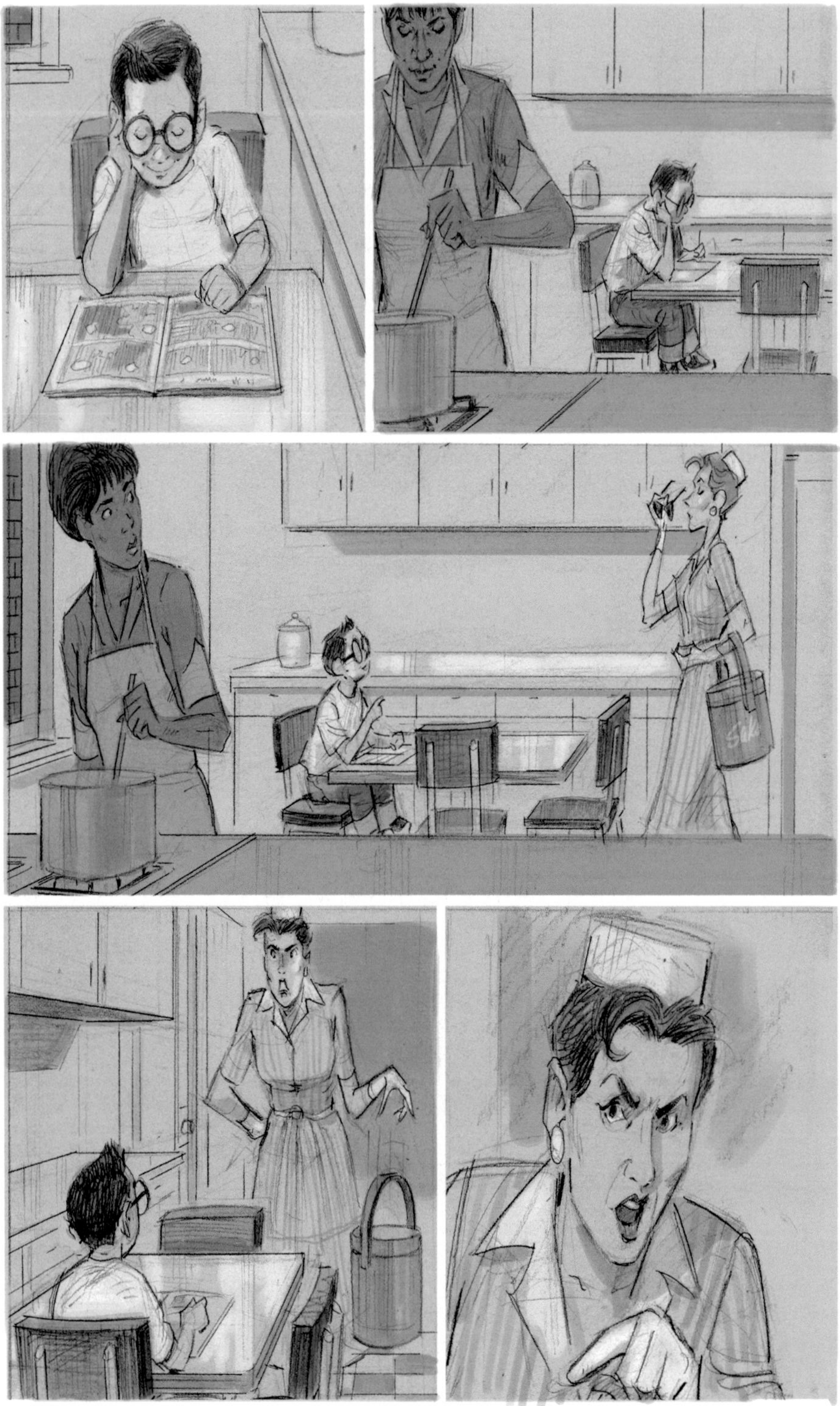

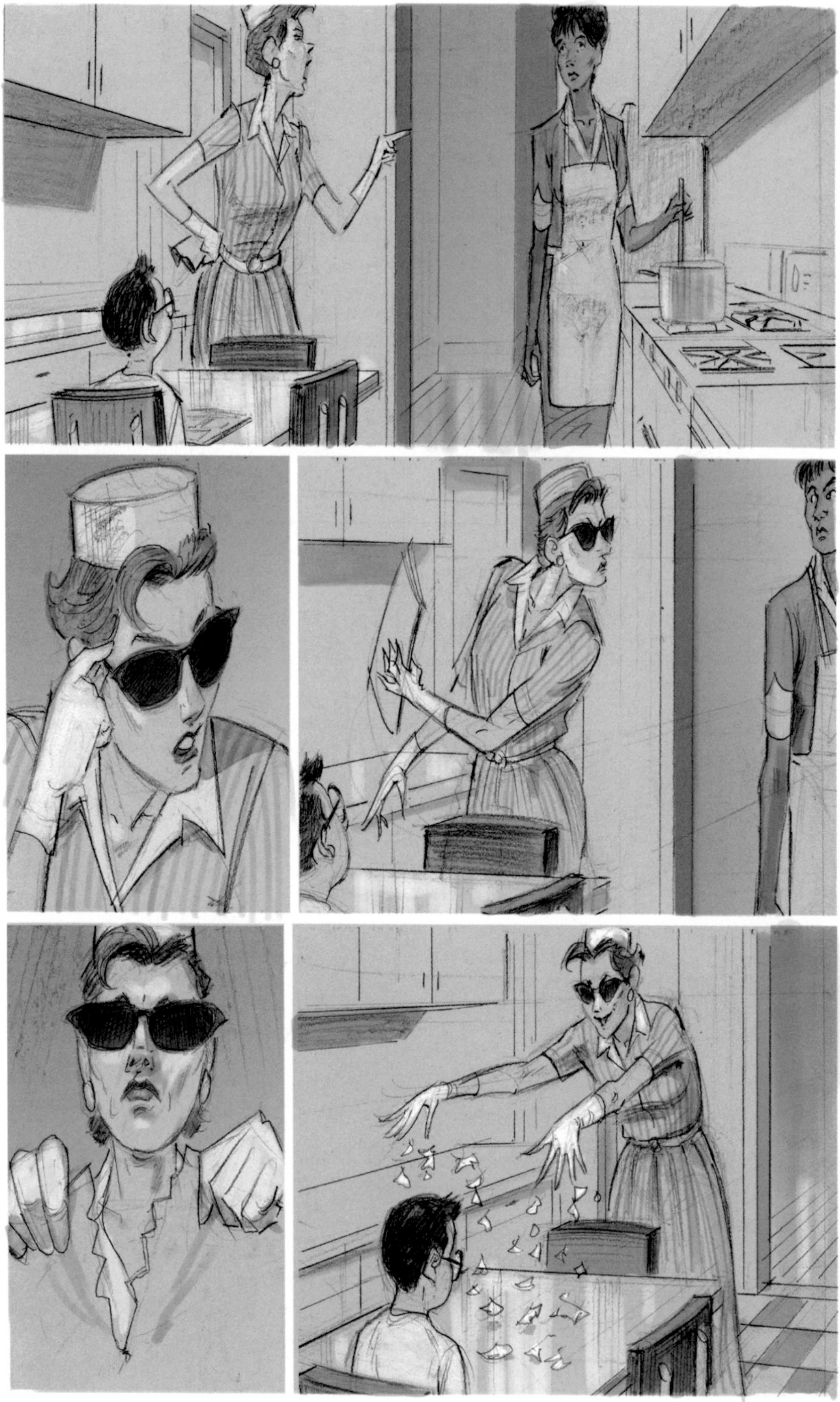

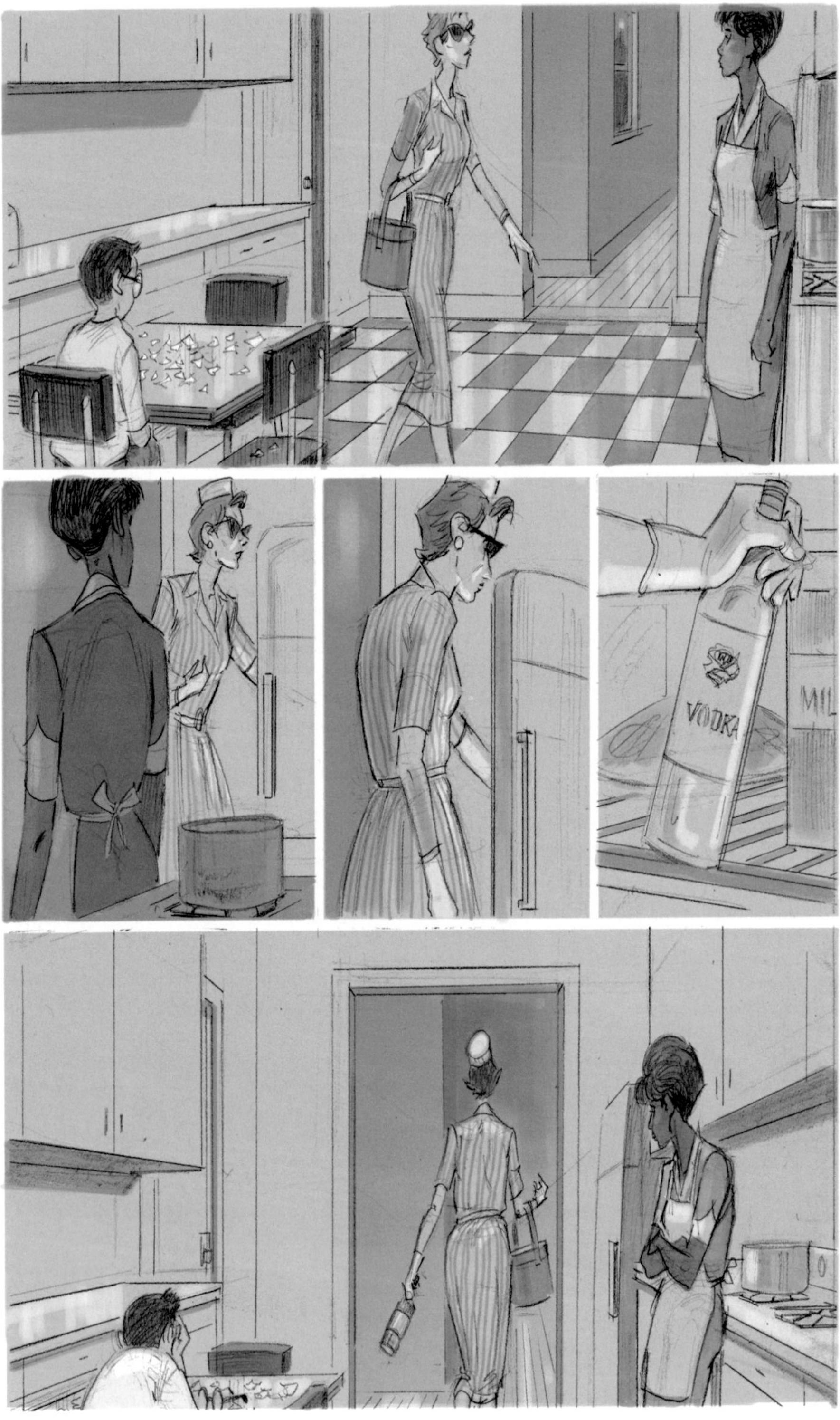
VODKA
MIL

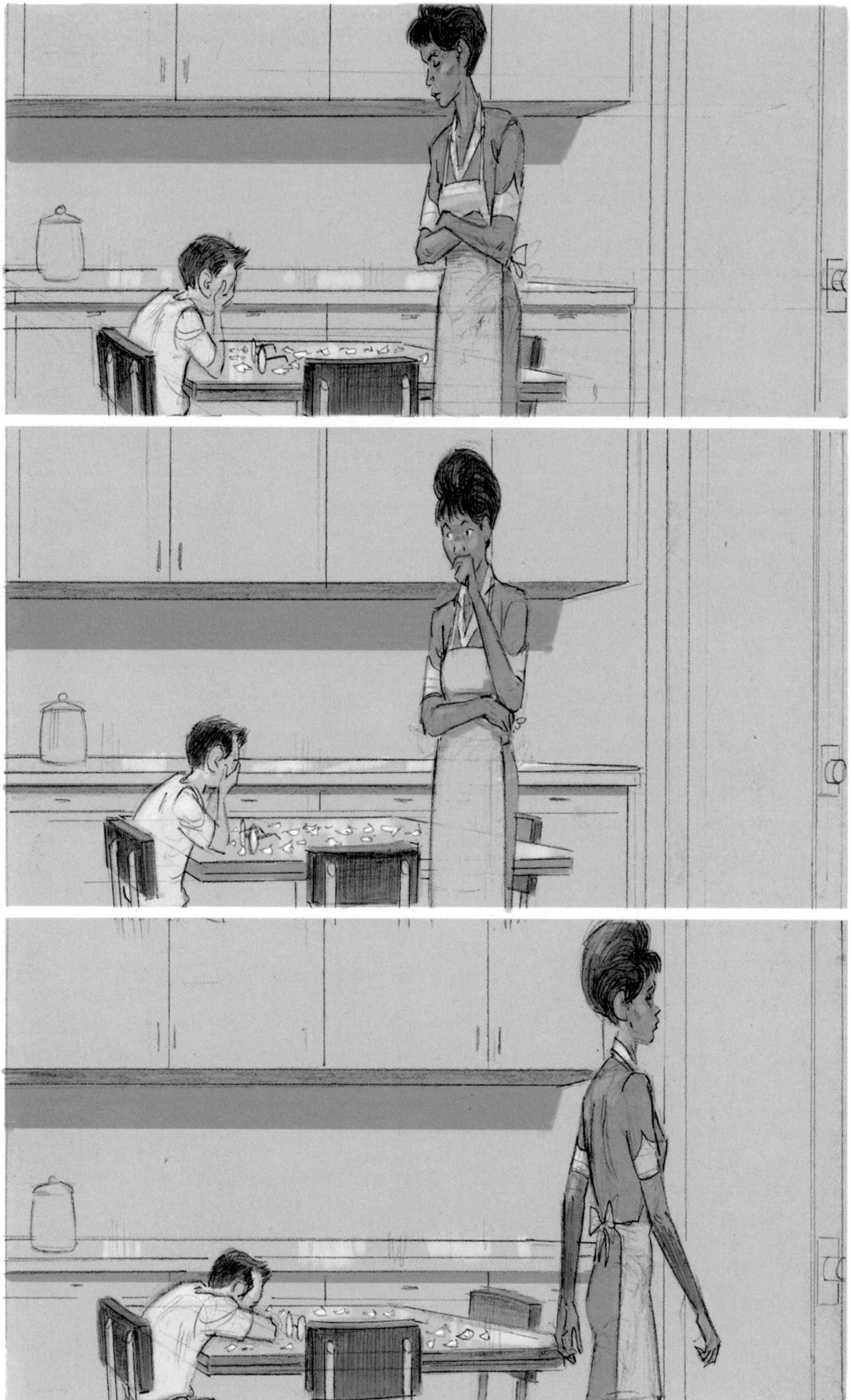

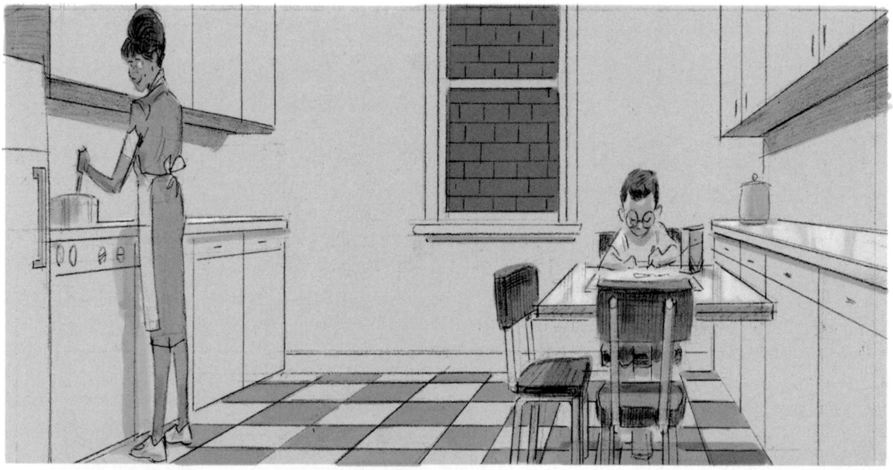

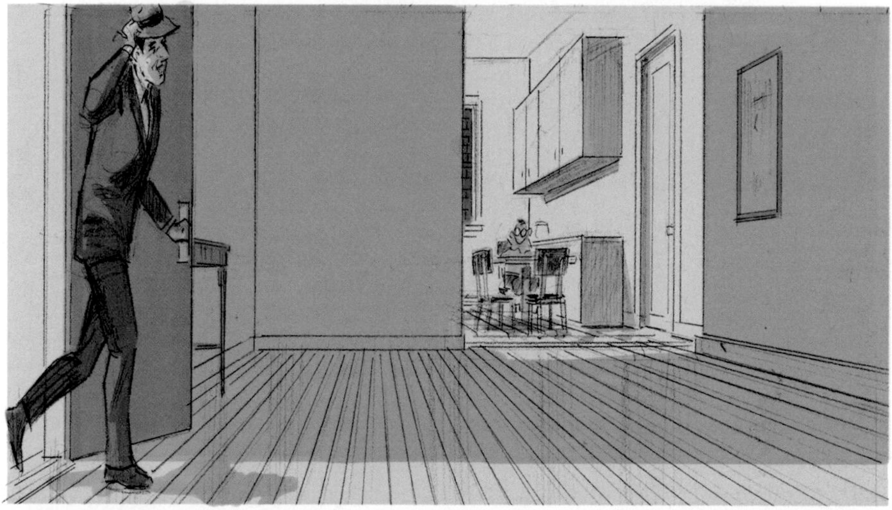

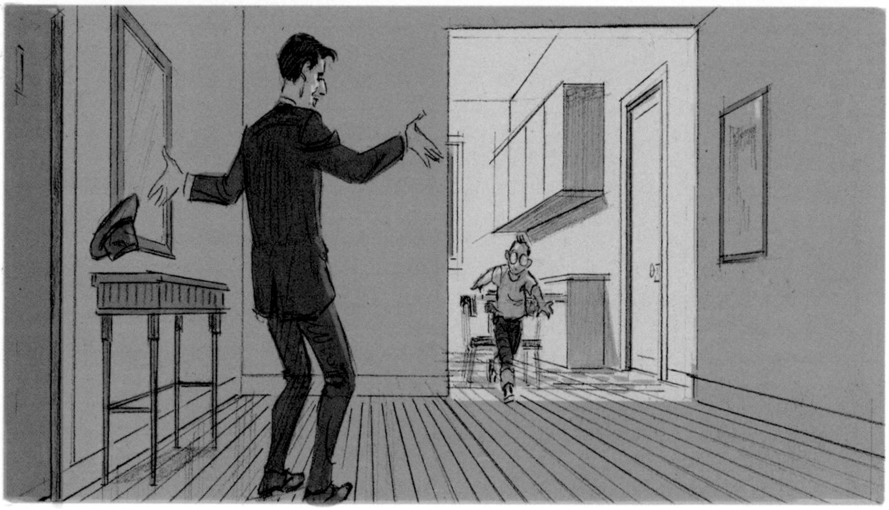

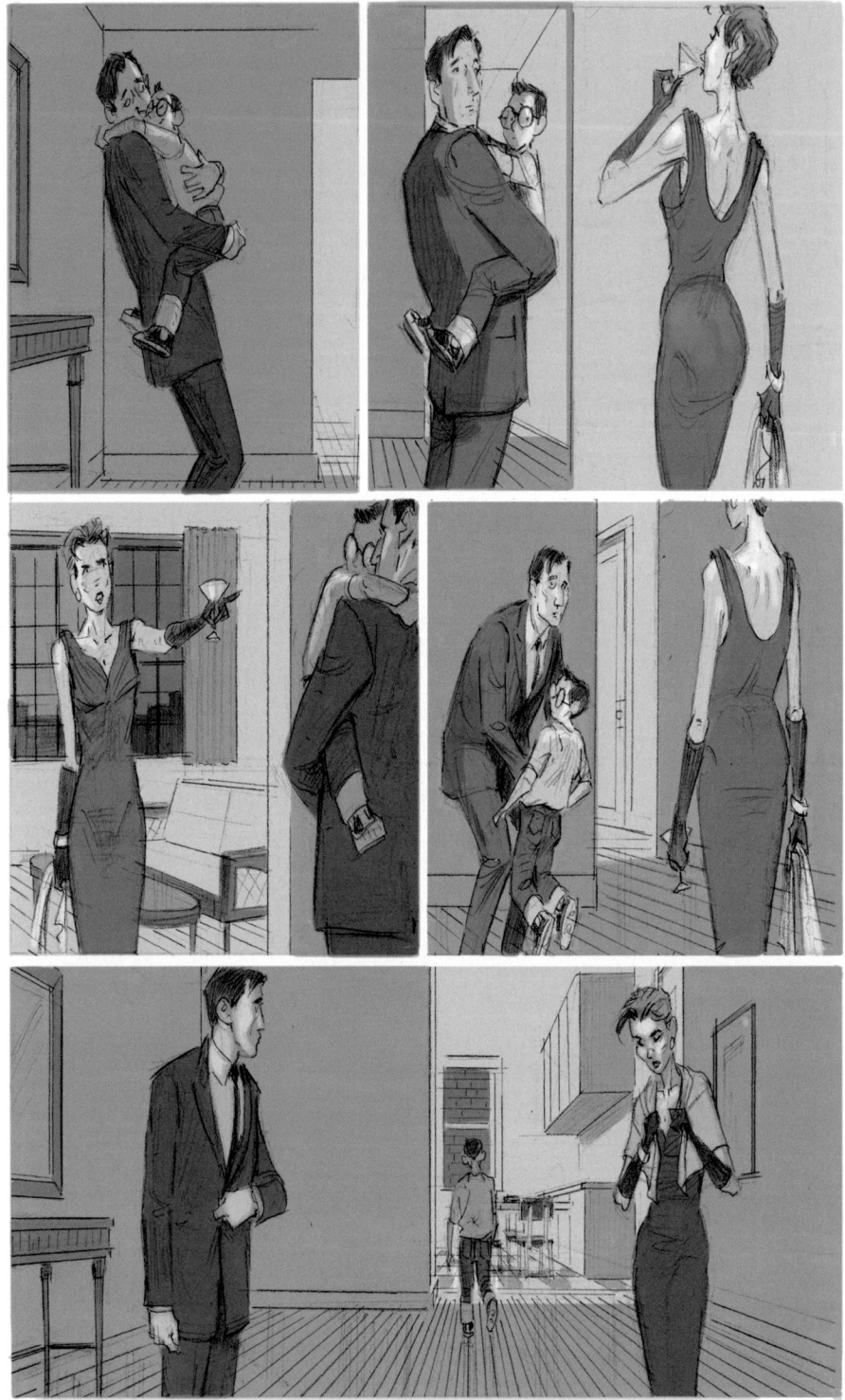

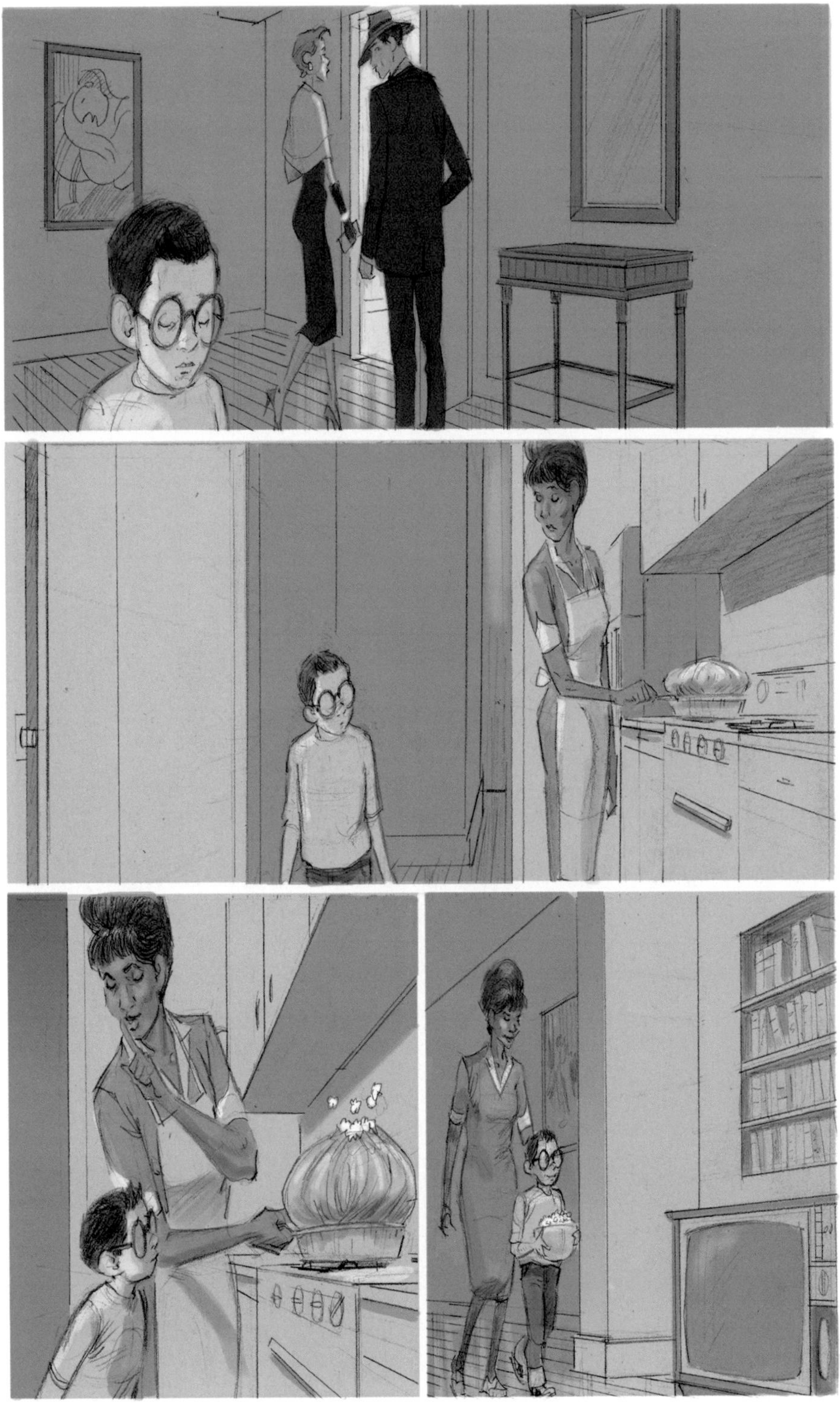

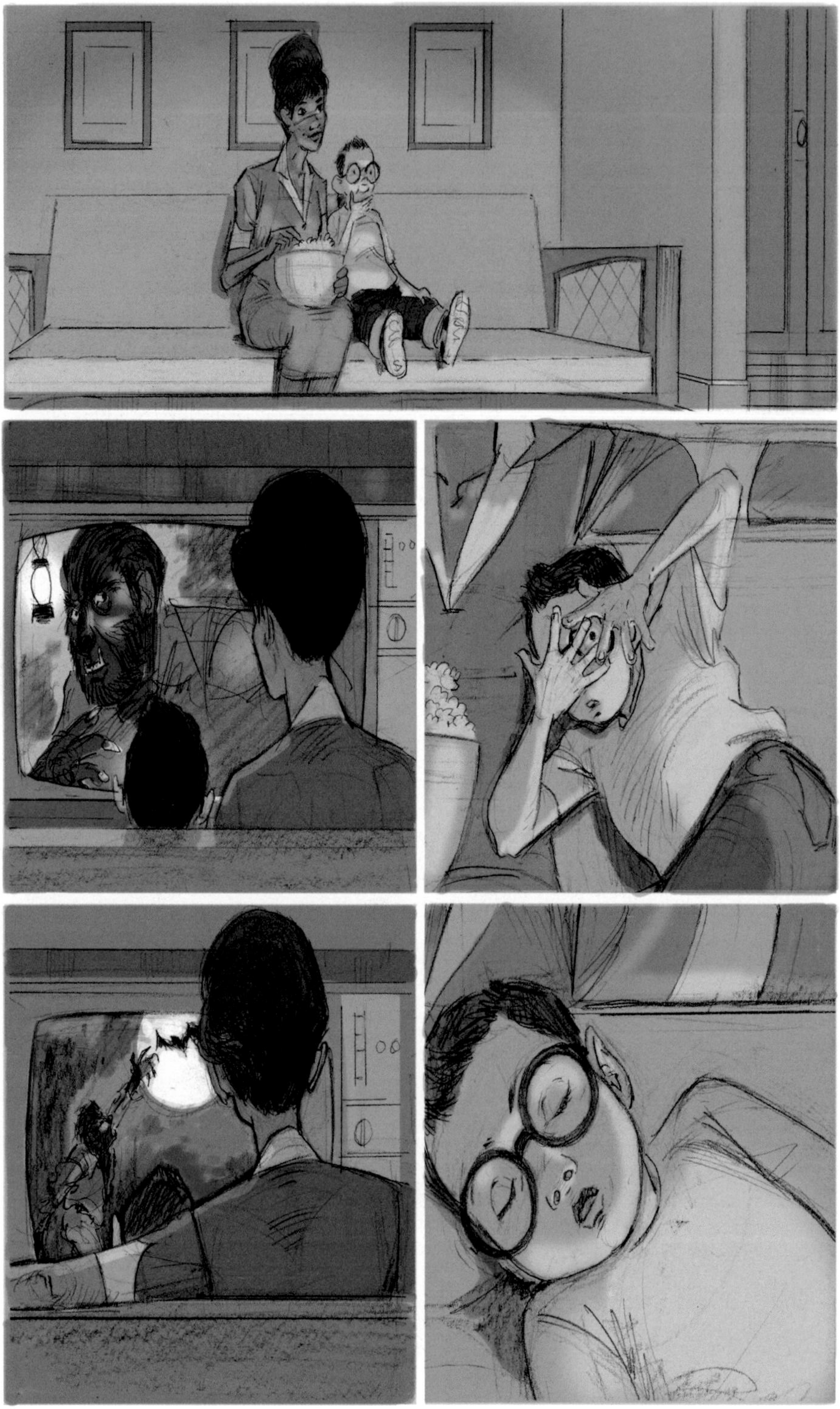

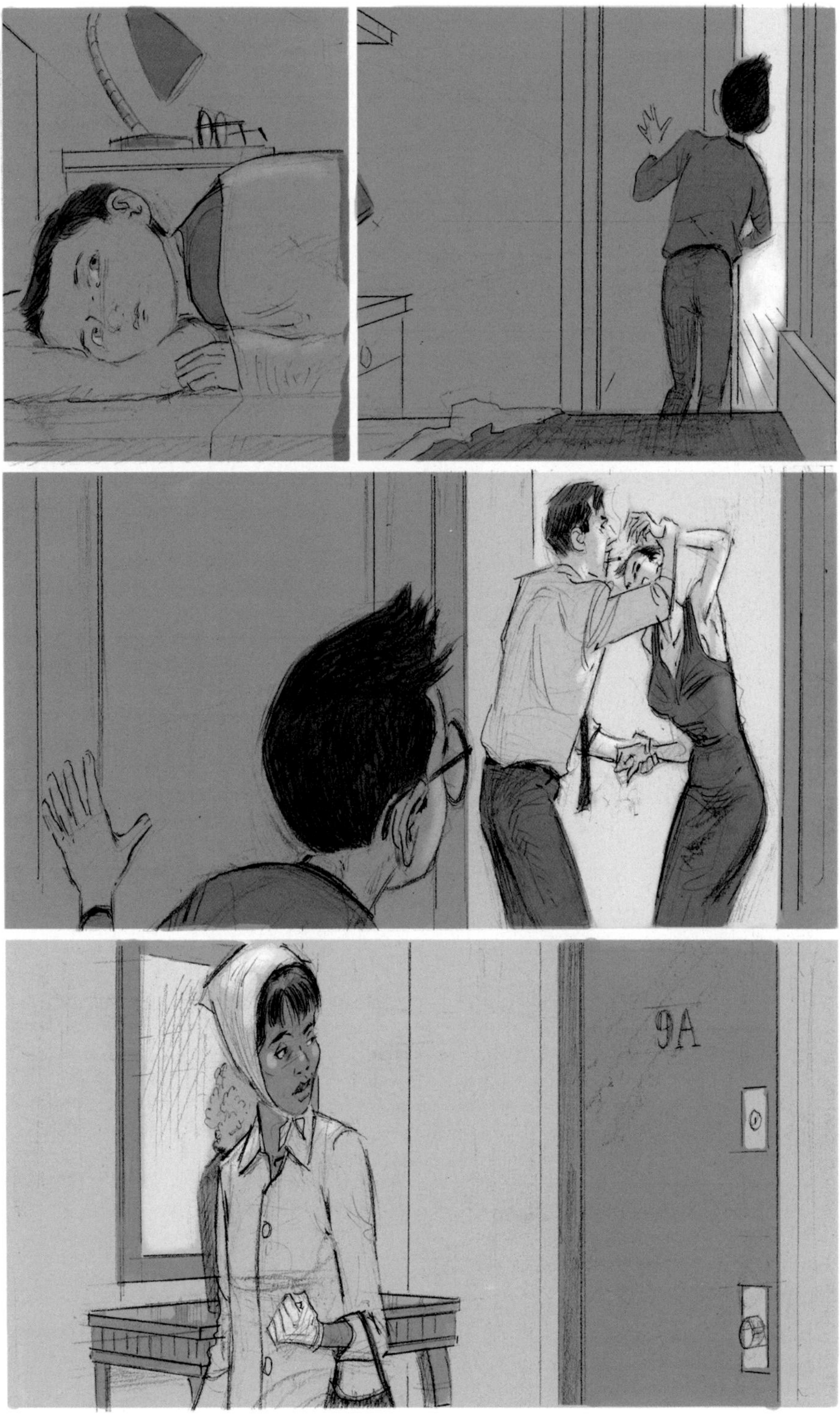
9A

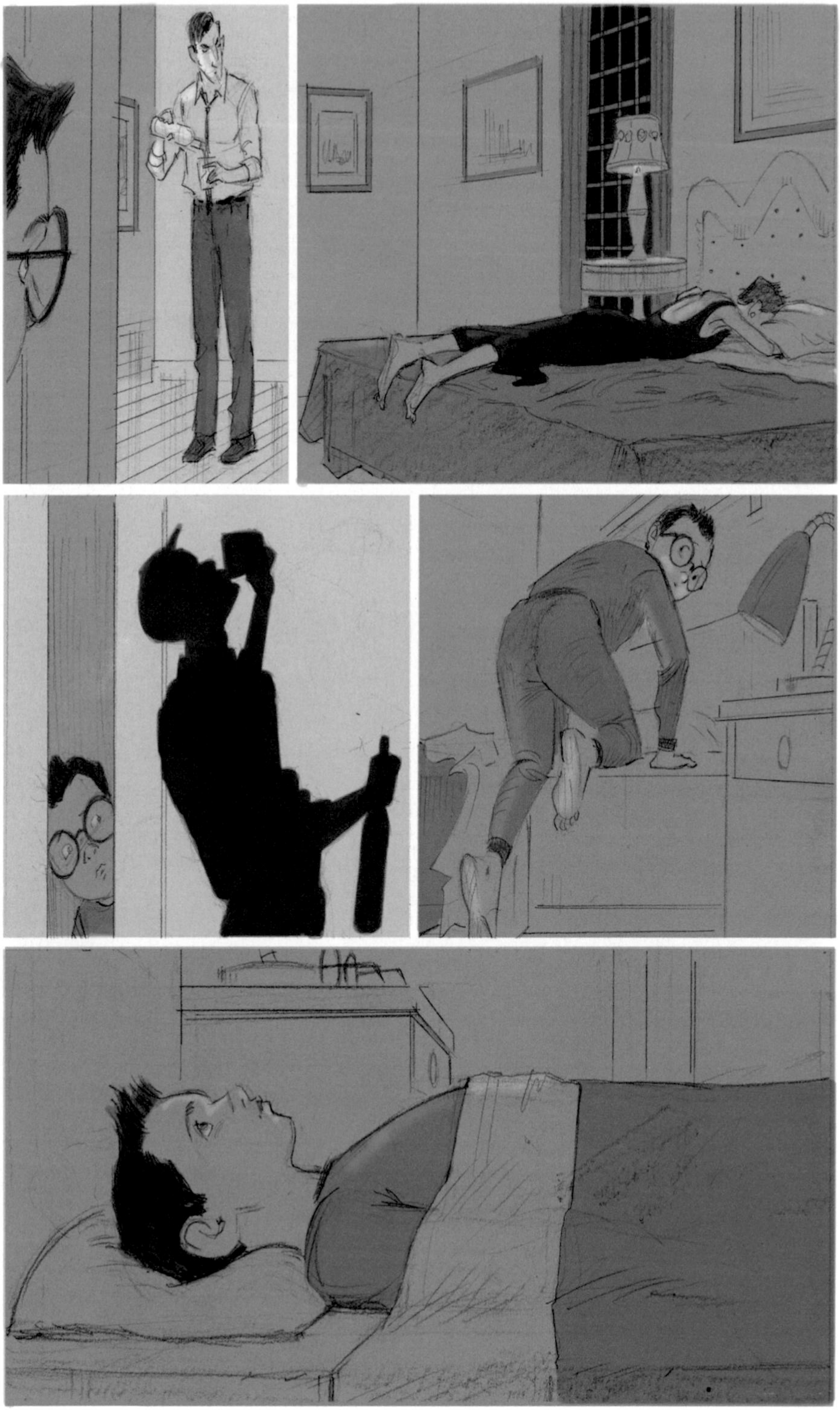

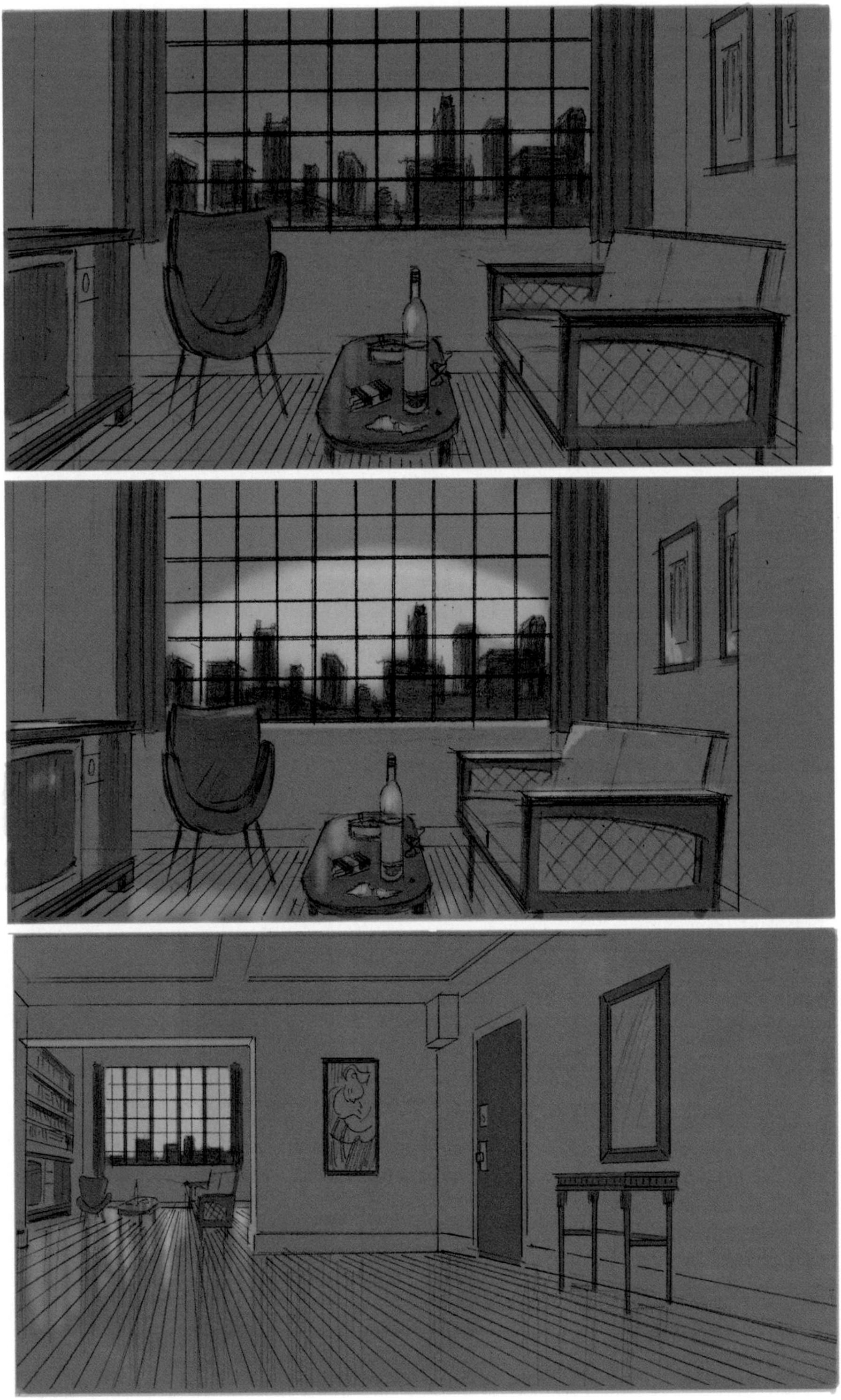

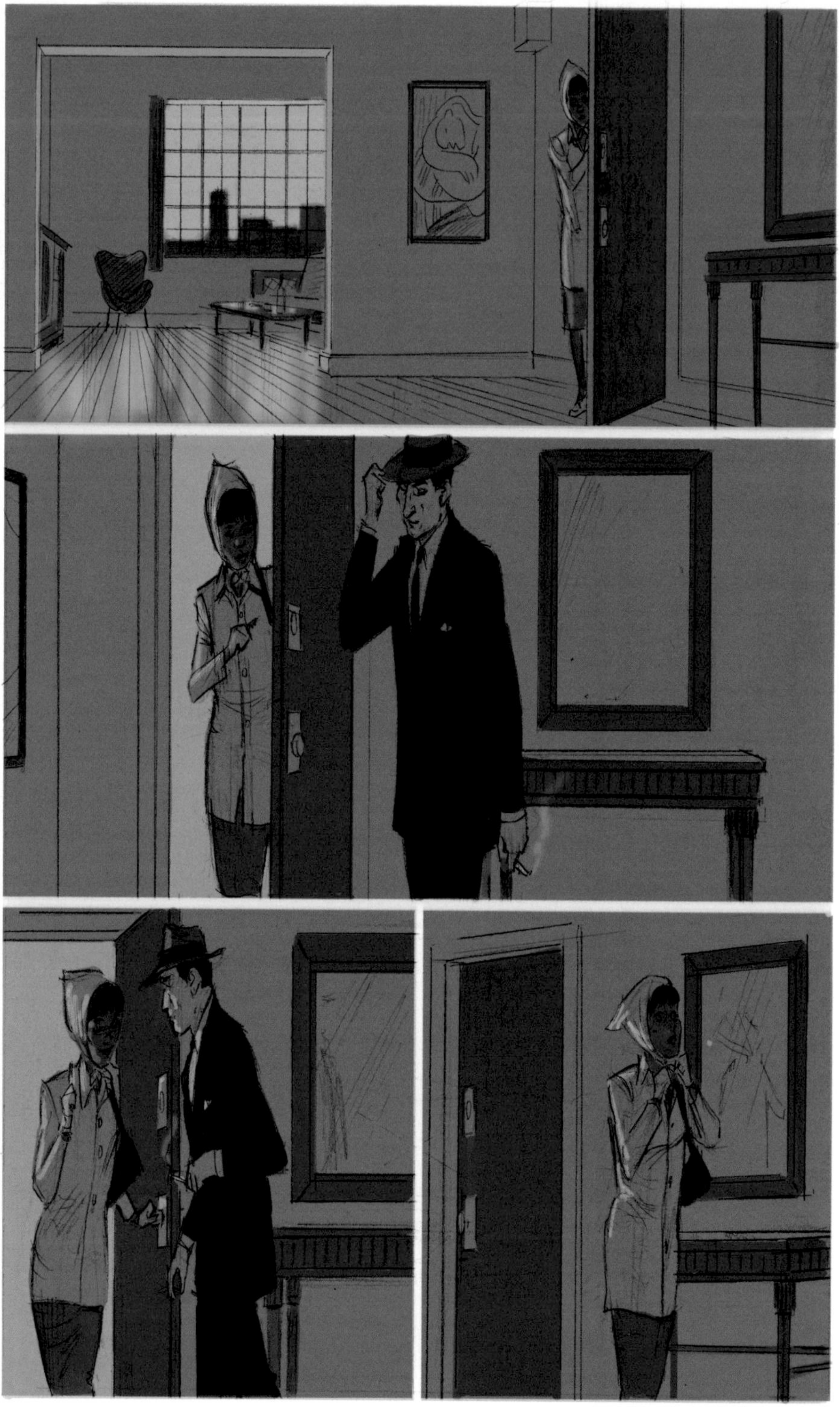

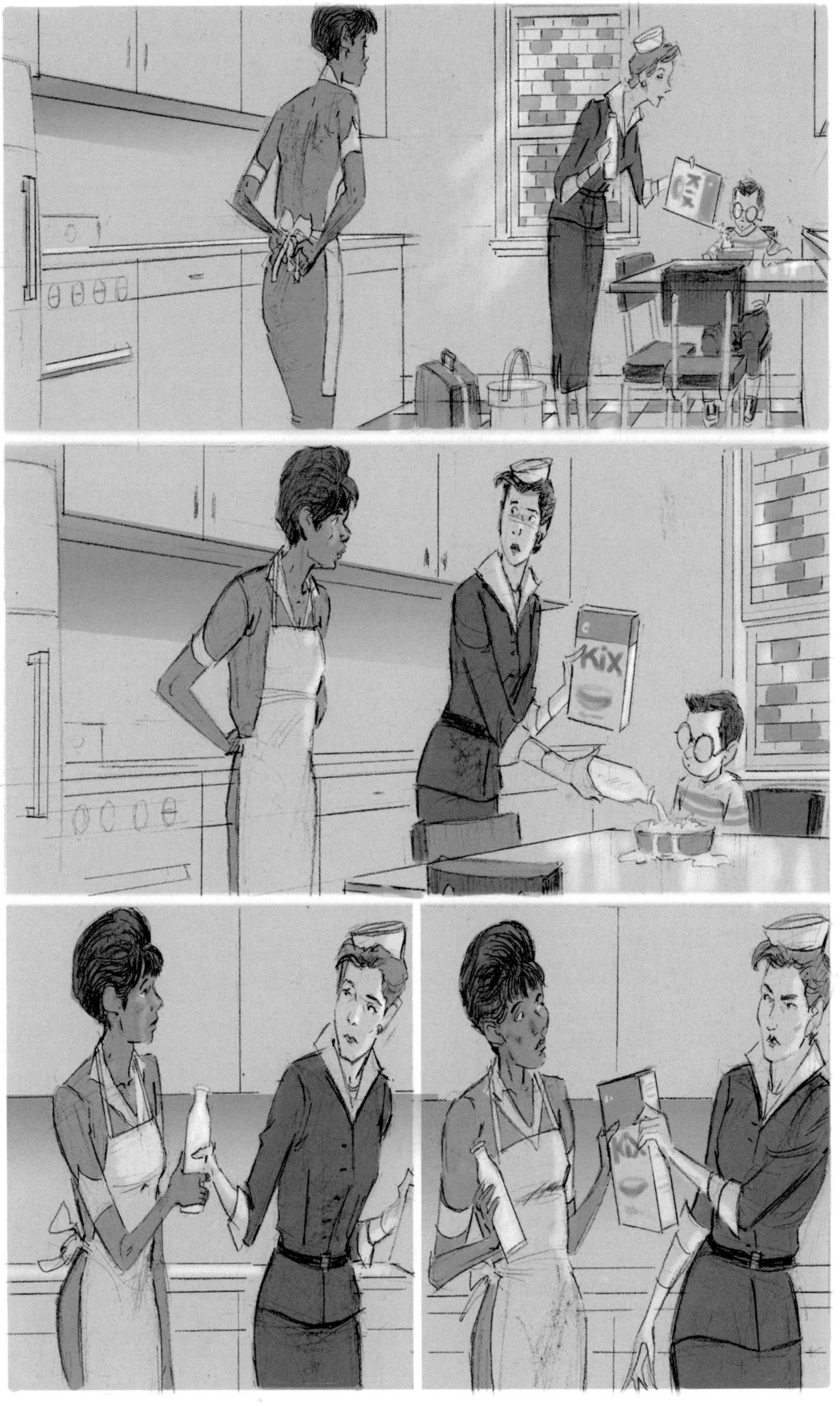
Kix
Kix
Kix

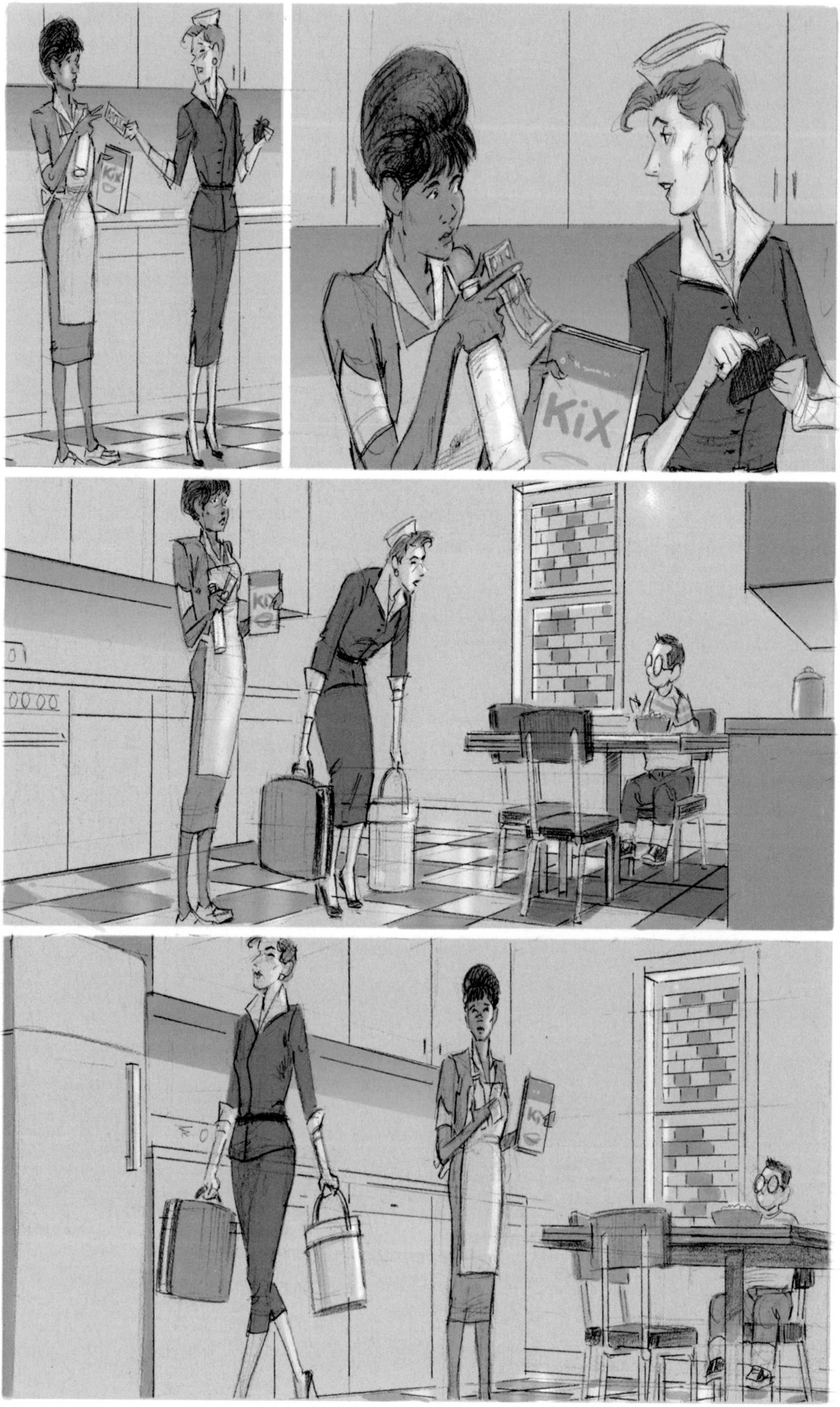
KiX

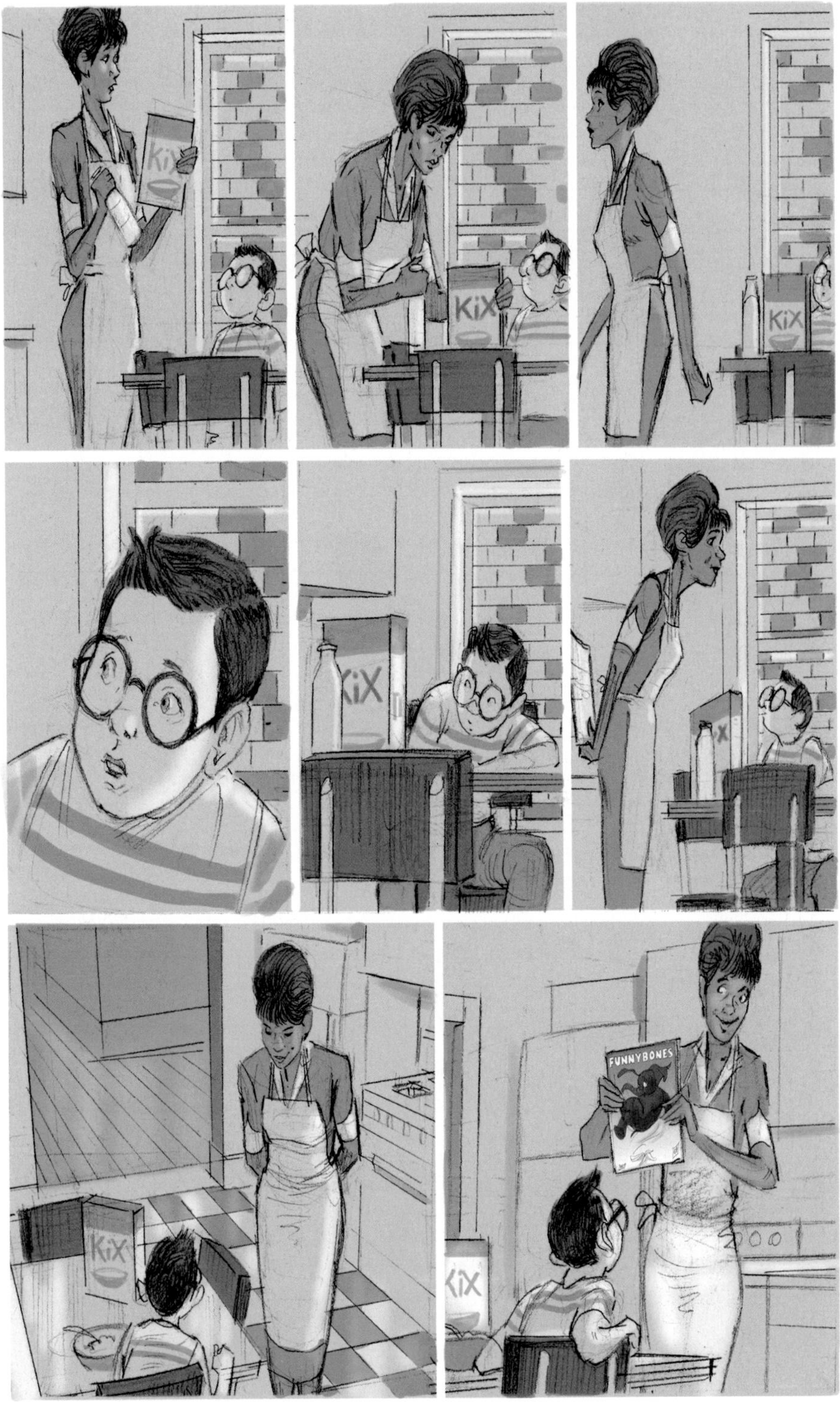
KiX
KiX
KiX
KiX
KiX
FUNNYBONES
KiX

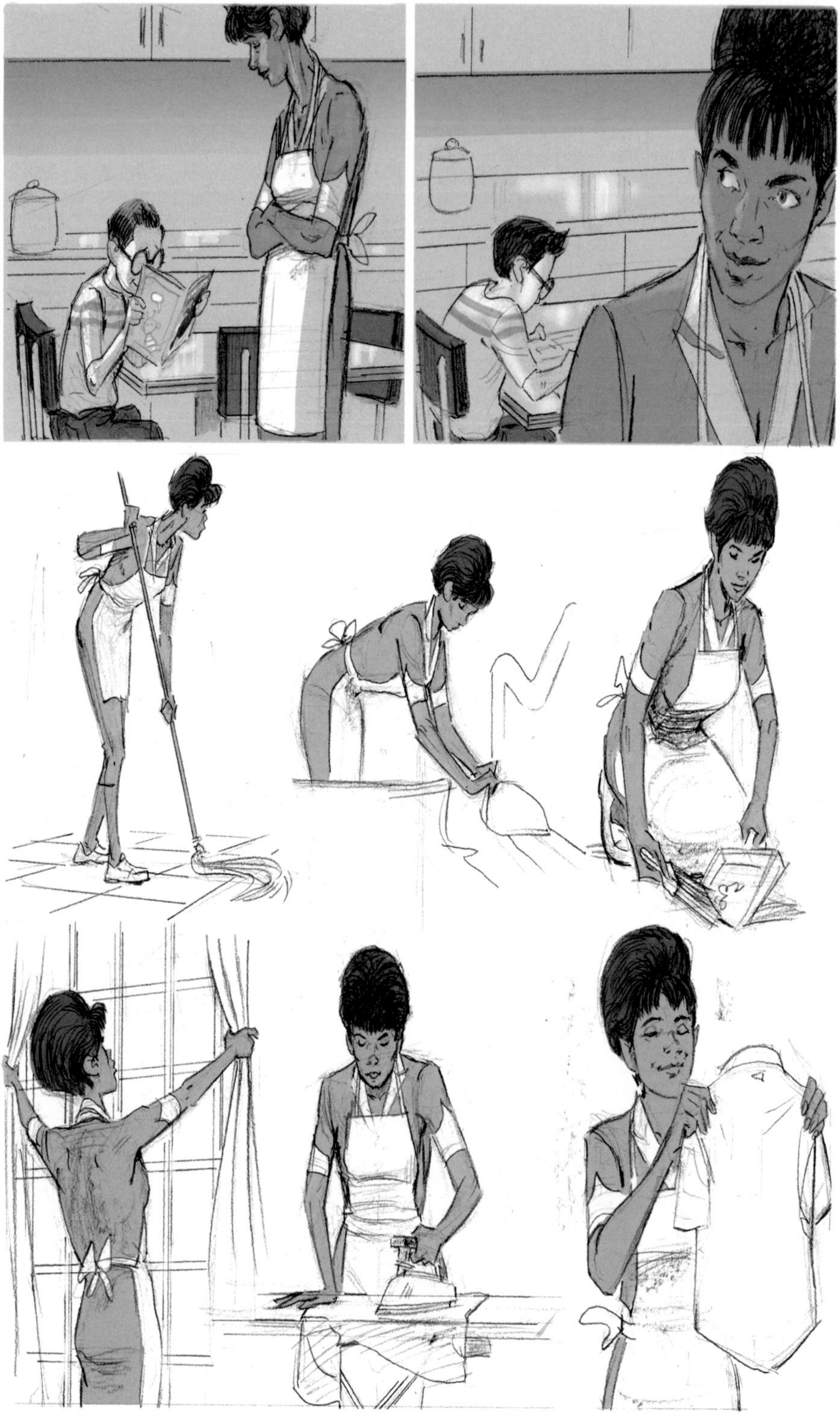

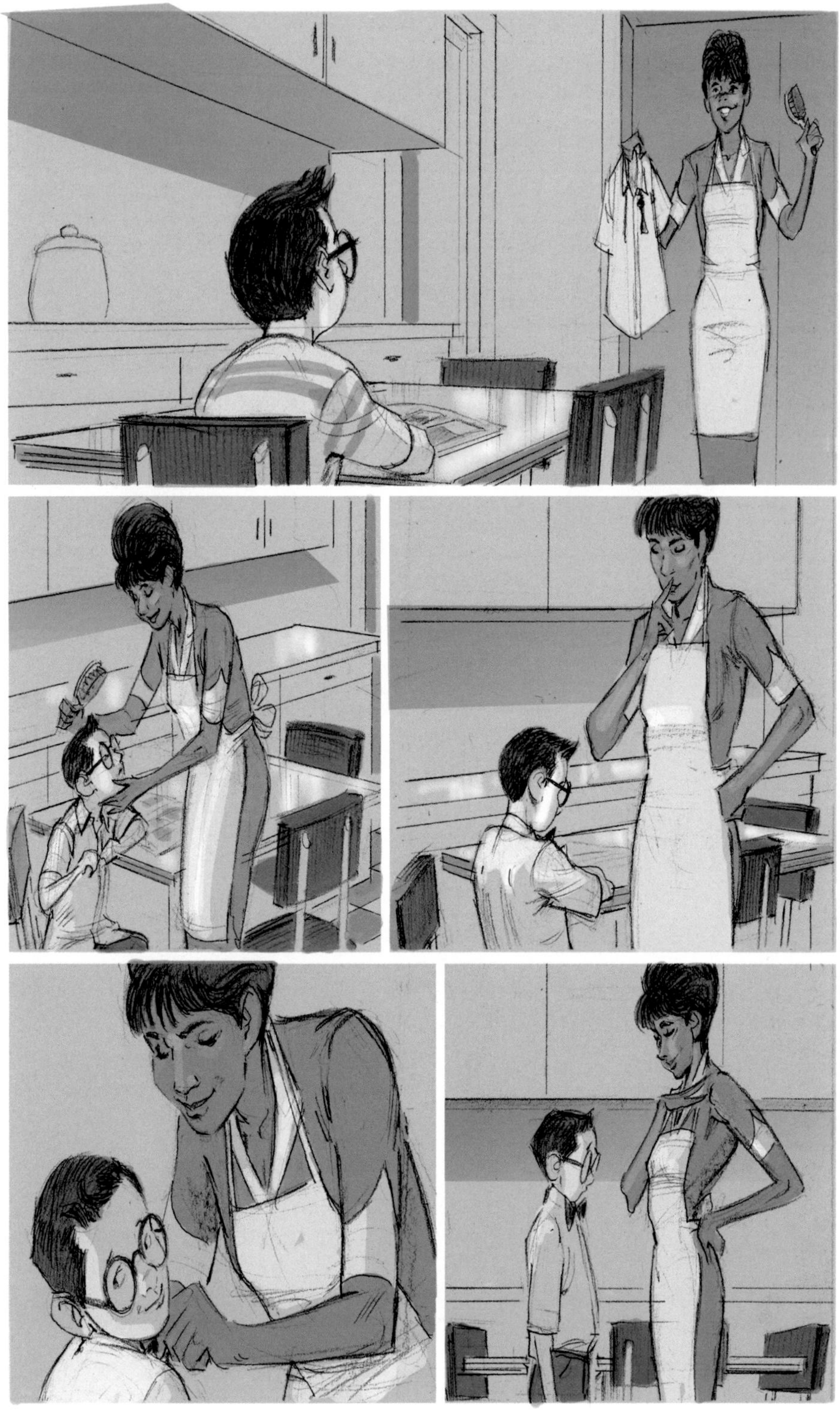

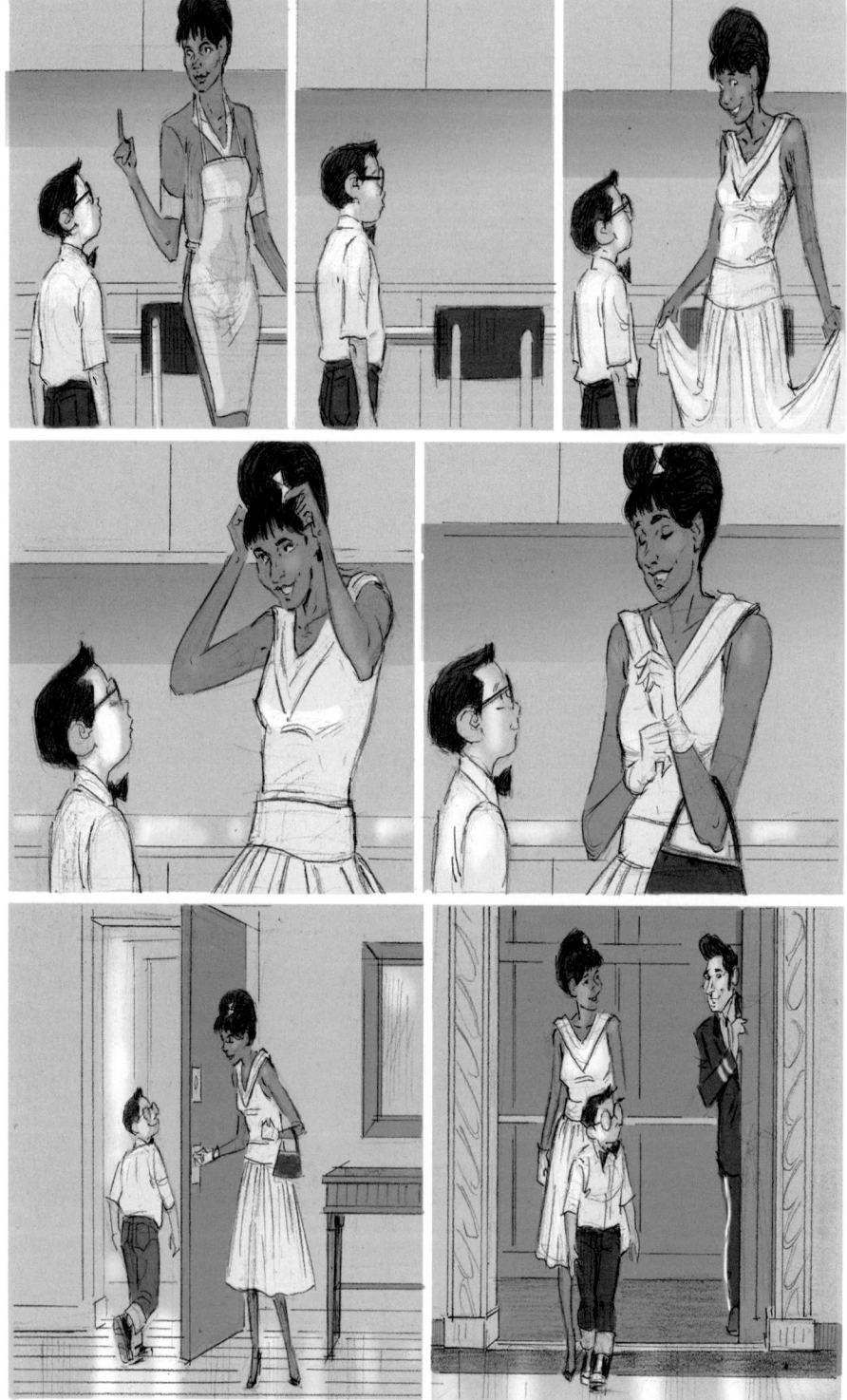

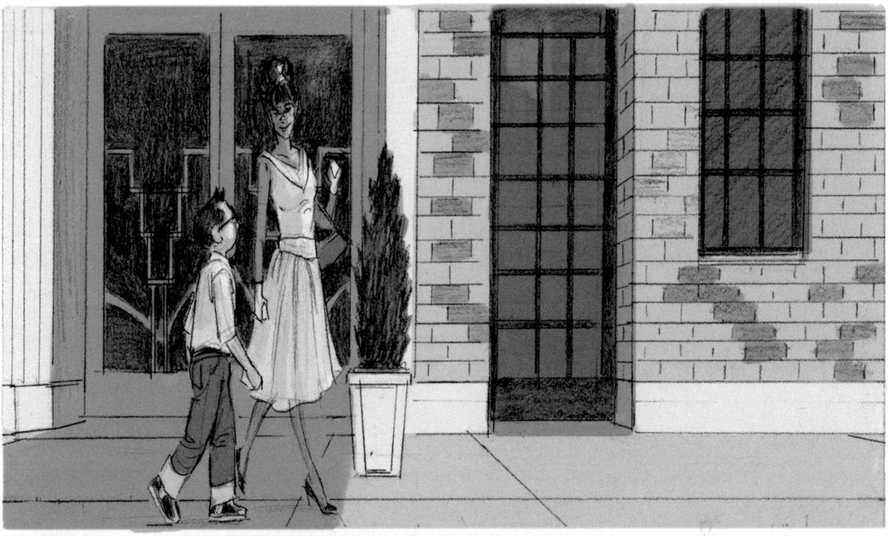
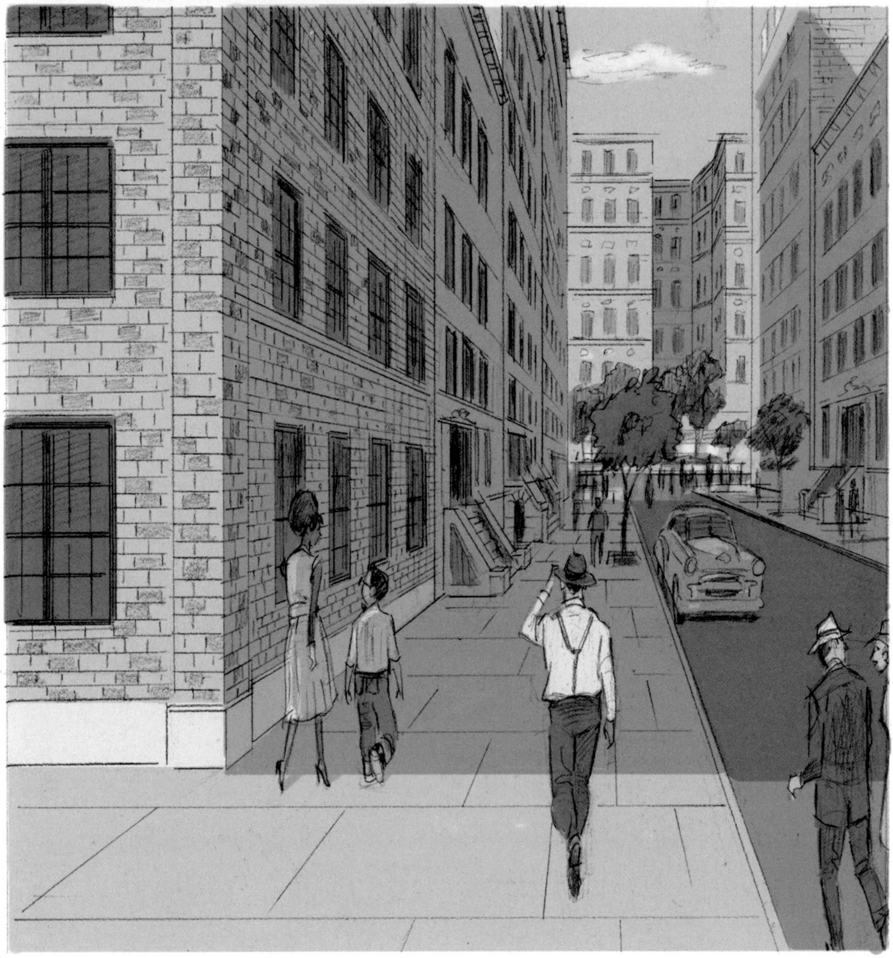

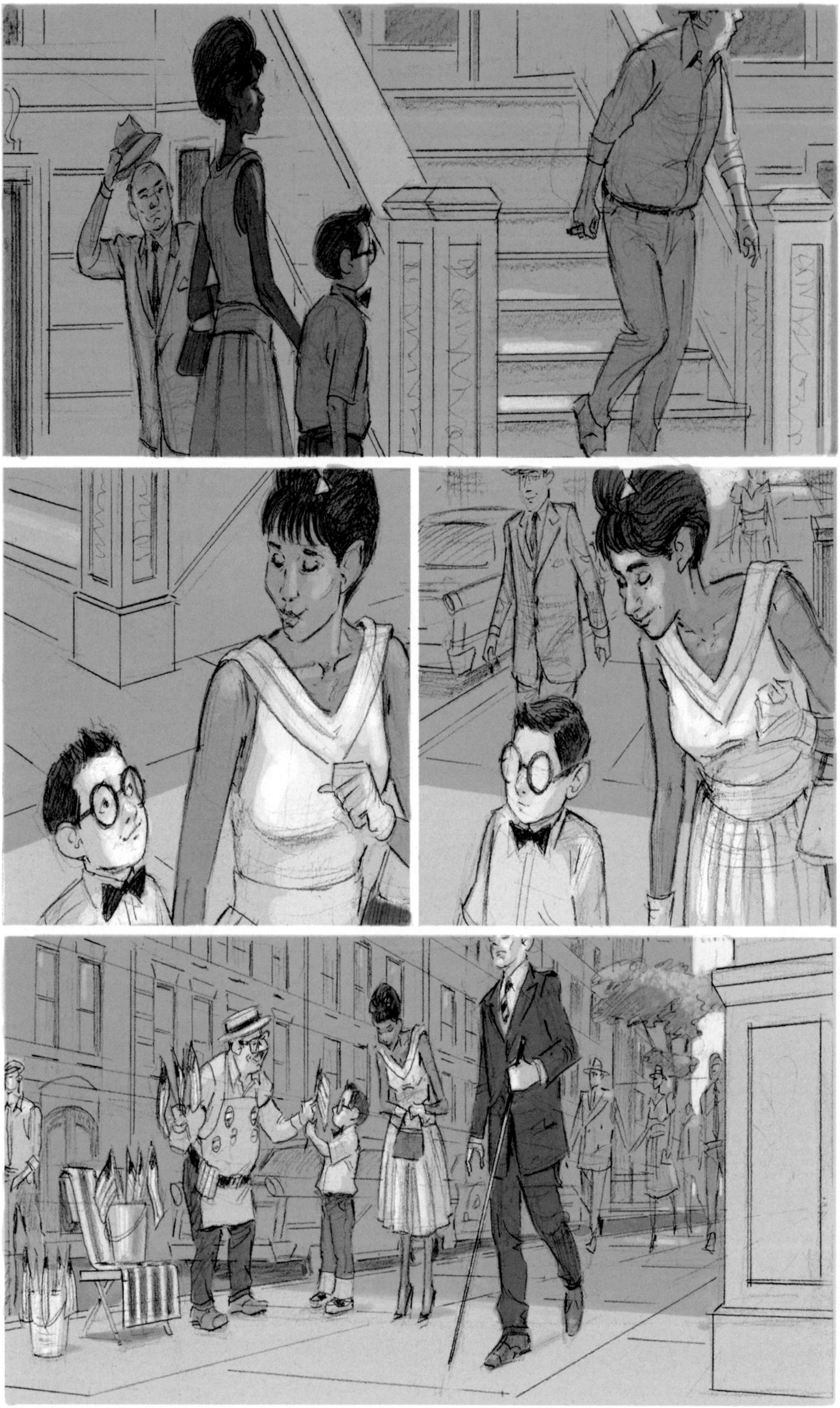

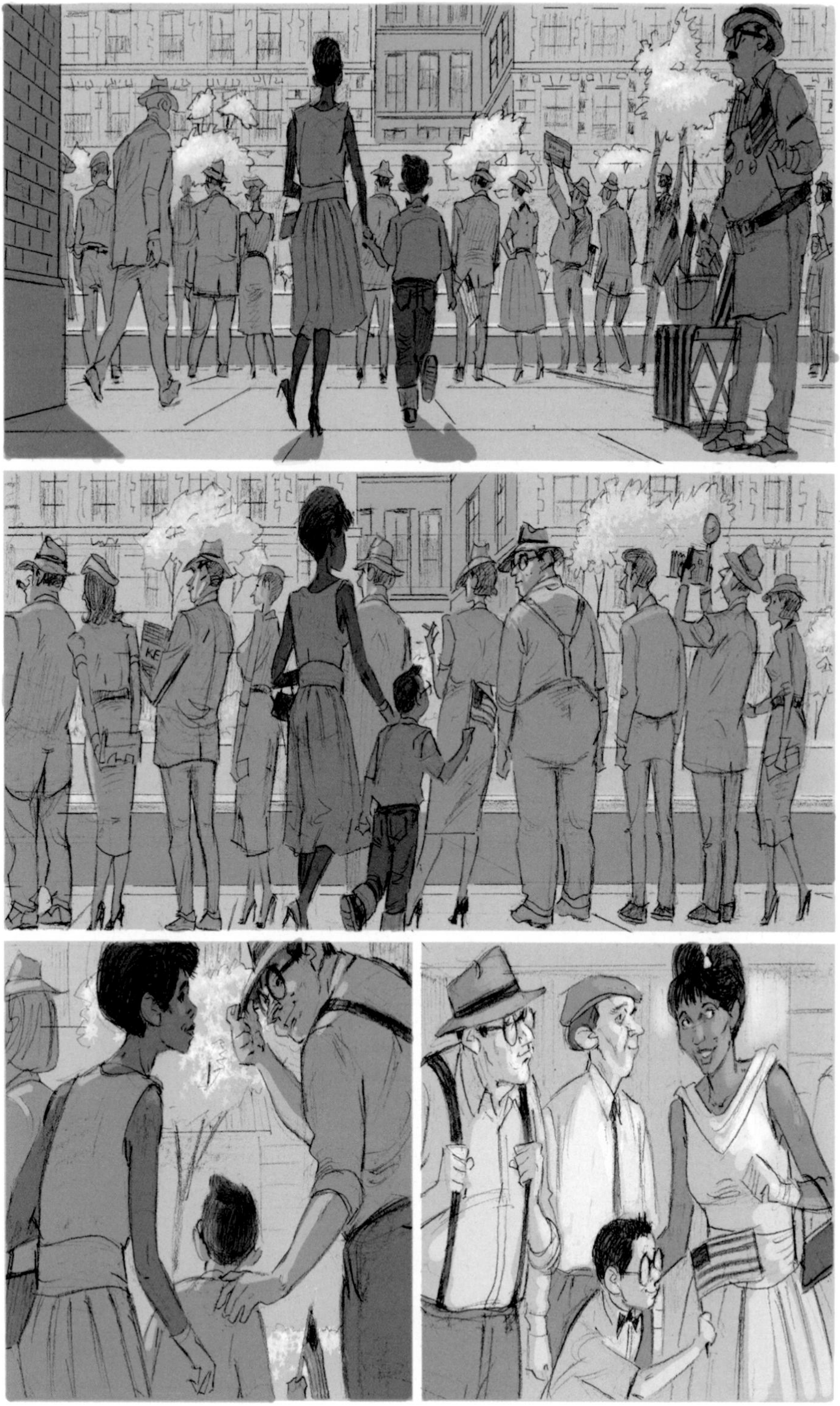

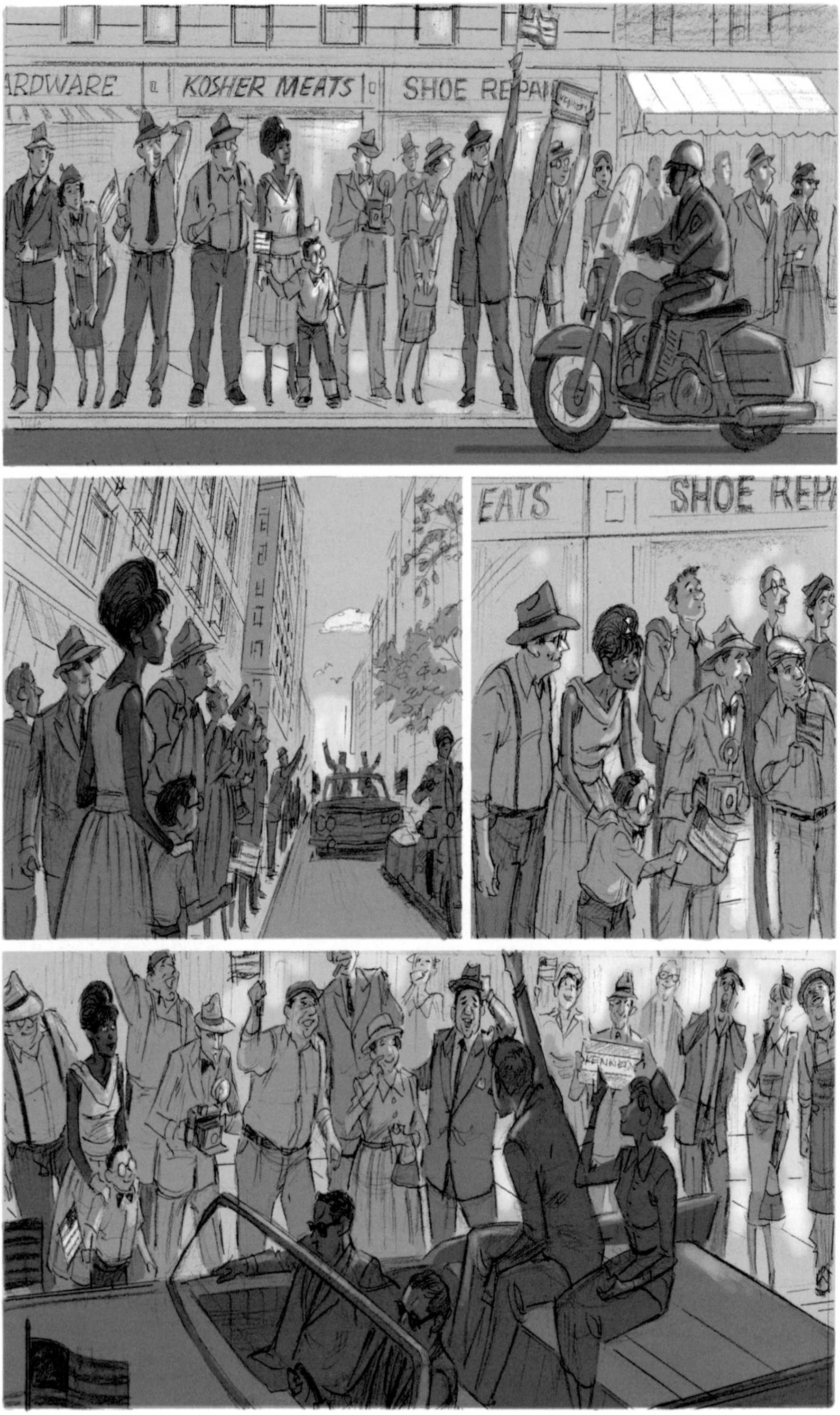
ARDWARE
KOSHER MEATS
SHOE REPA
EATS
SHOE REPA

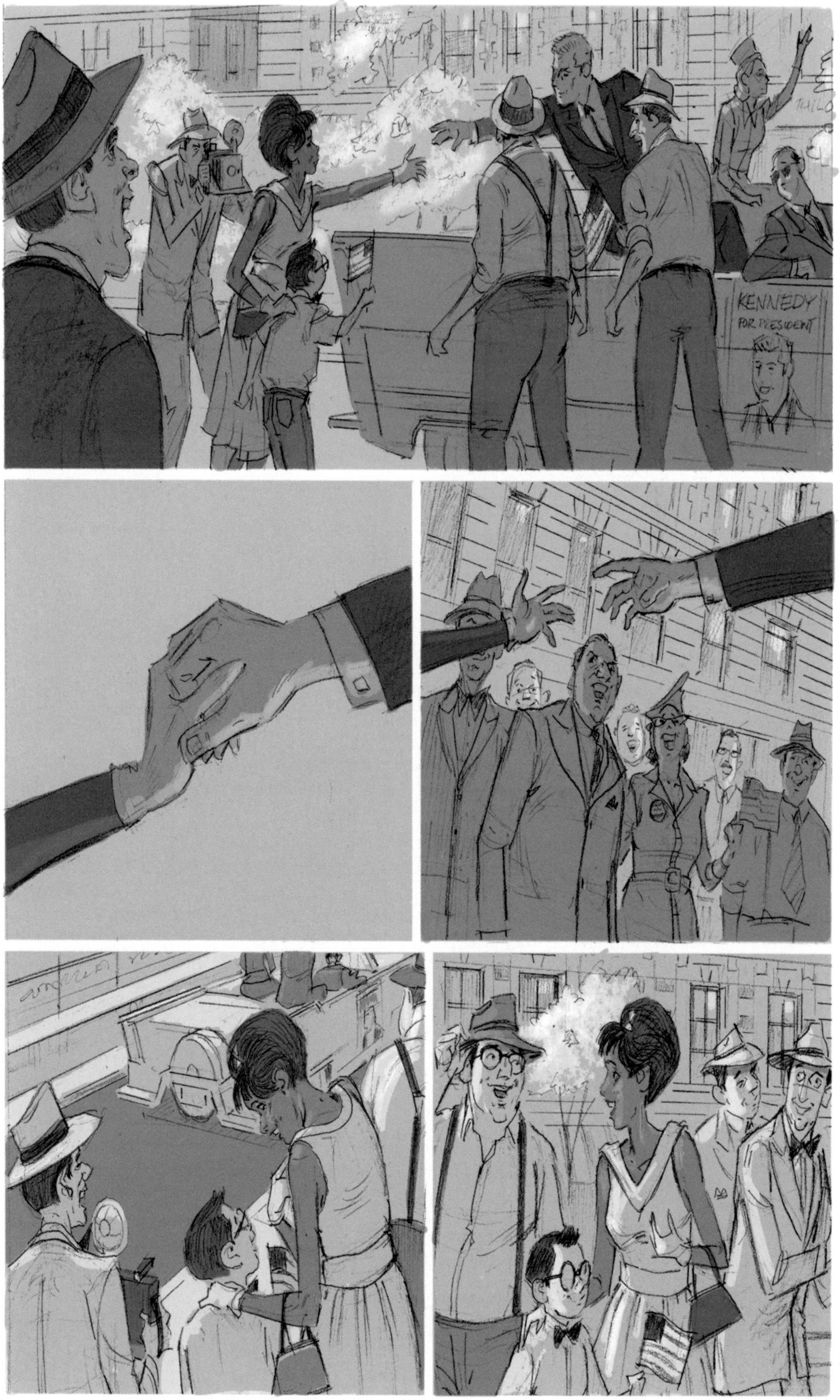
KENNEDY
FOR PRESIDENT

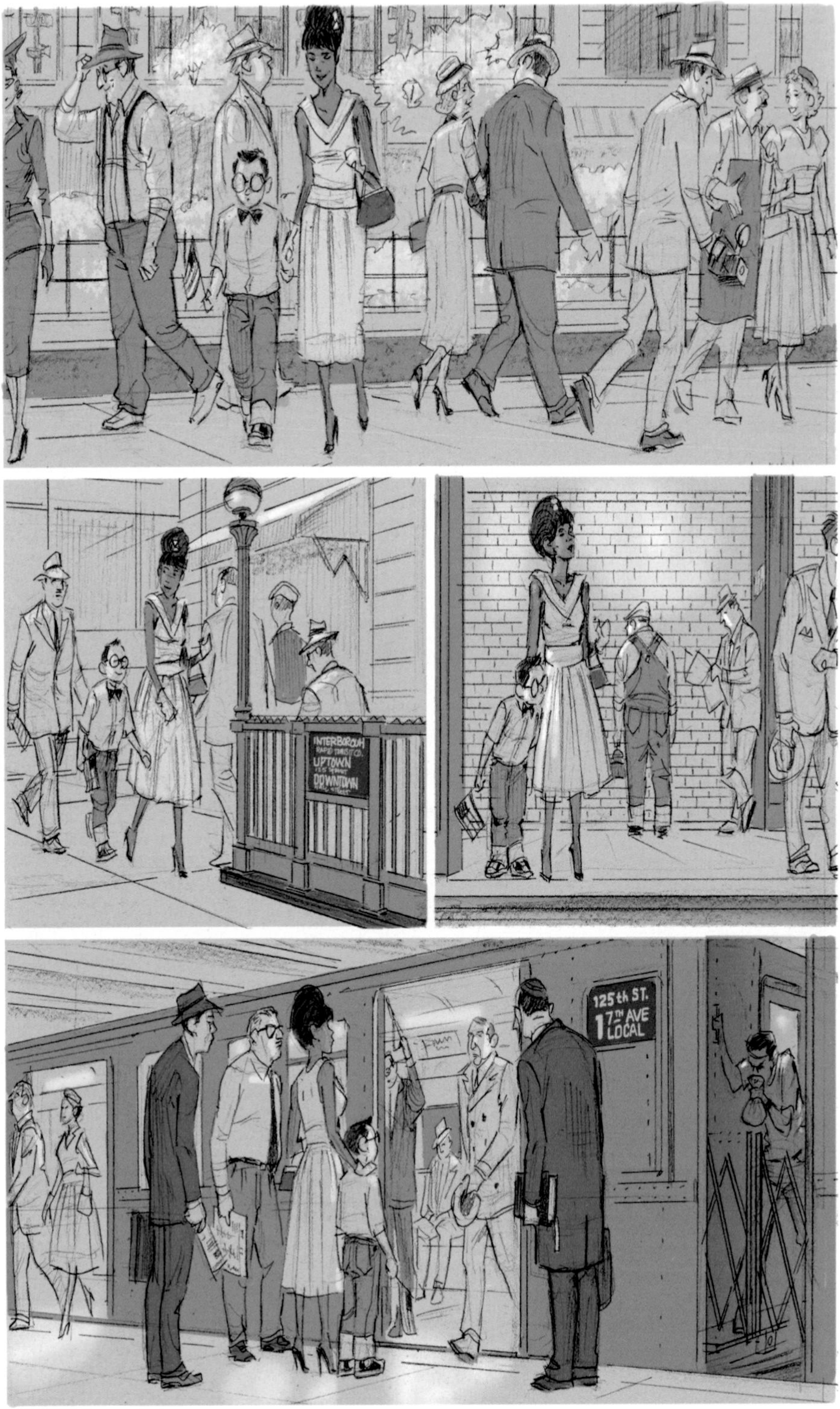

INTERBOROUH
UPTOWN
DOWNTOWN
125th ST.
1 7TH AVE LOCAL

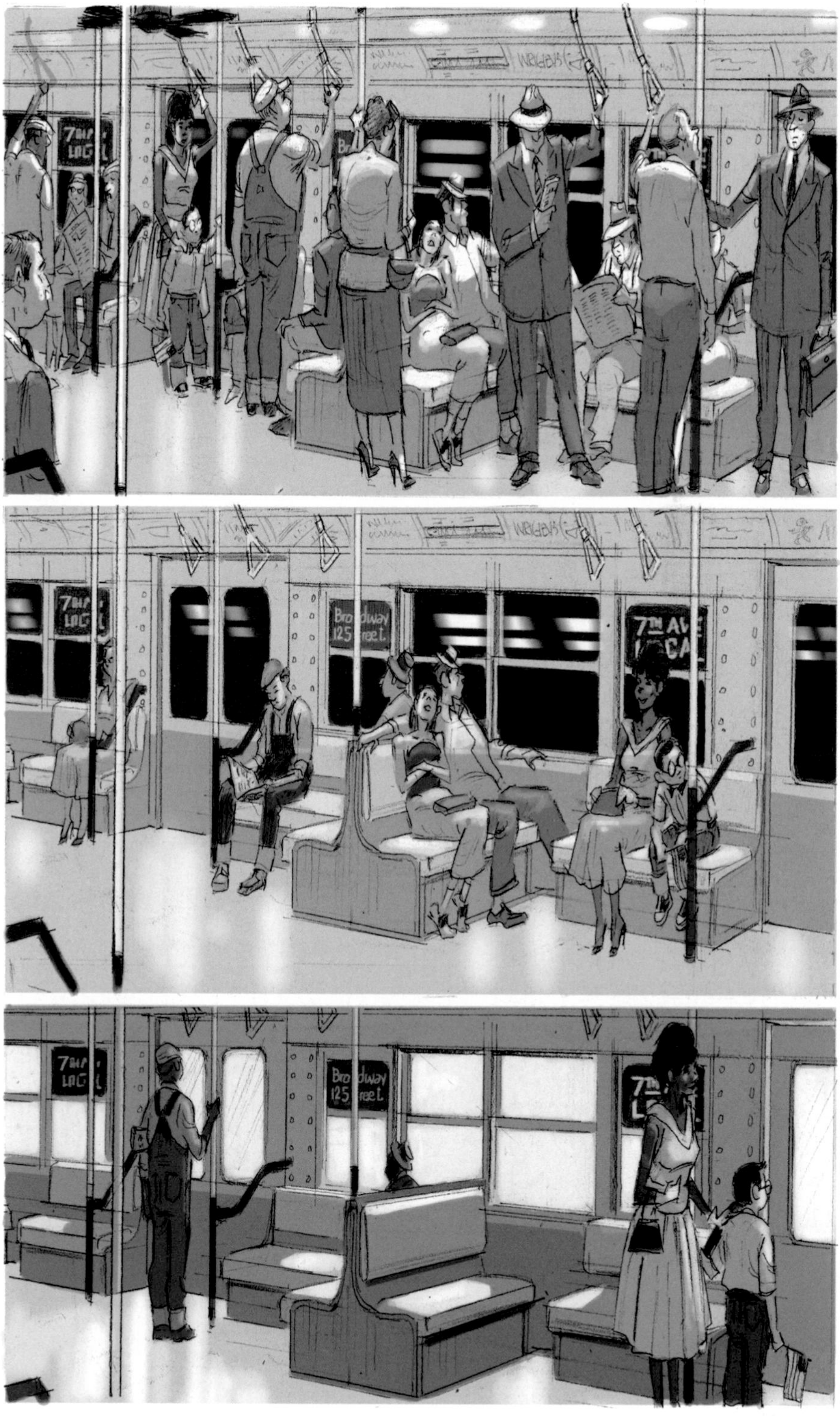
Broadway
125 Street

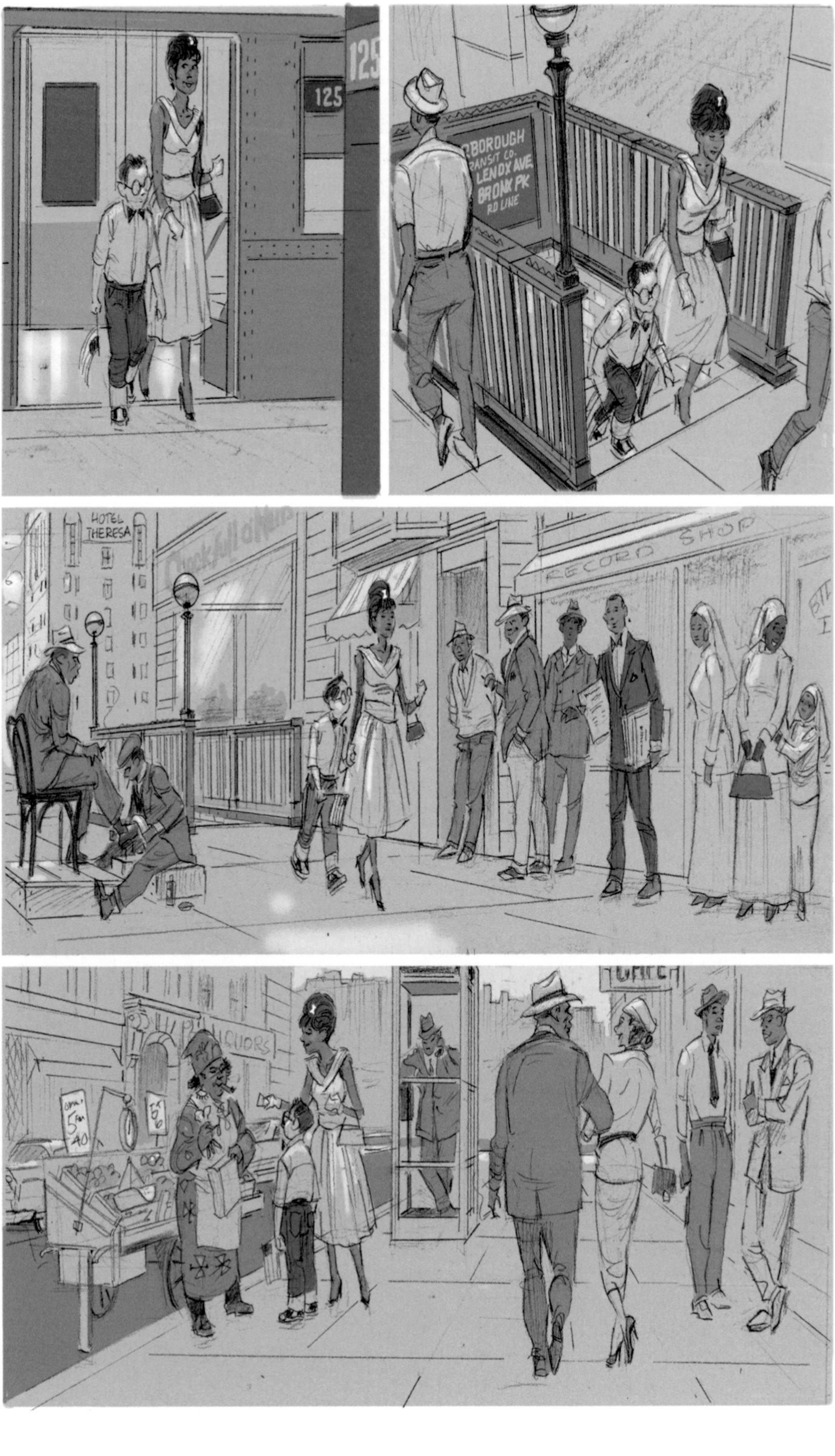
125
125
RBOROUGH
RANSIT CO.
LENOX AVE.
BRONX PK
RD LINE
HOTEL THERESA
RECORD SHOP
LIQUORS

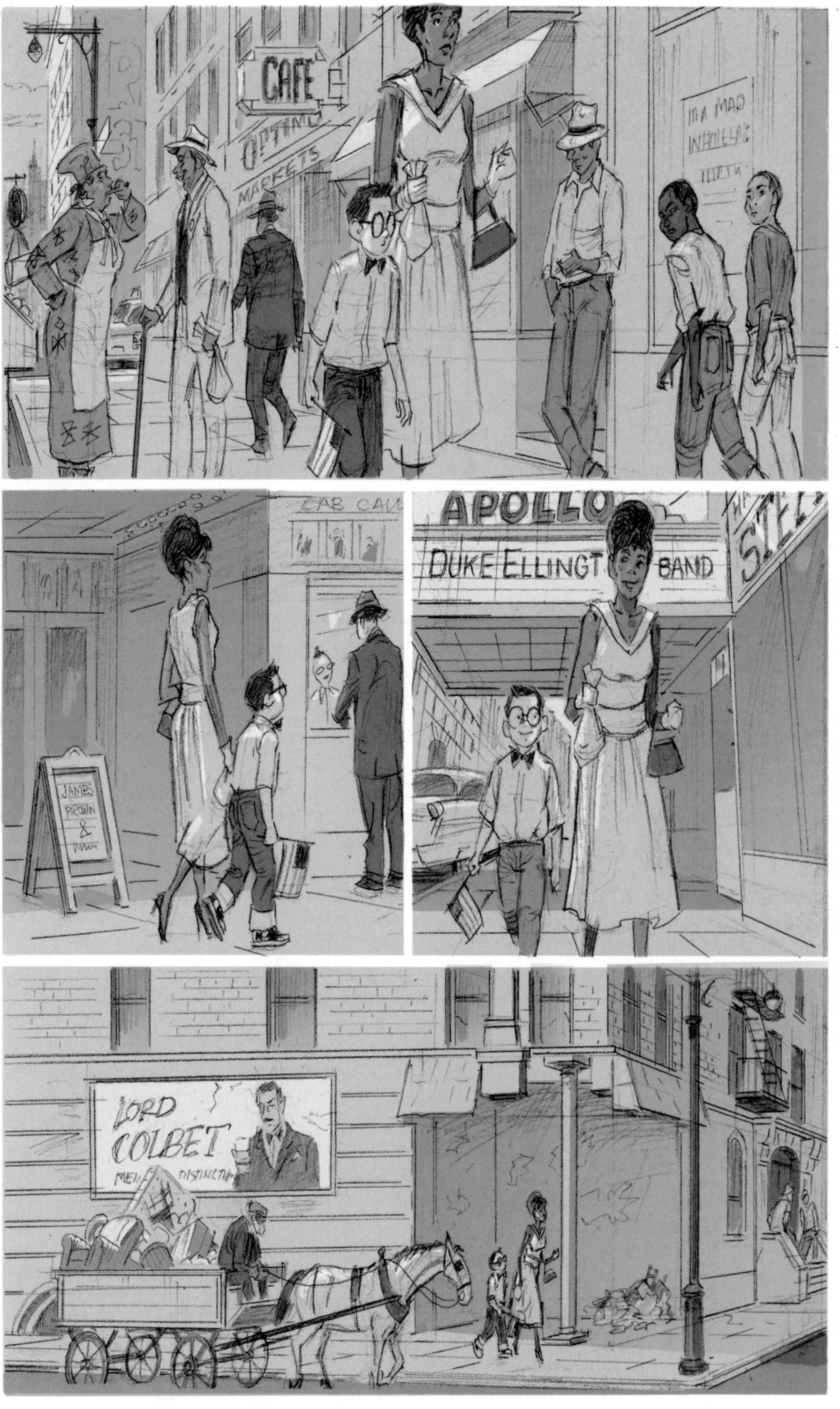
CAFE
MARKETS
APOLLO
DUKE ELLINGT
BAND
JAMES
BROWN
&
LORD
COLBET

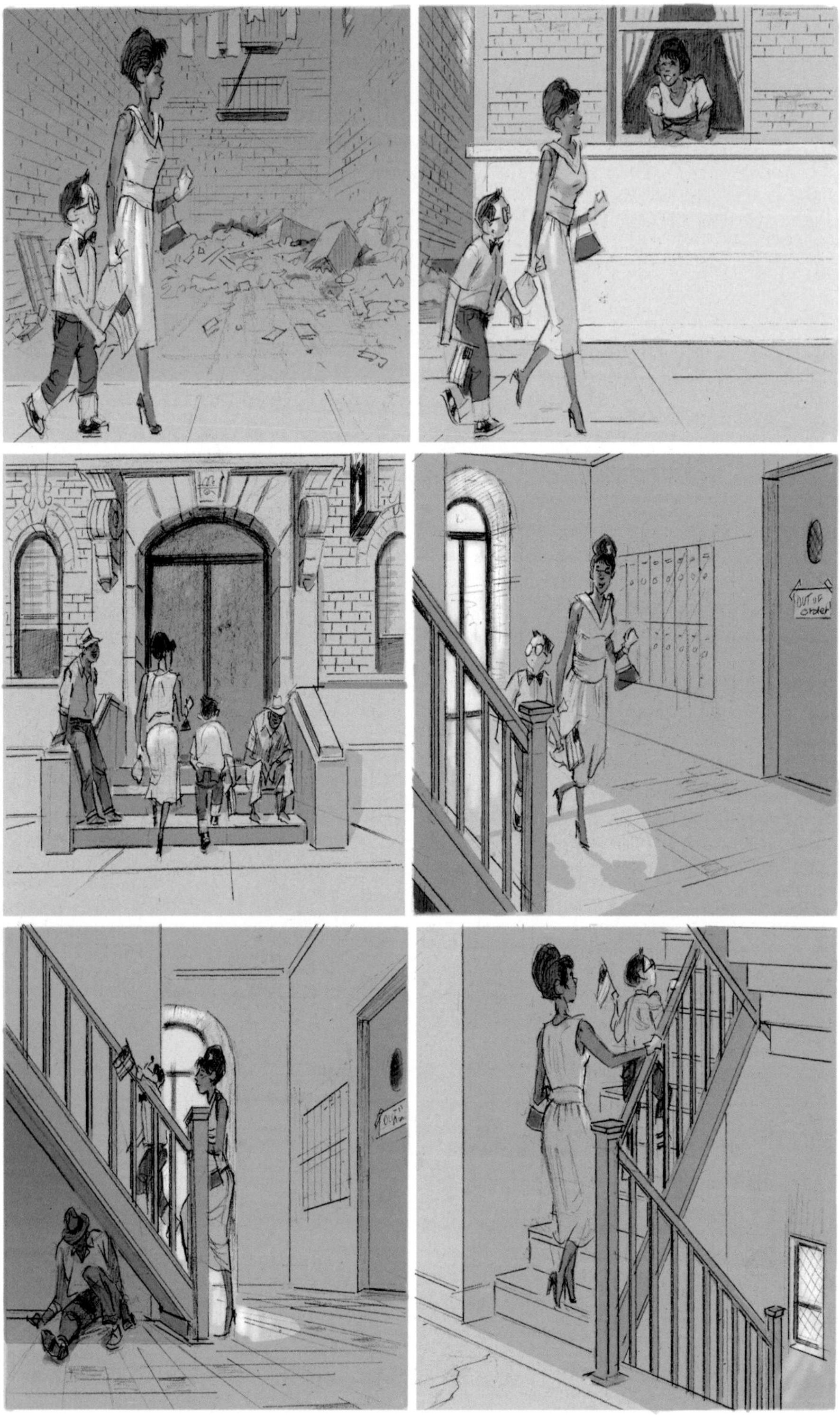
OUT OF order

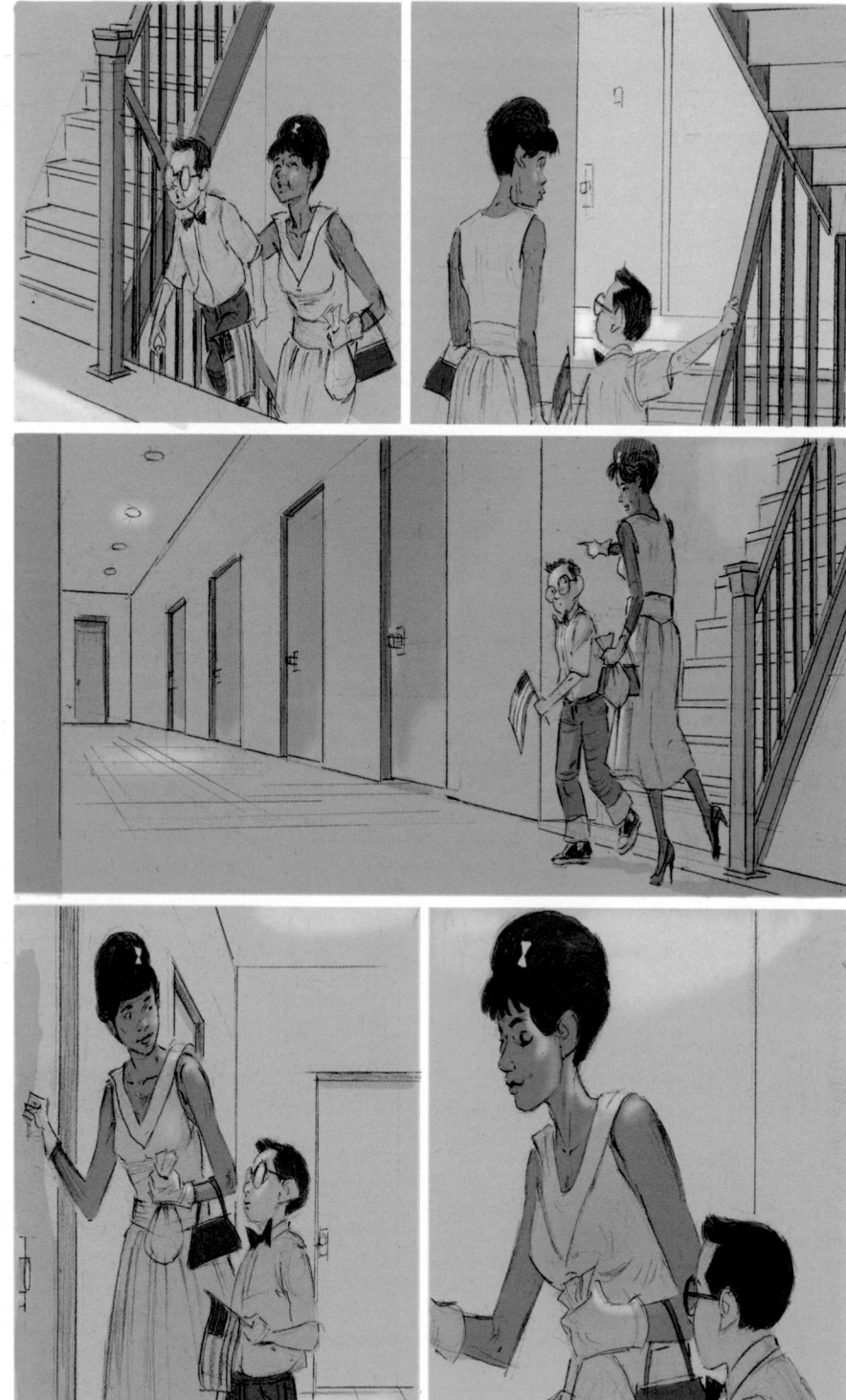

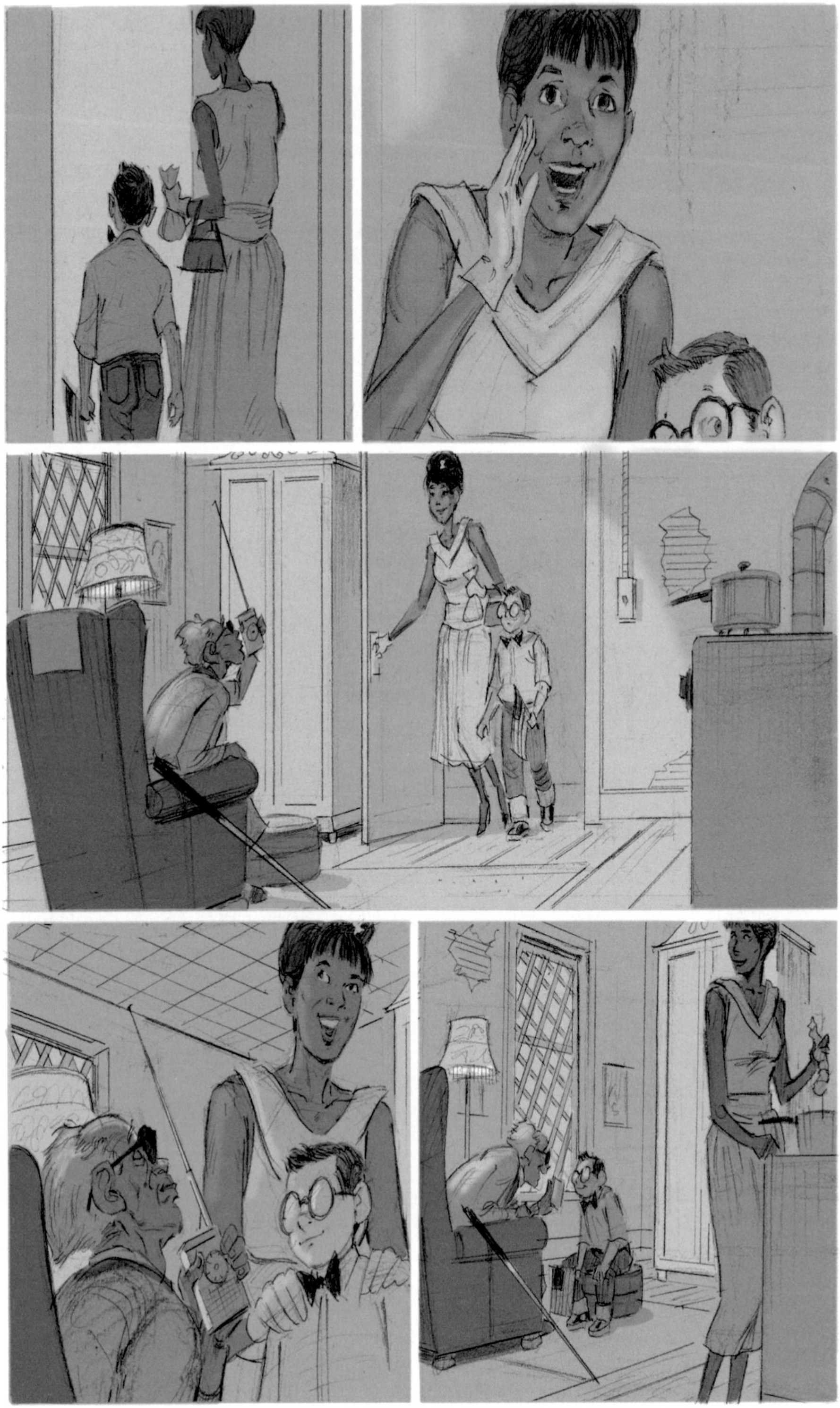

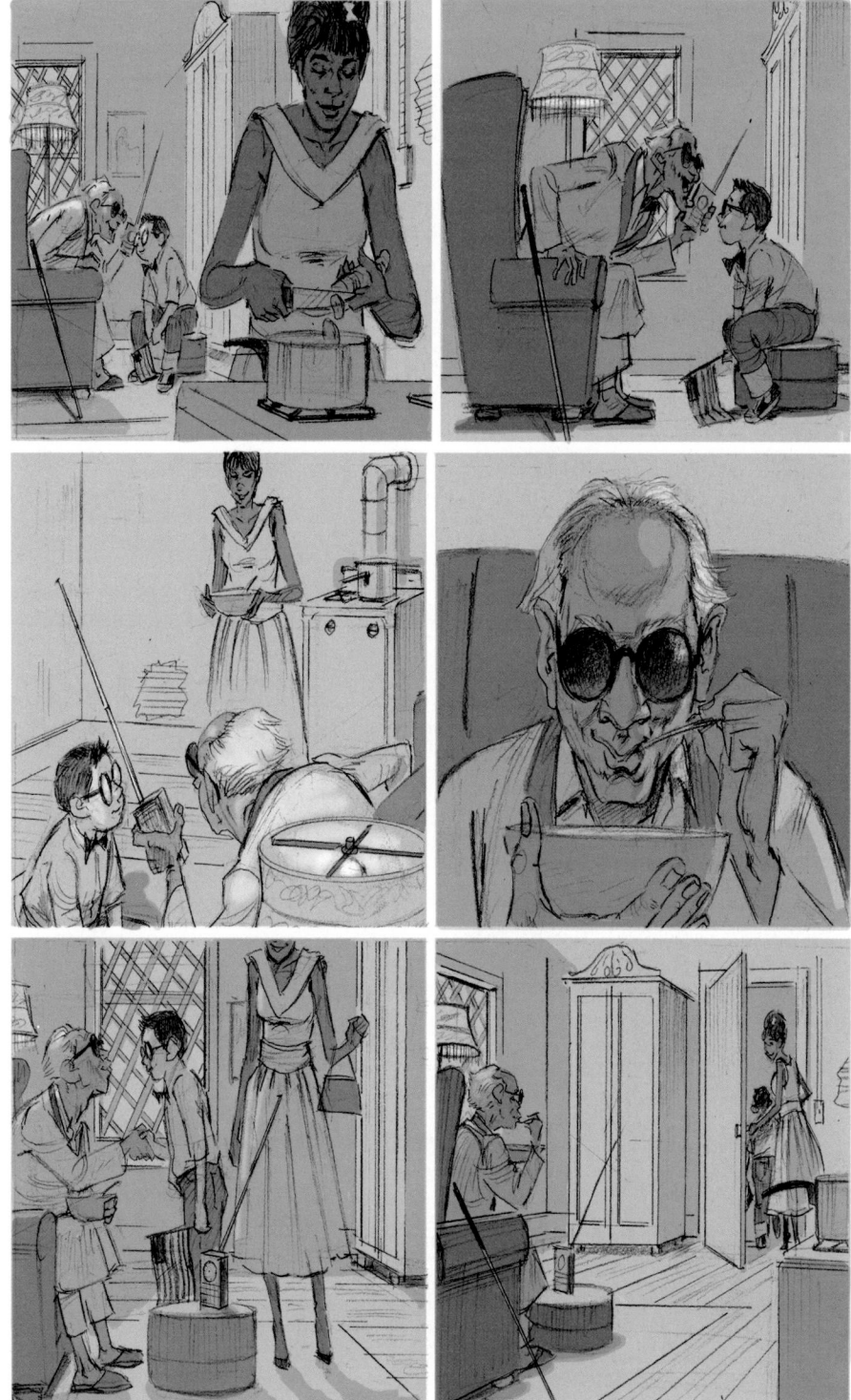

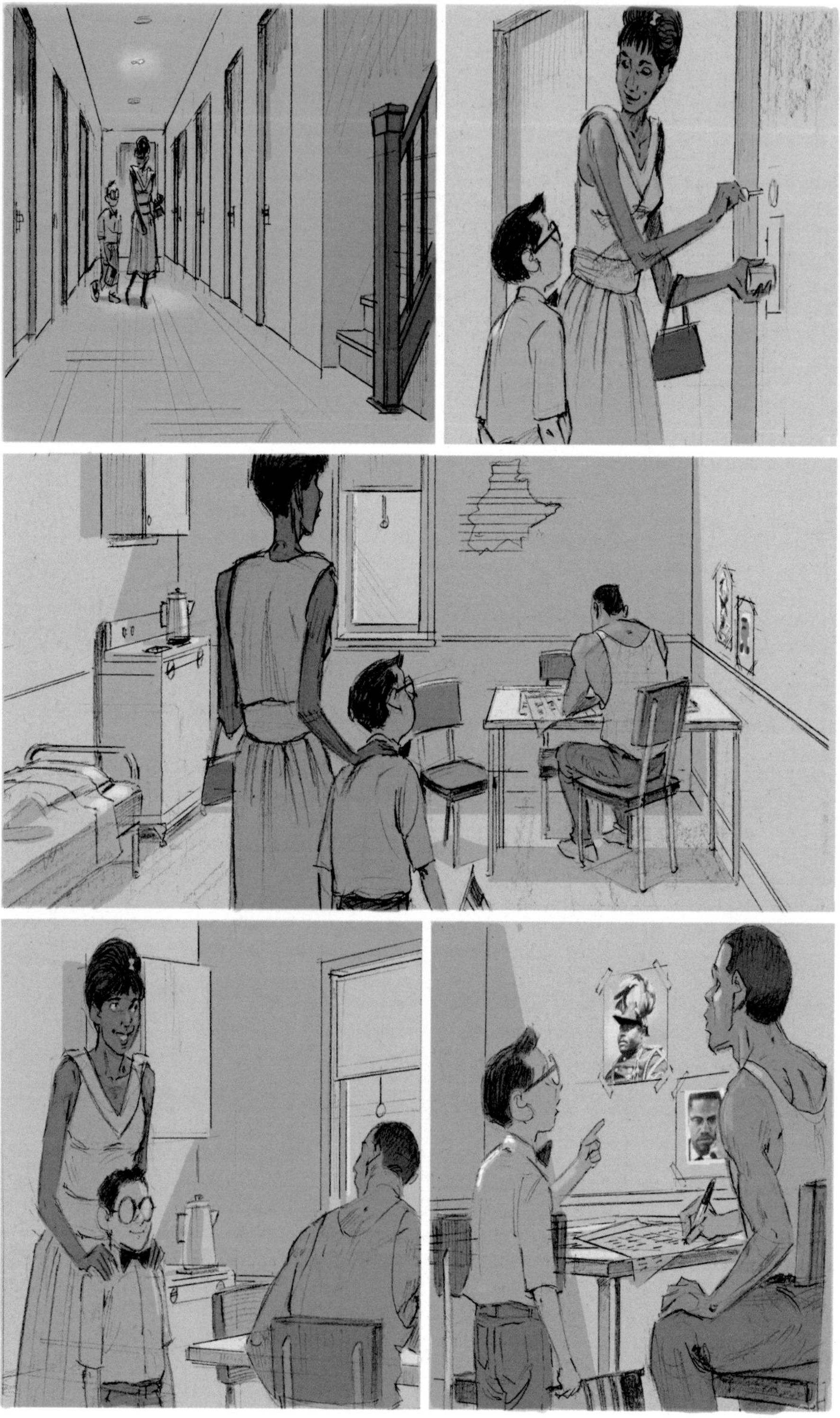

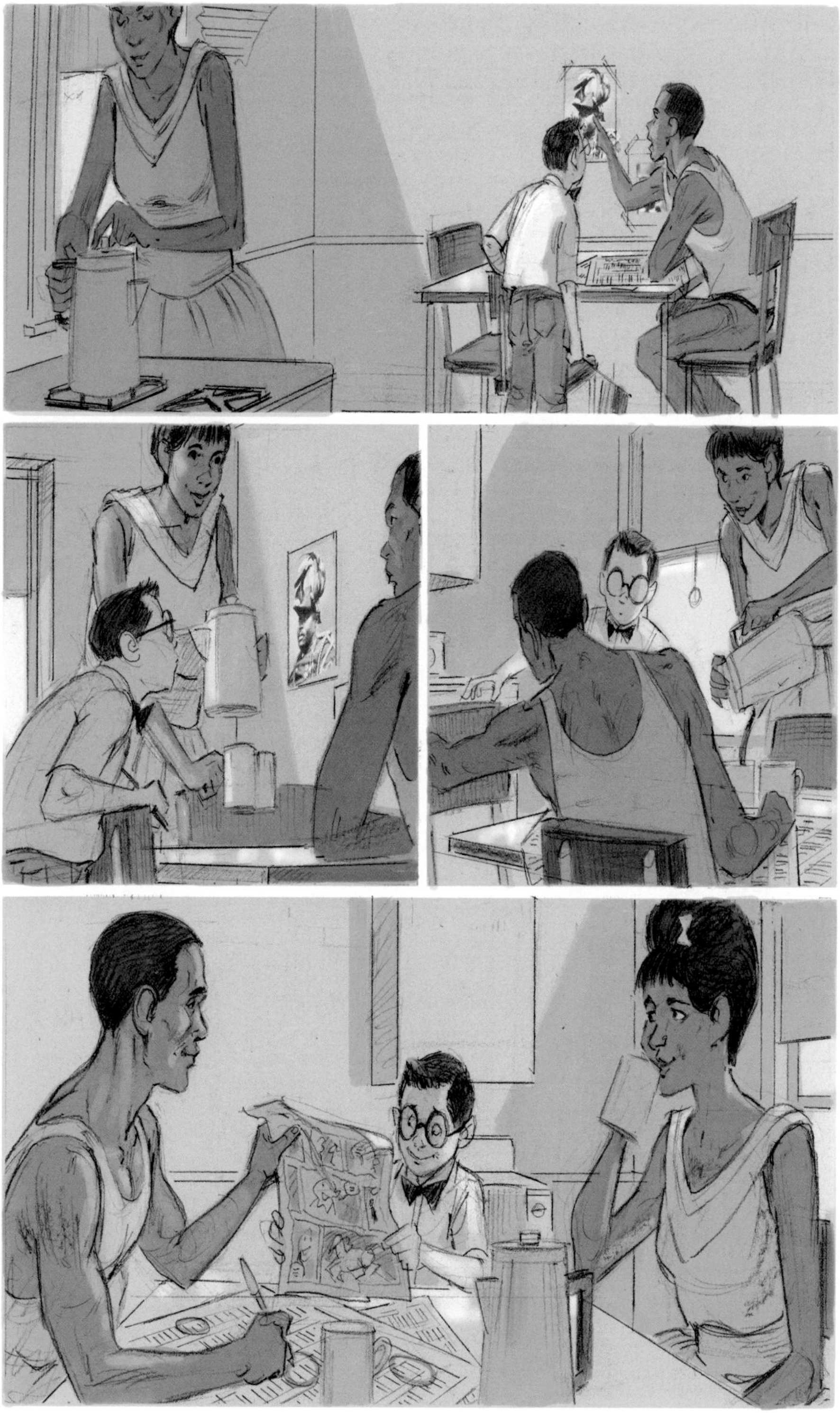

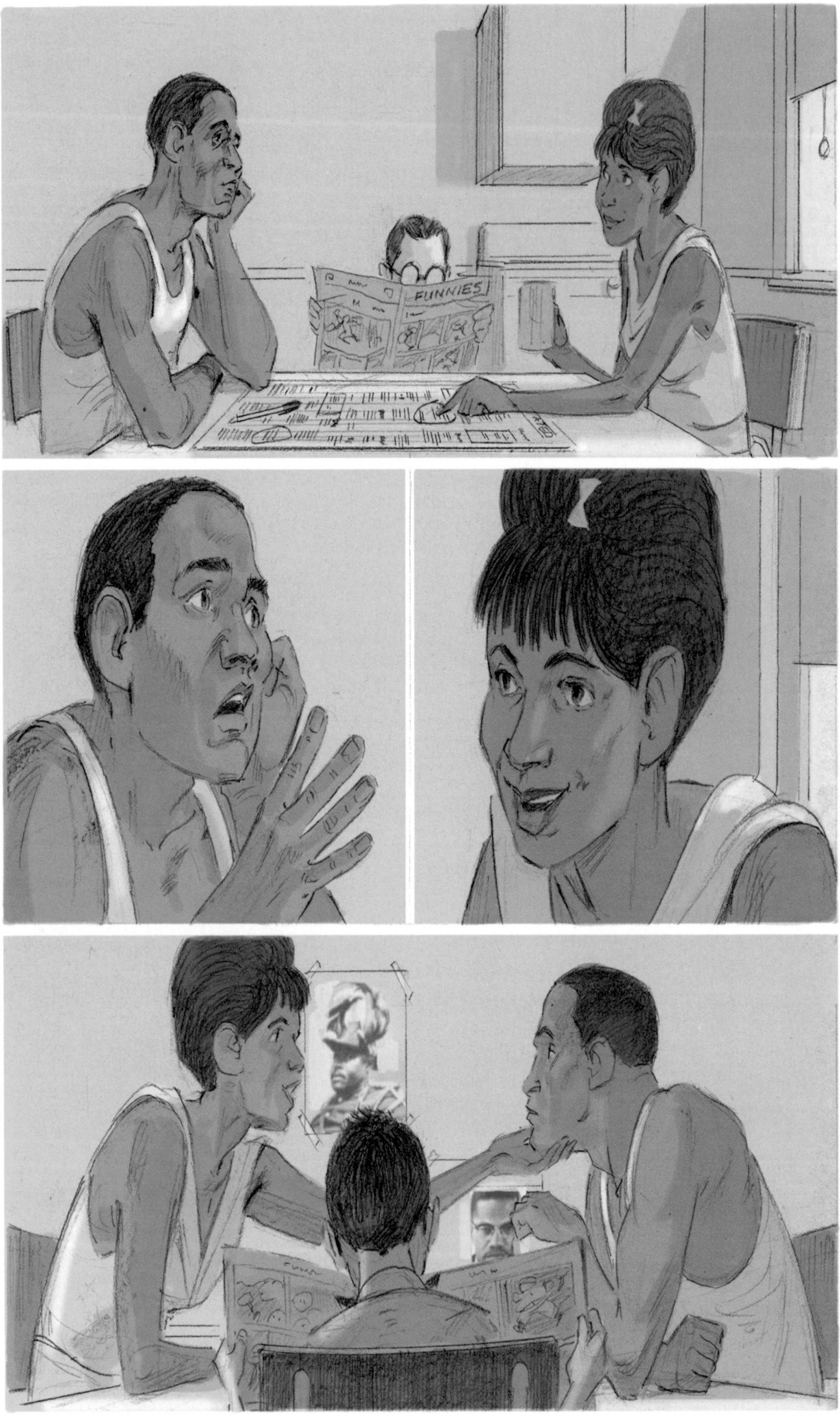
FUNNIES

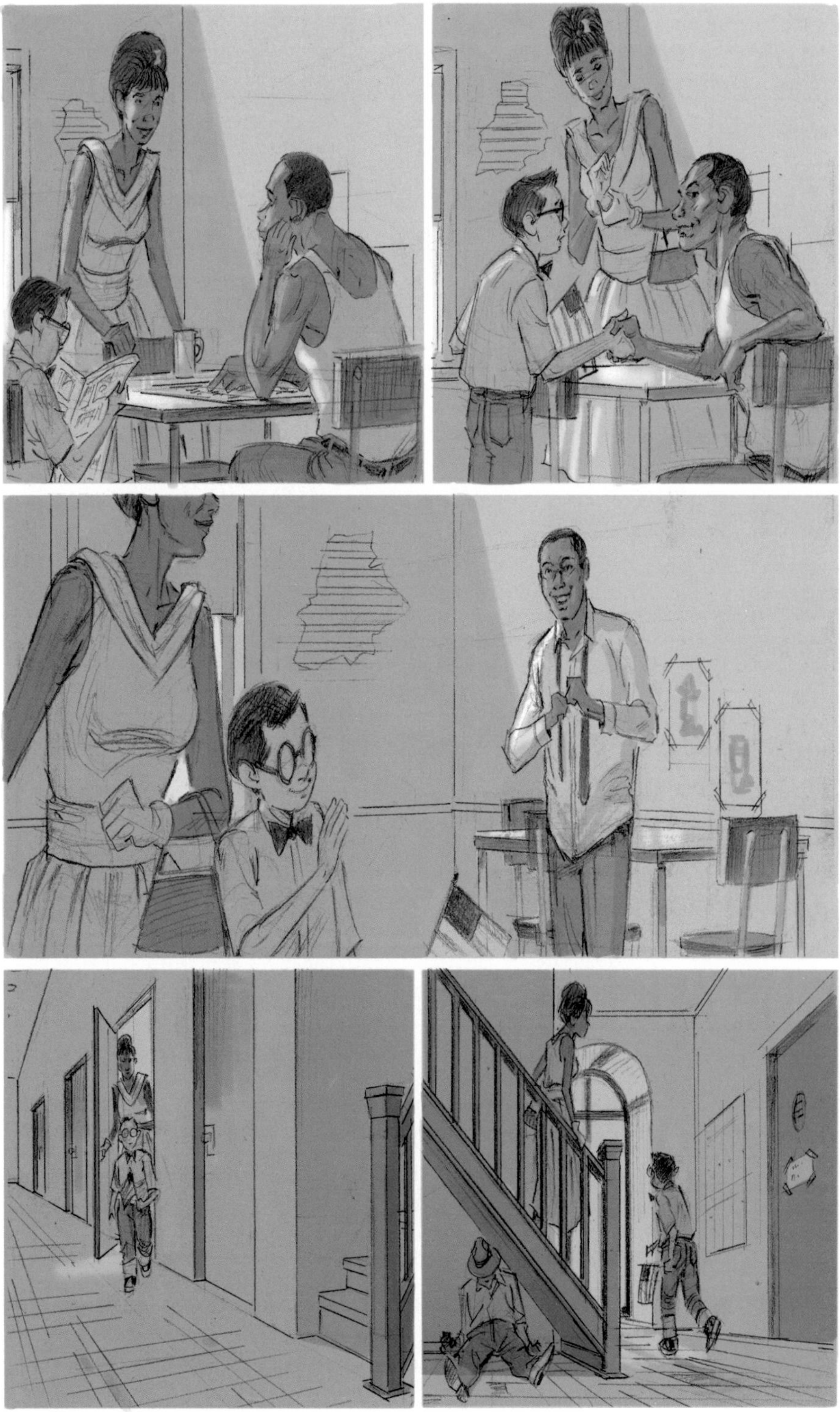

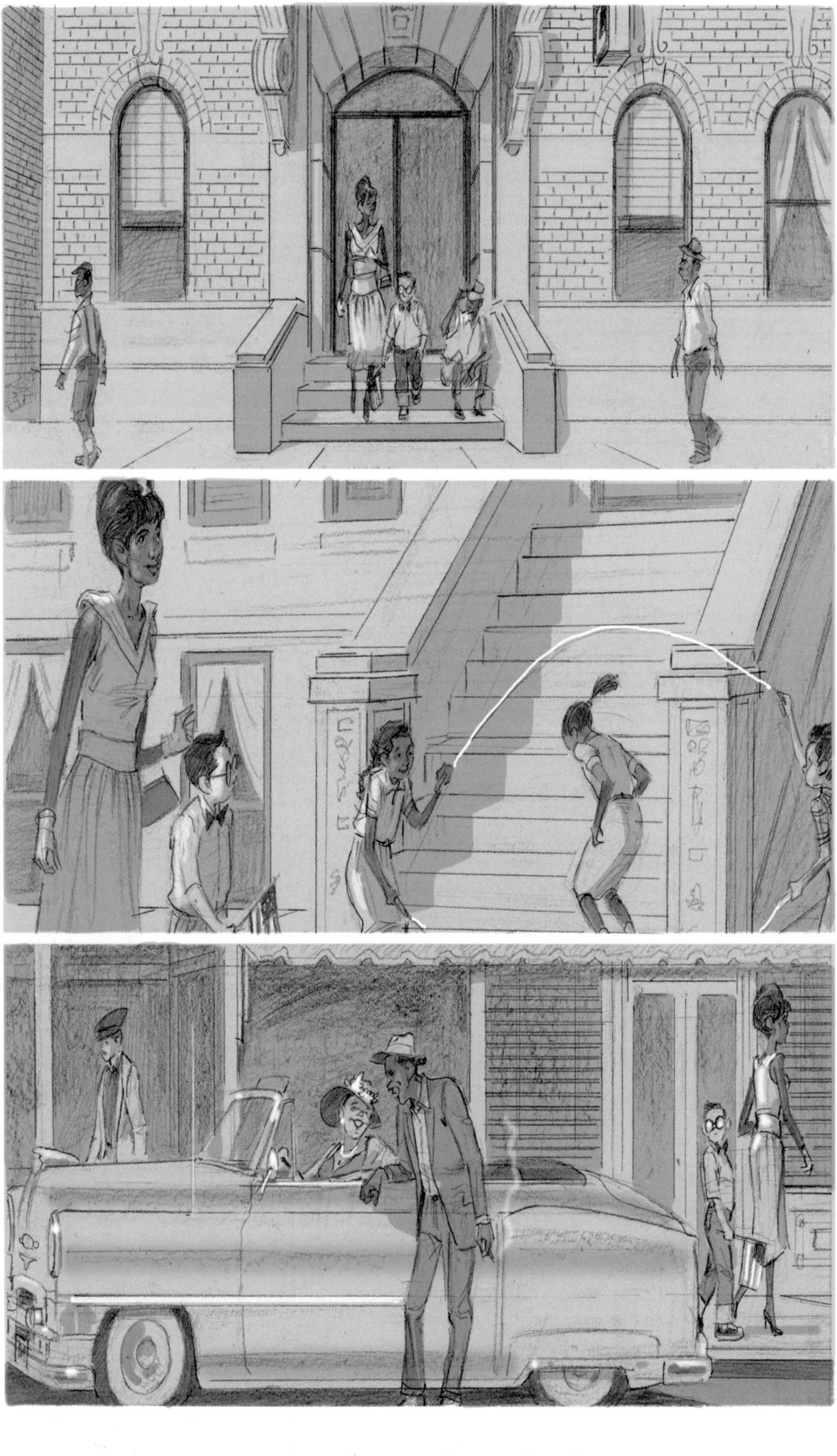

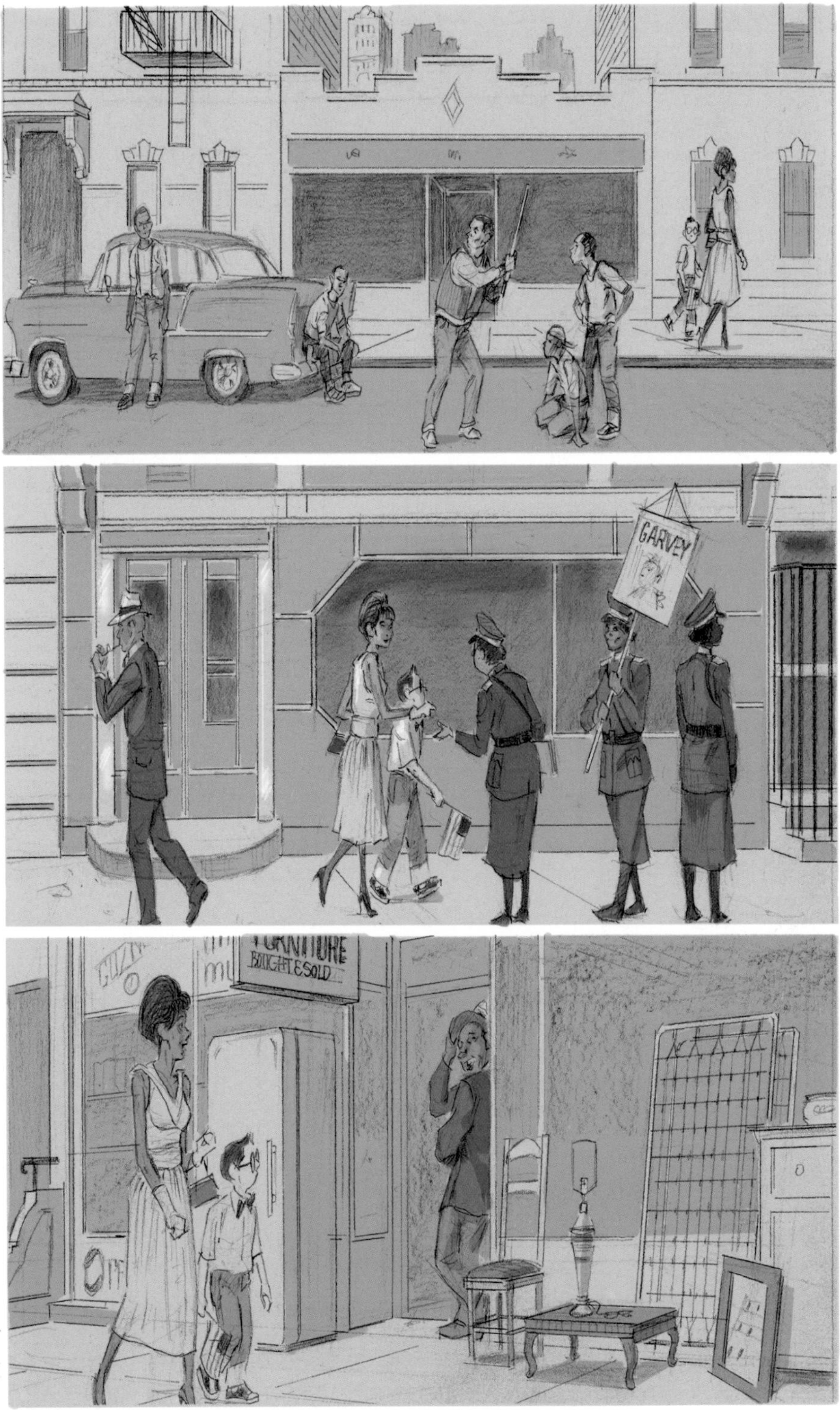
GARVEY
BOUGHT & SOLD

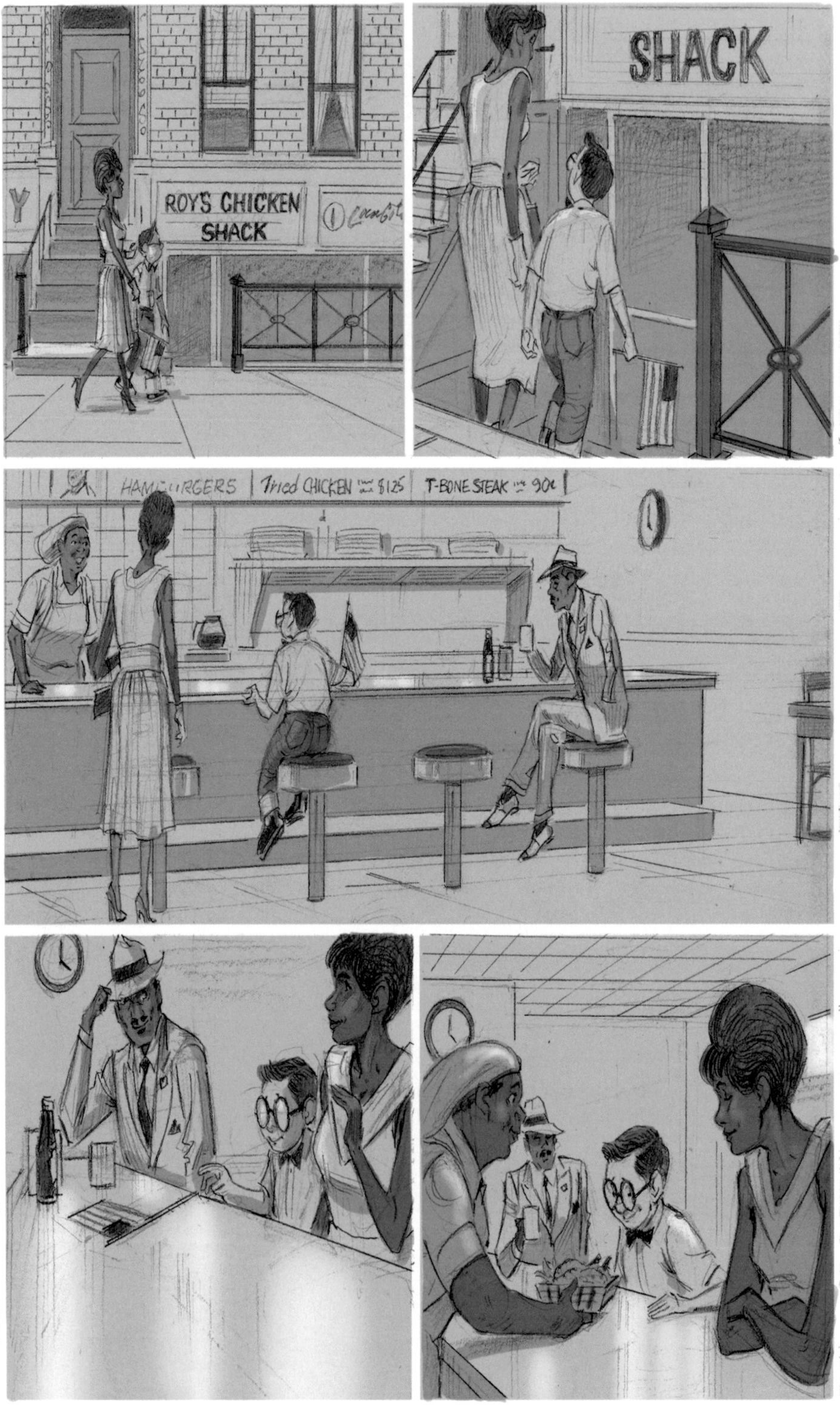
ROY'S CHICKEN
SHACK
SHACK
T-BONE STEAK

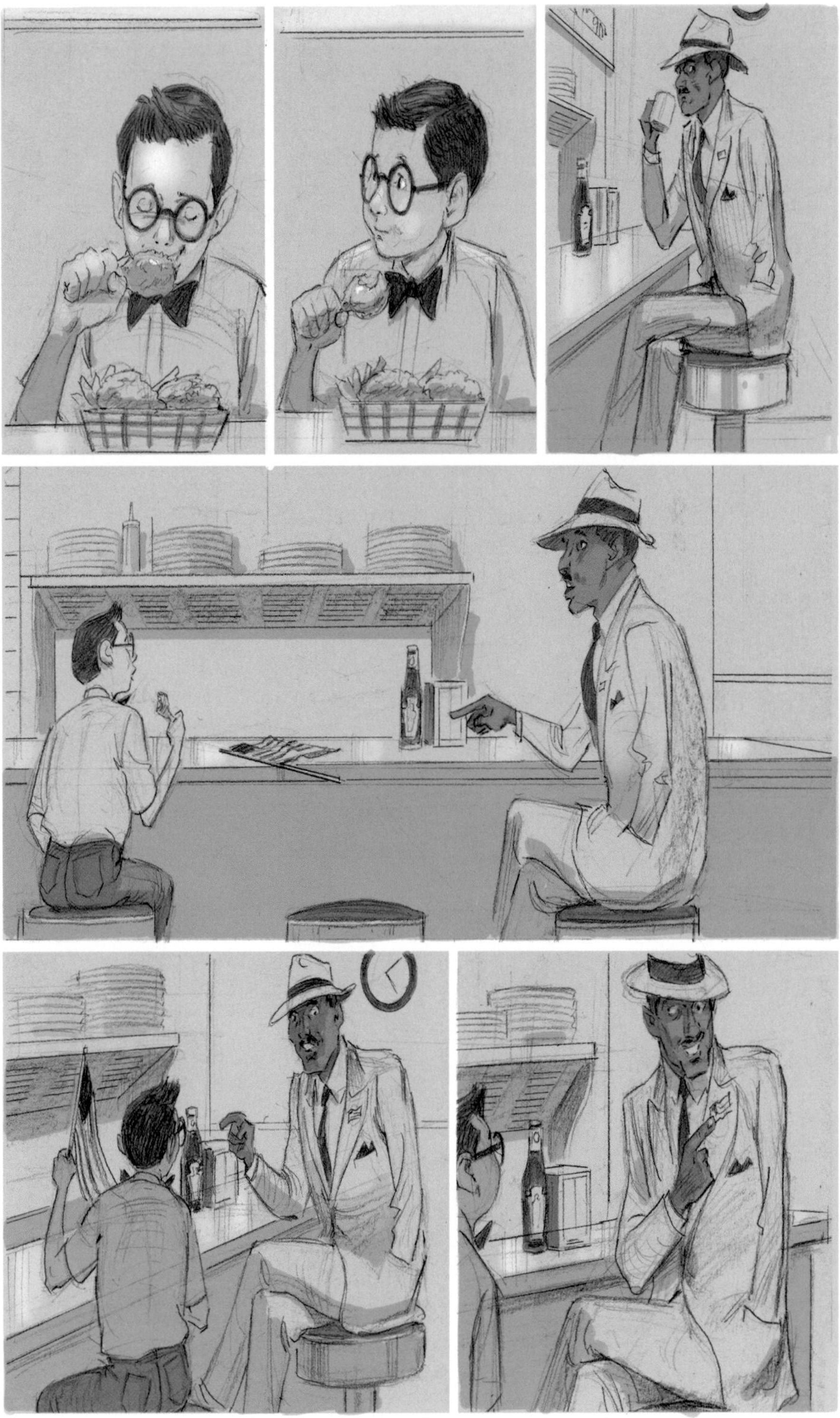

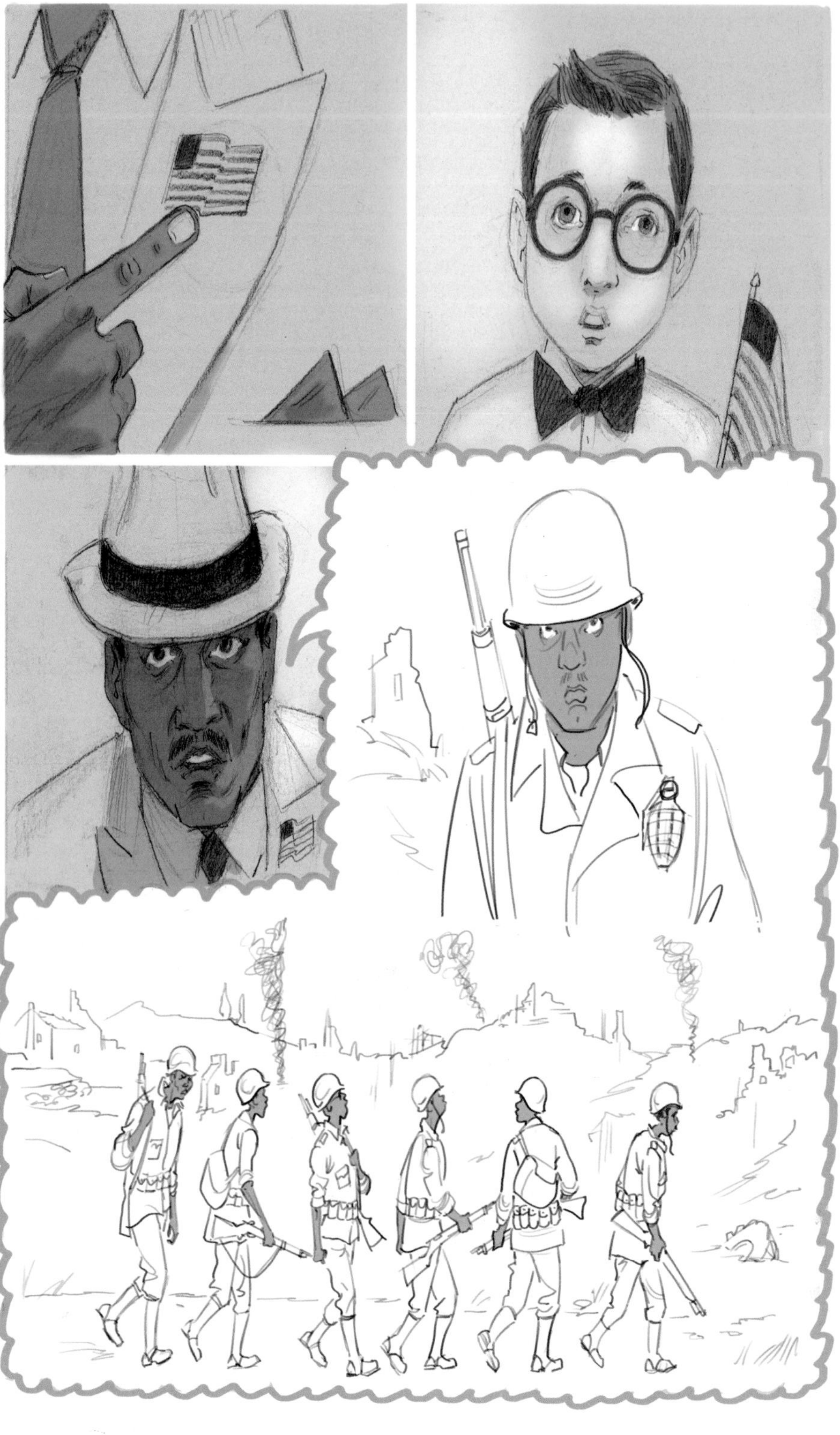

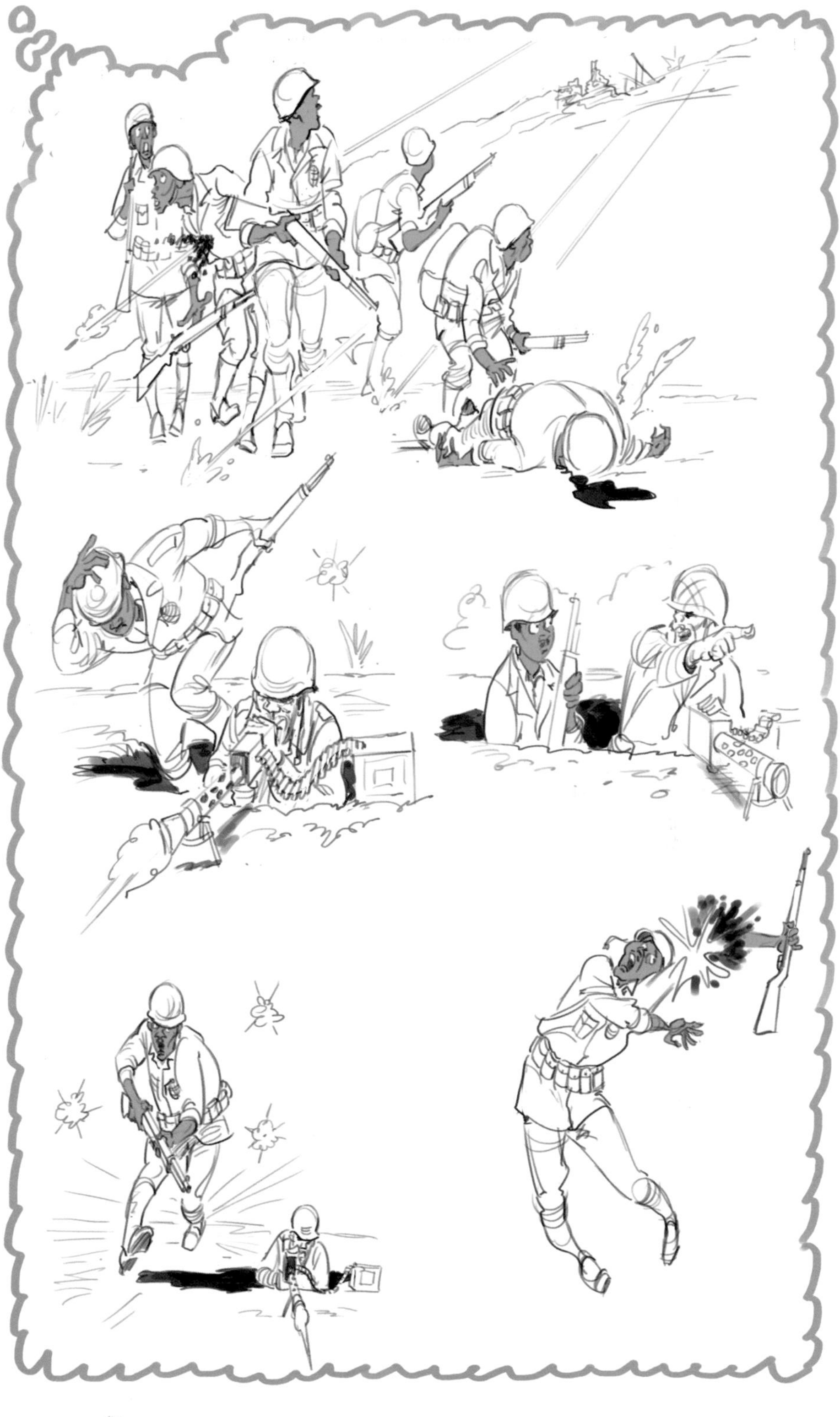

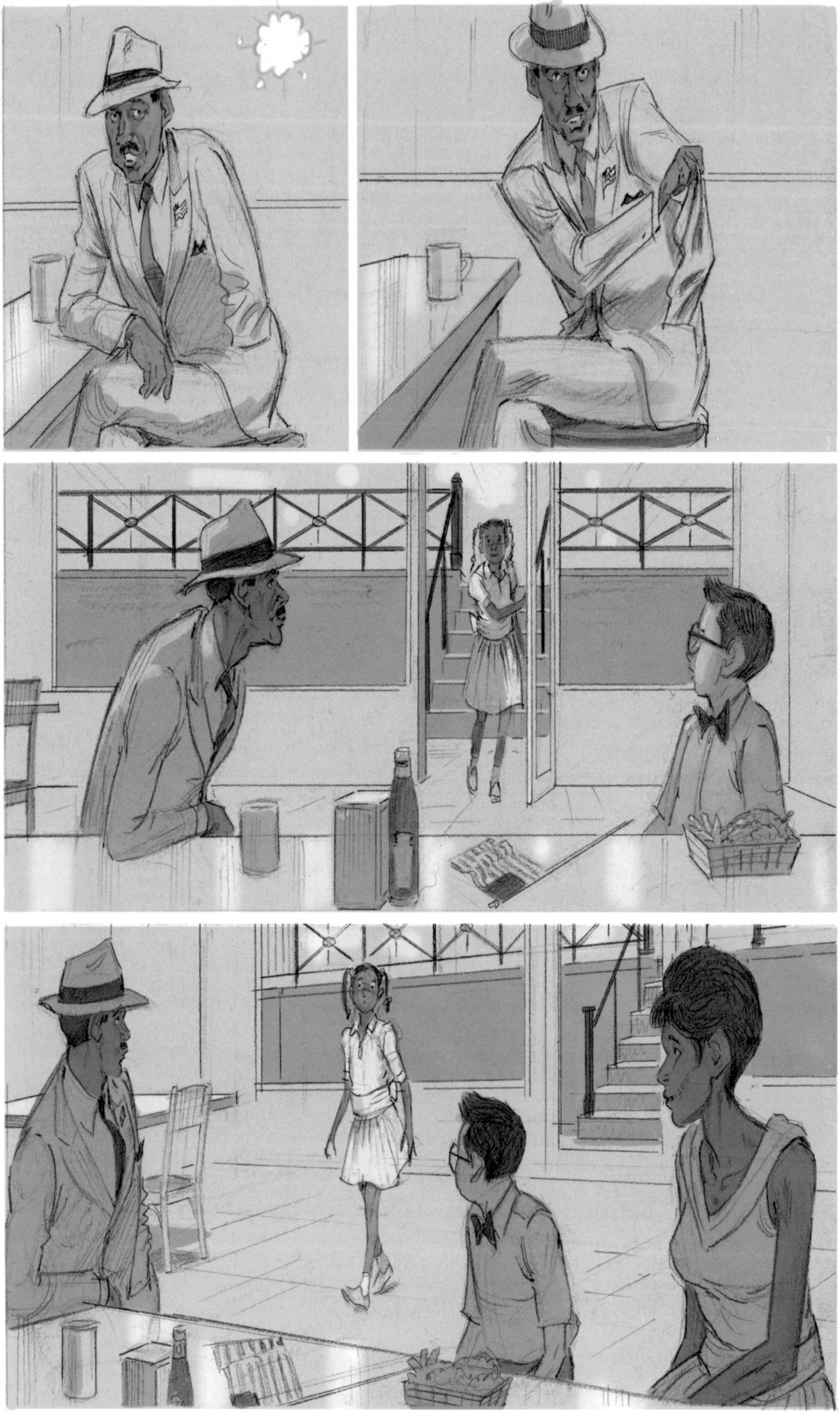

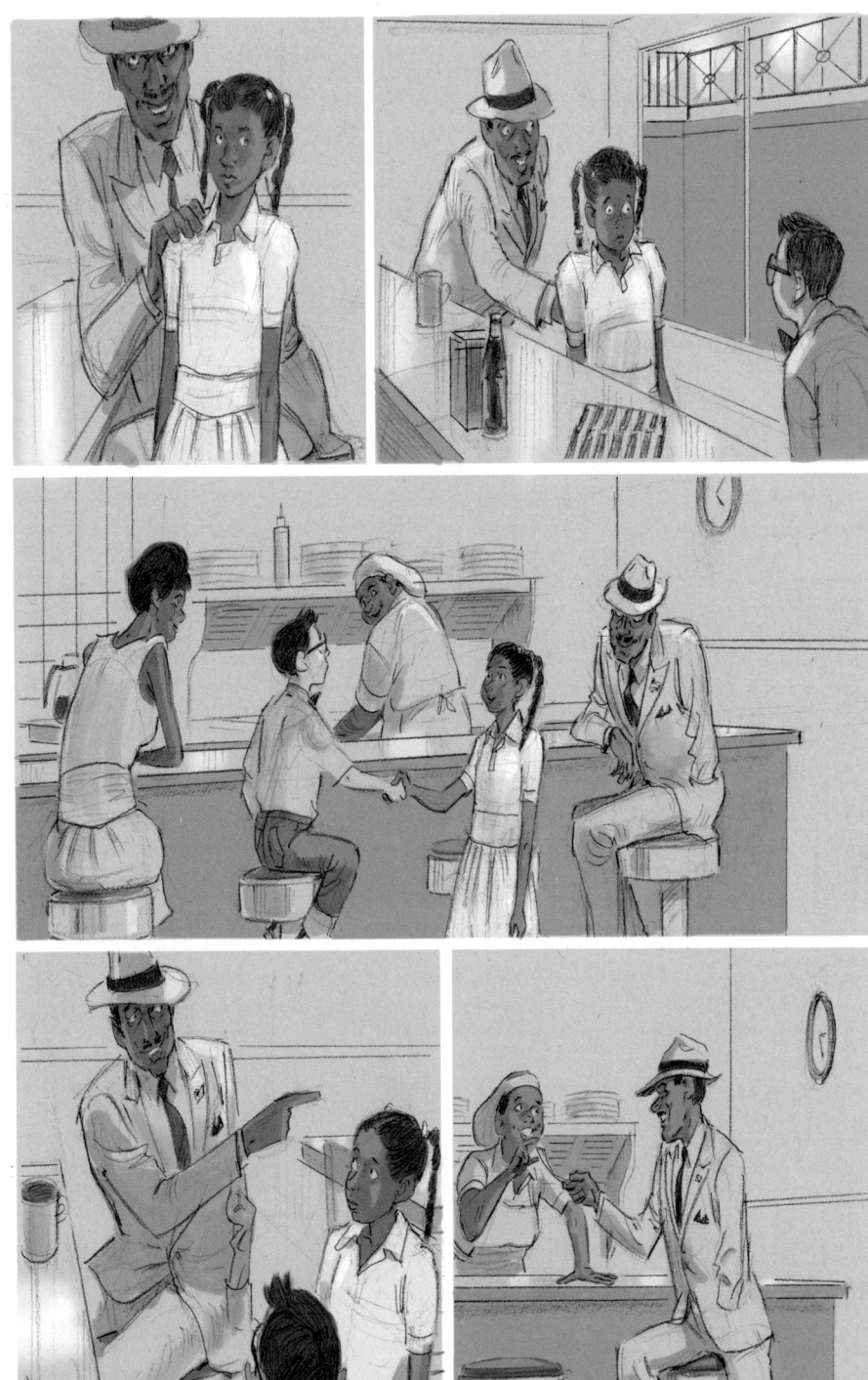

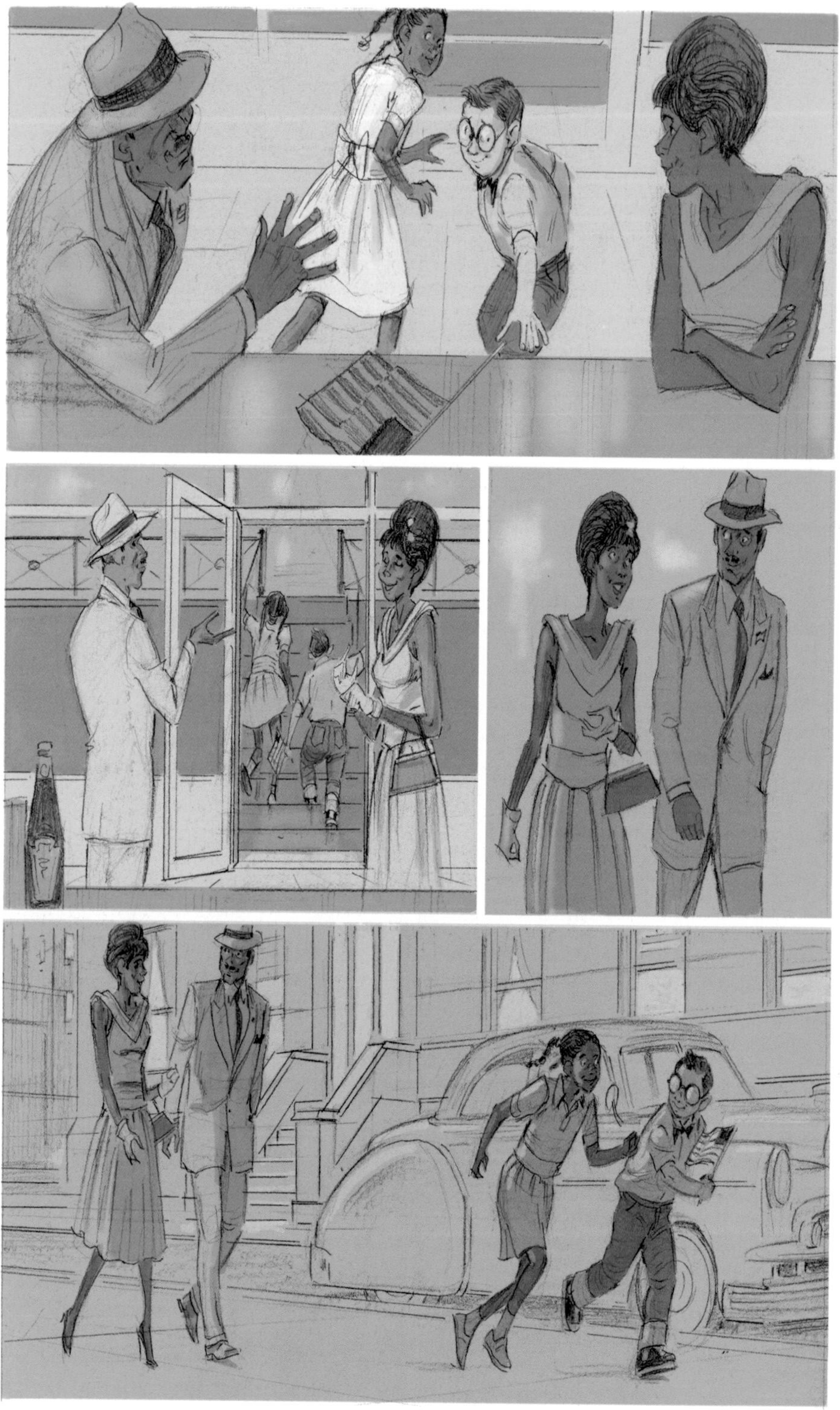

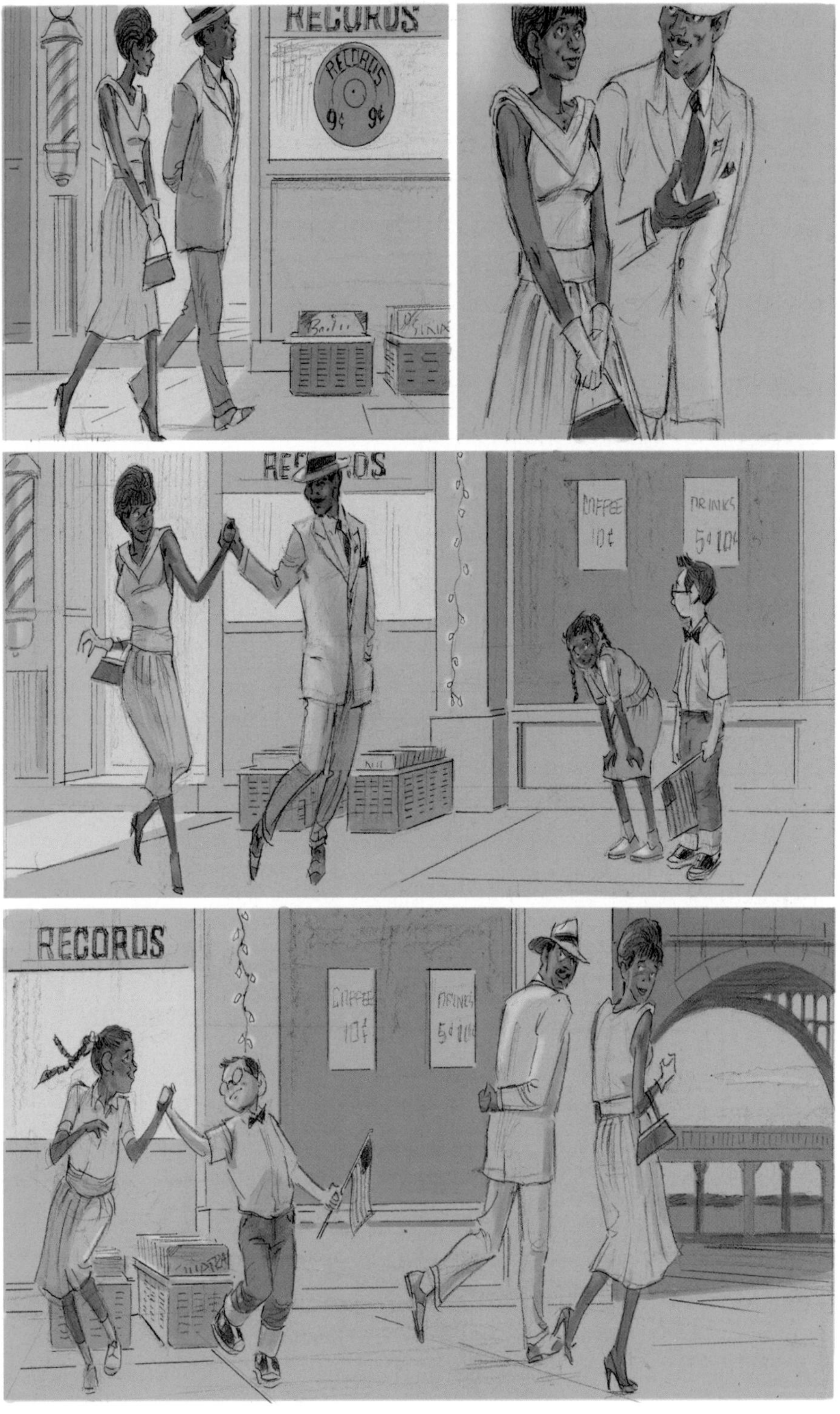

RECORDS
RECORDS
9¢ 9¢
COFFEE
10¢
DRINKS
5¢ 10¢
RECORDS

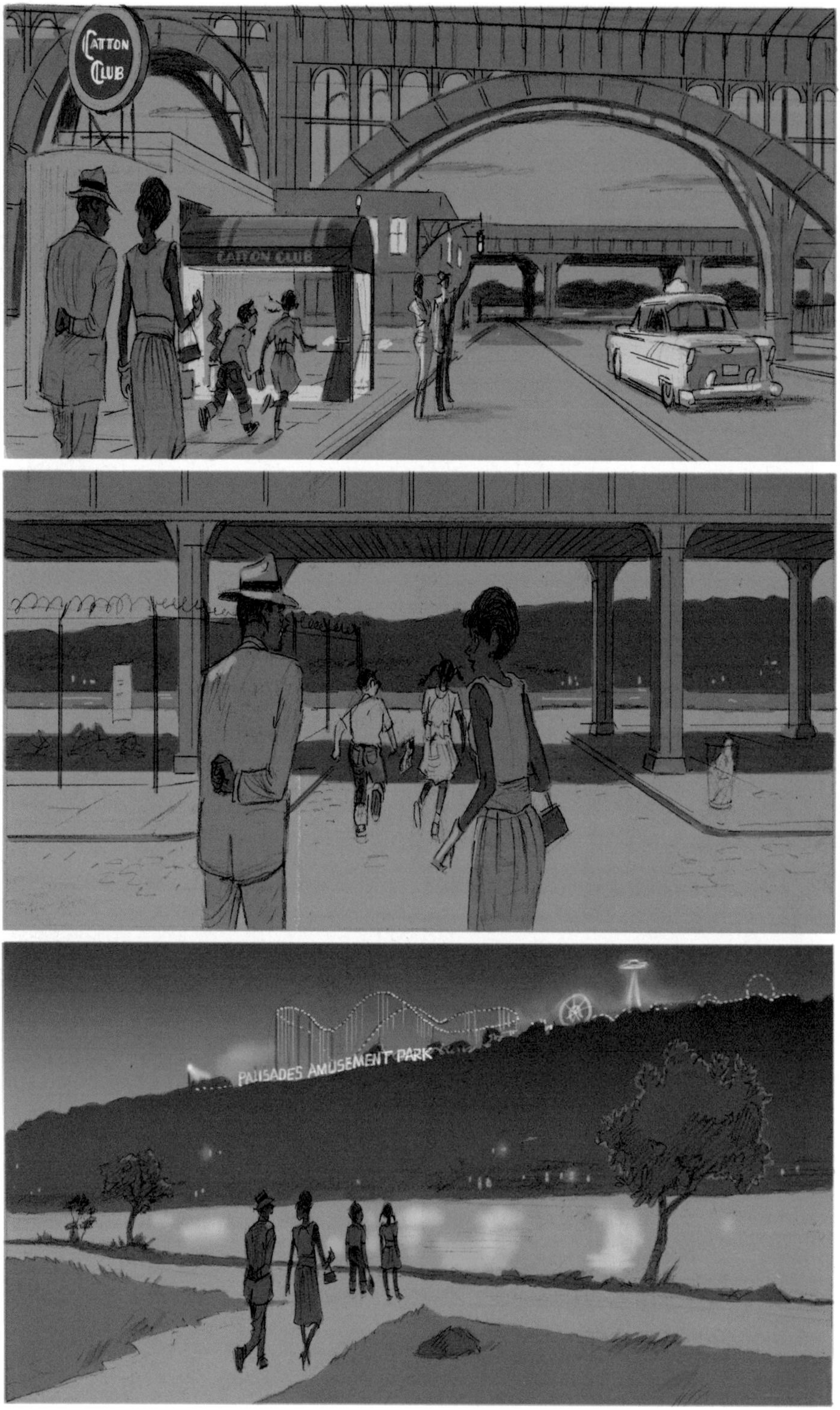
CATTON CLUB
CATTON CLUB
PALISADES AMUSEMENT PARK

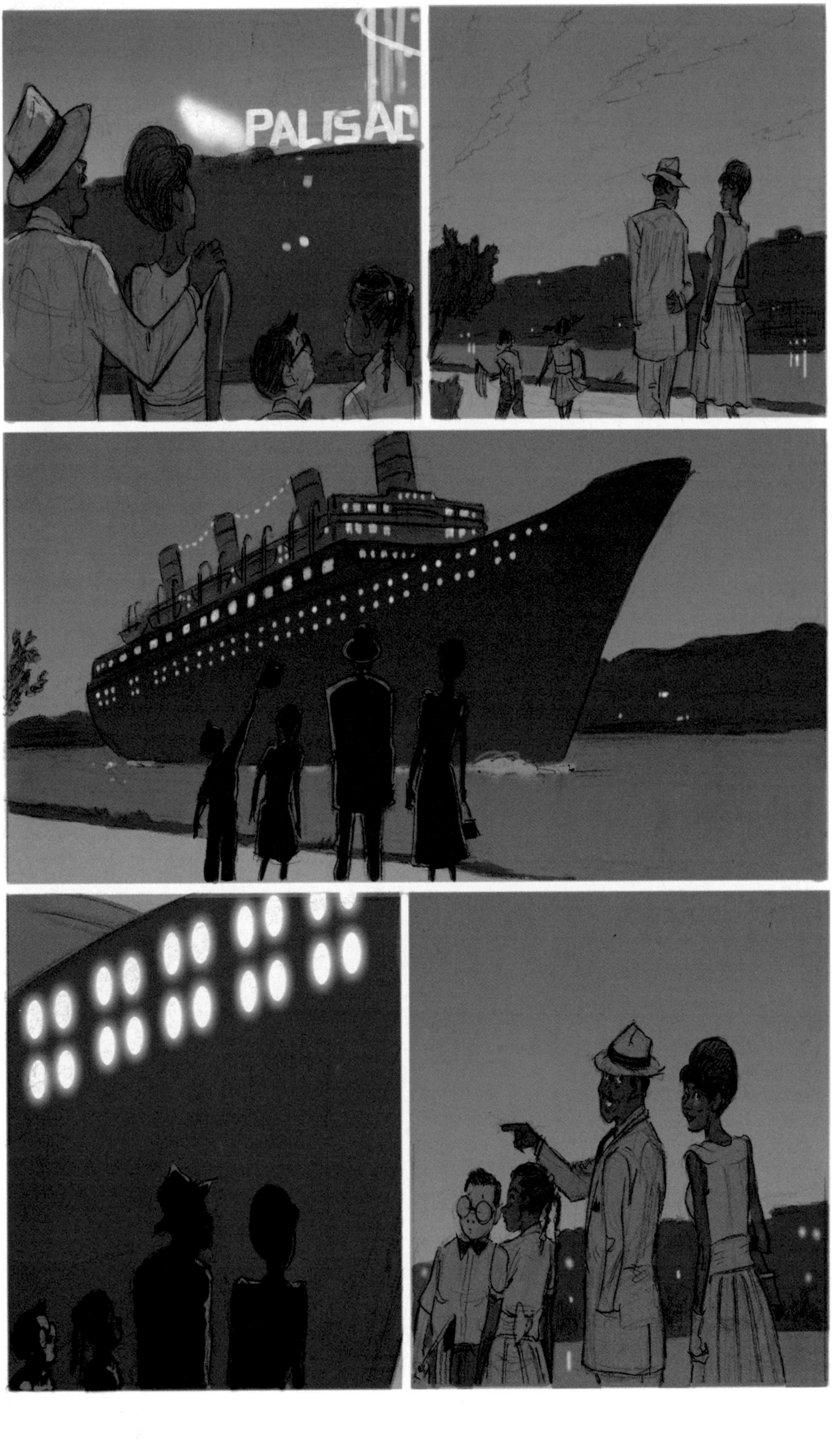
PALISAD

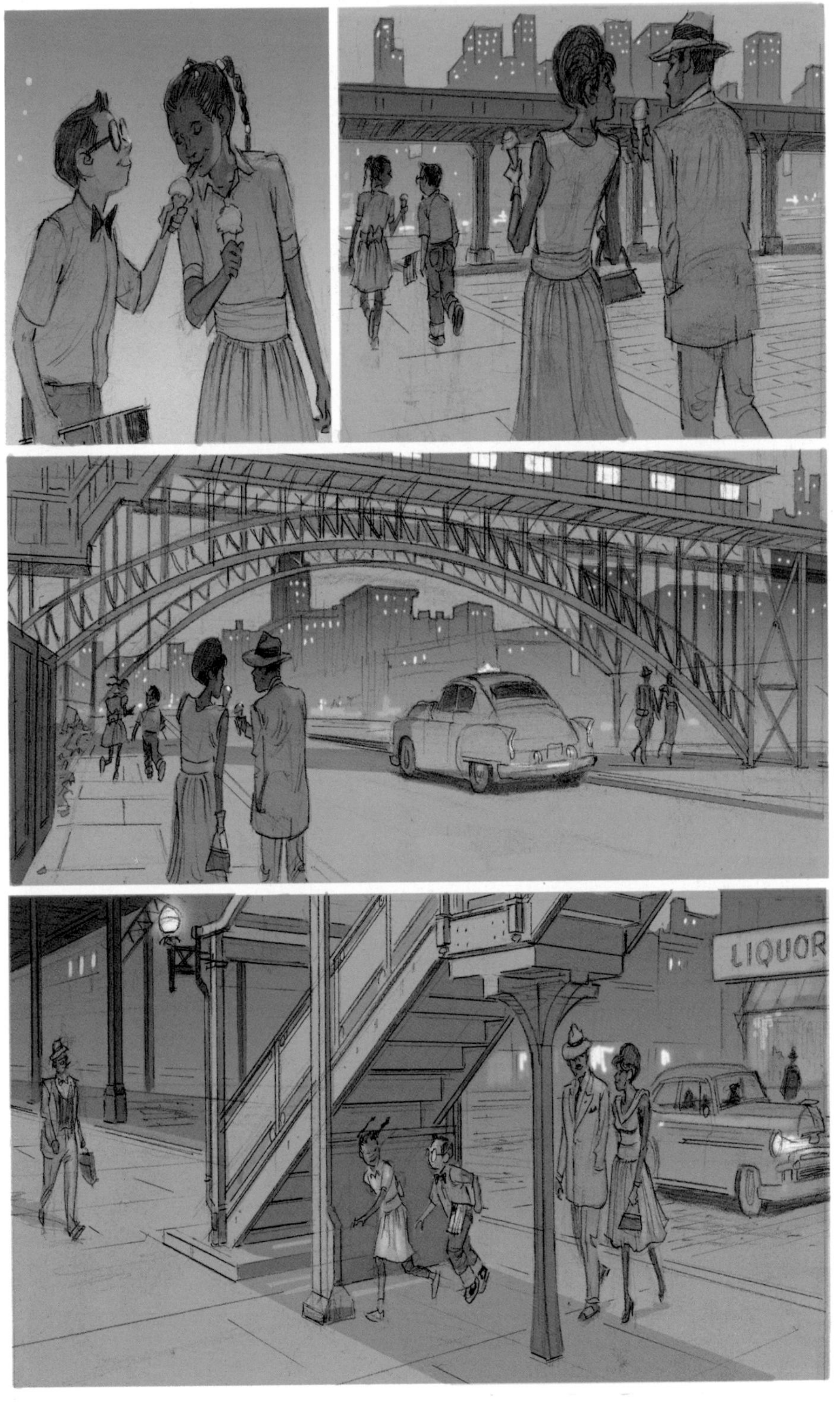
LIQUOR

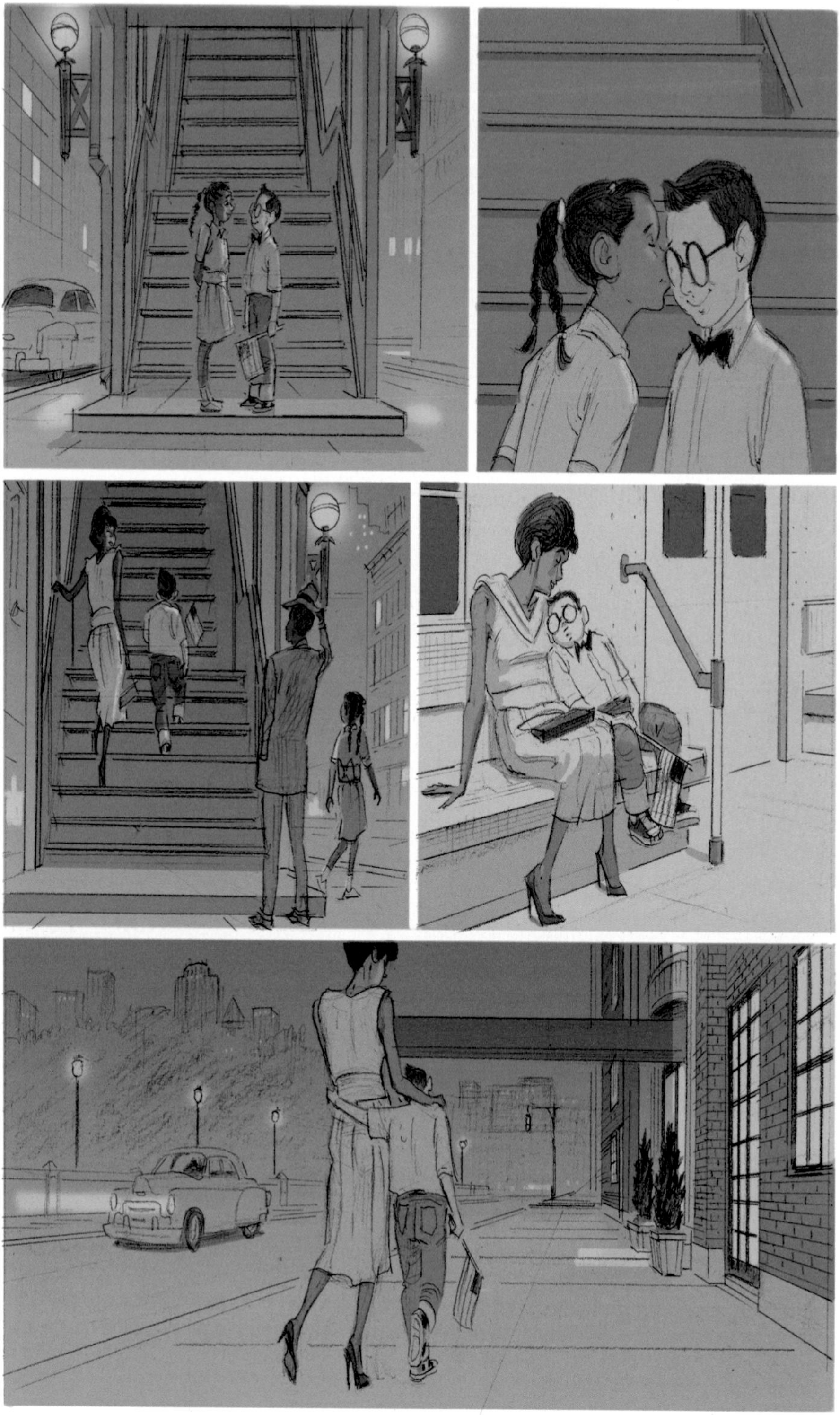

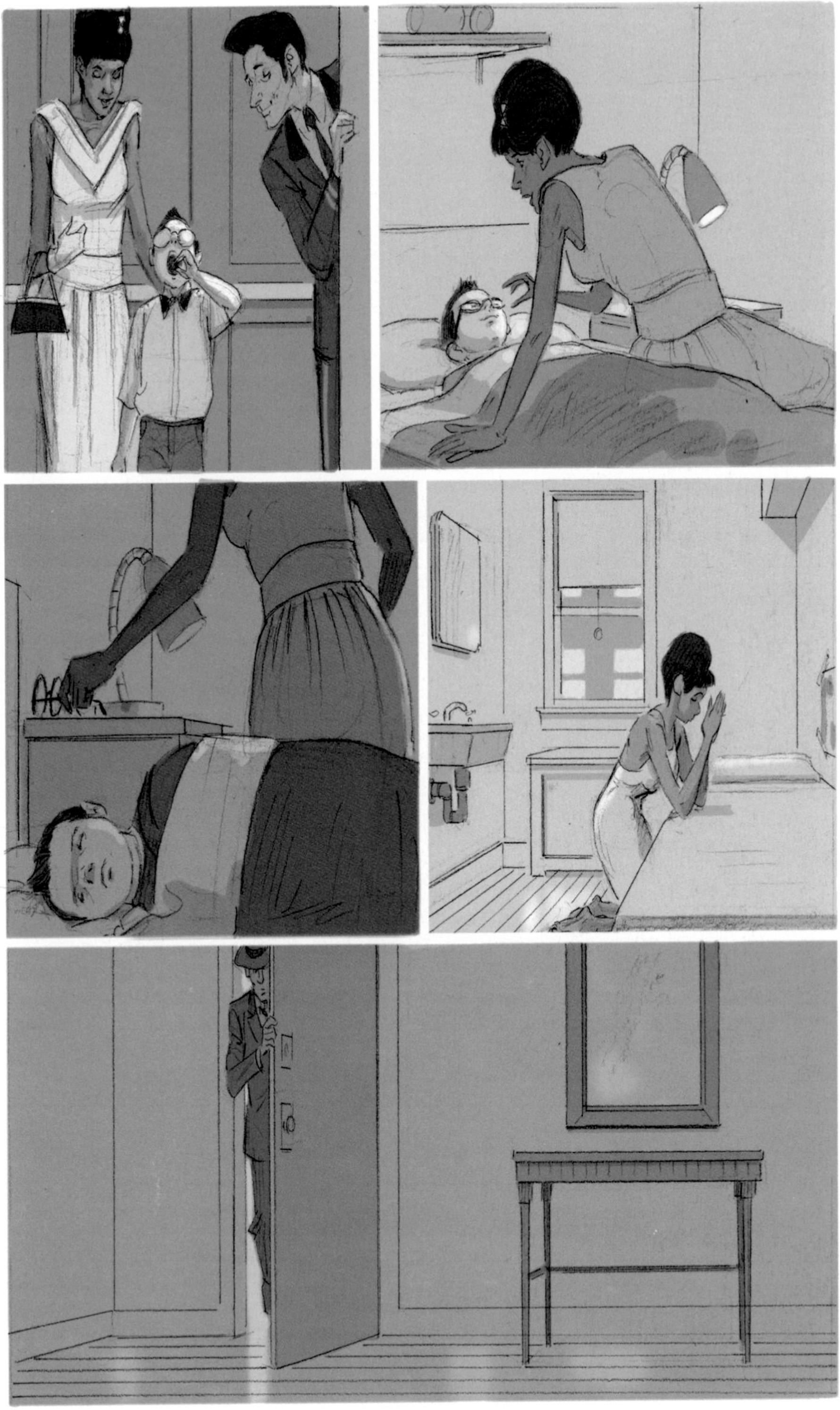

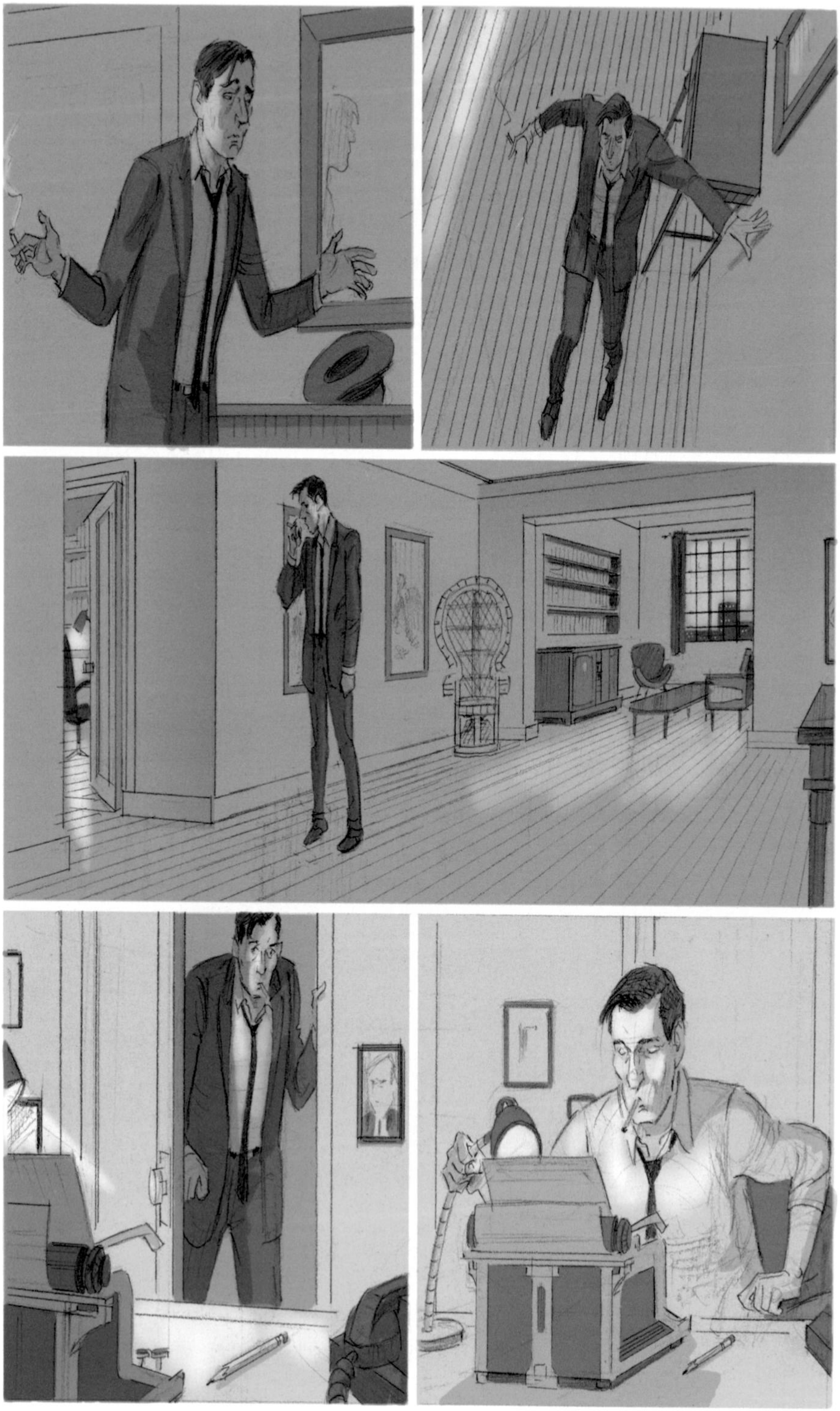

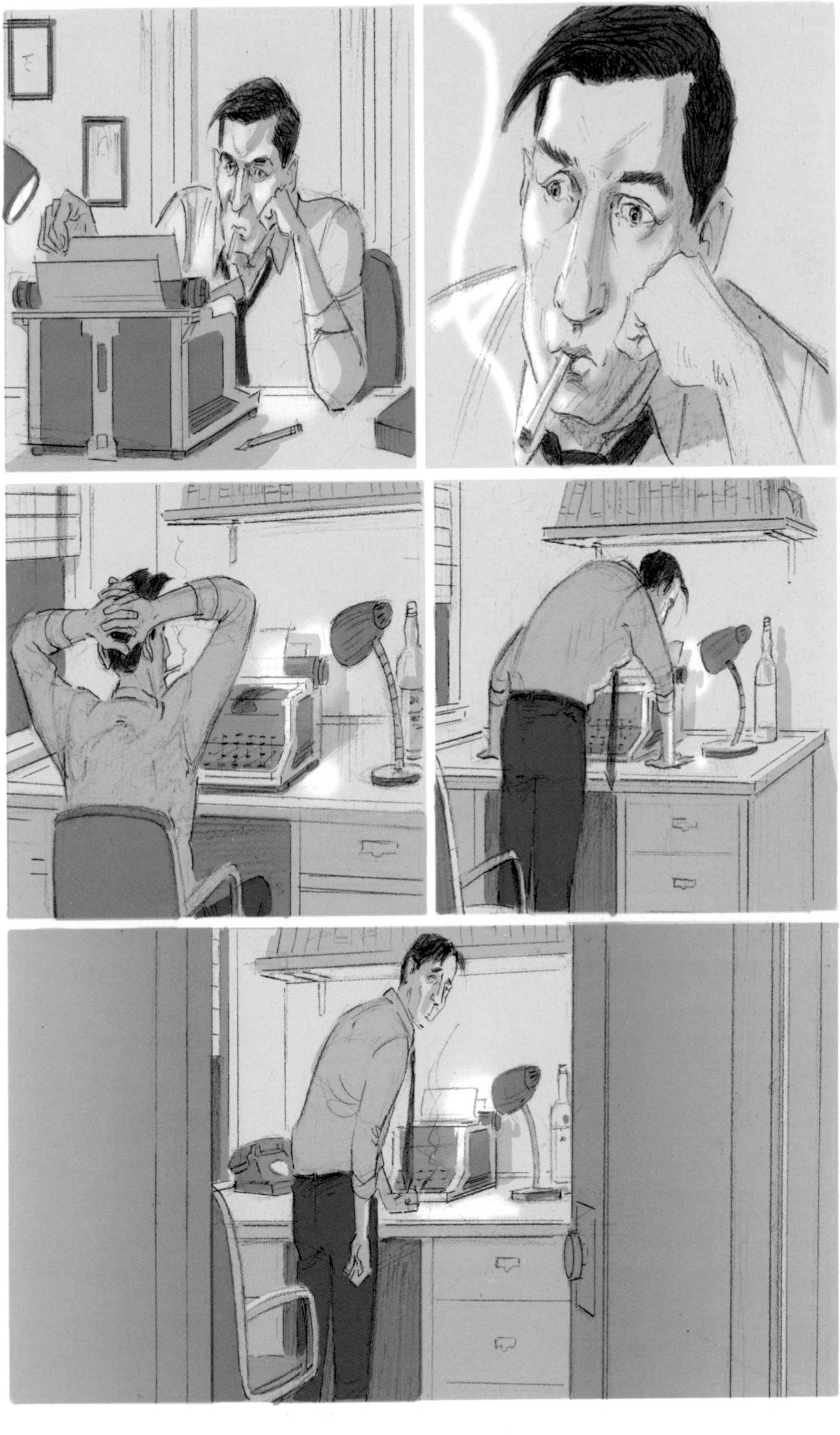

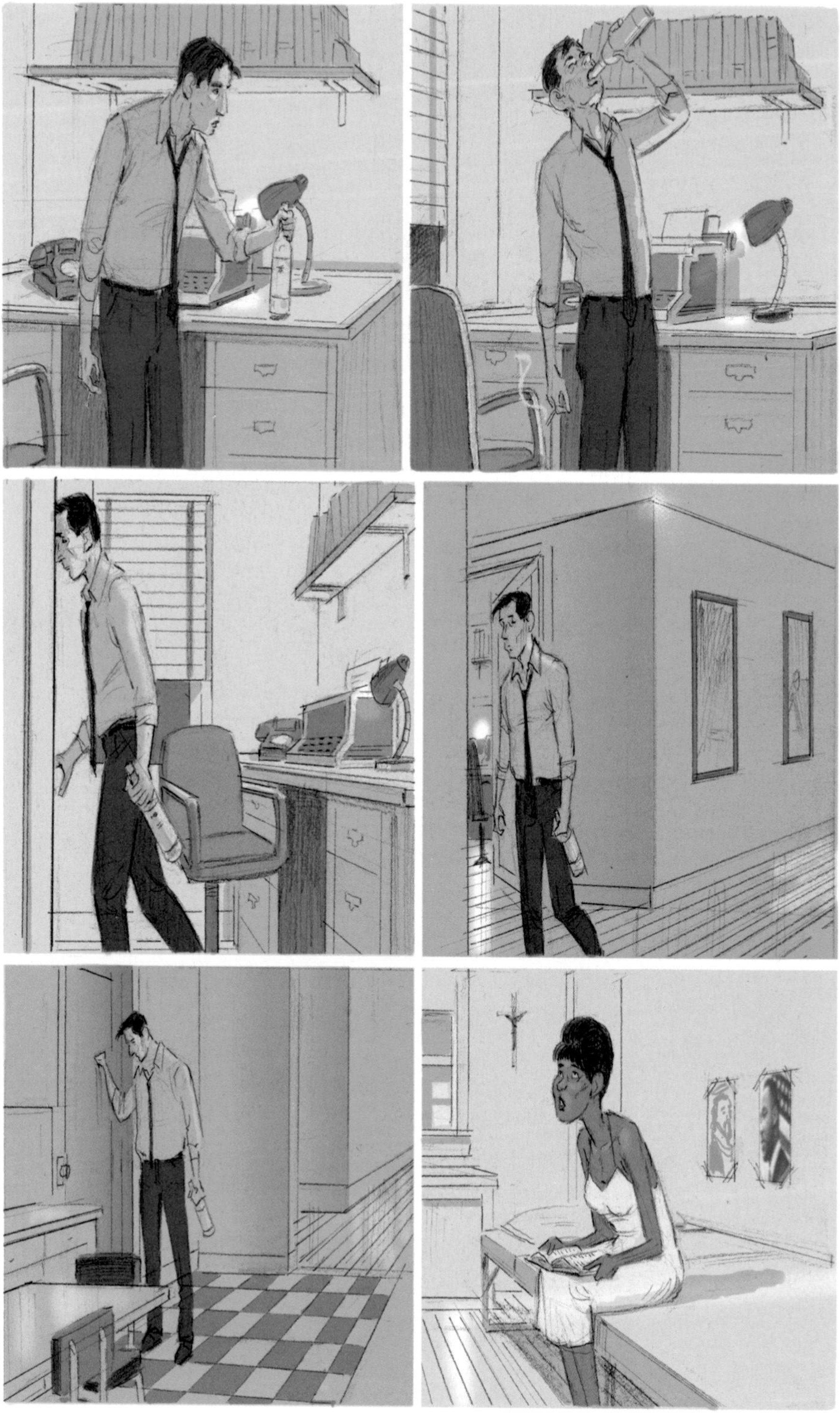

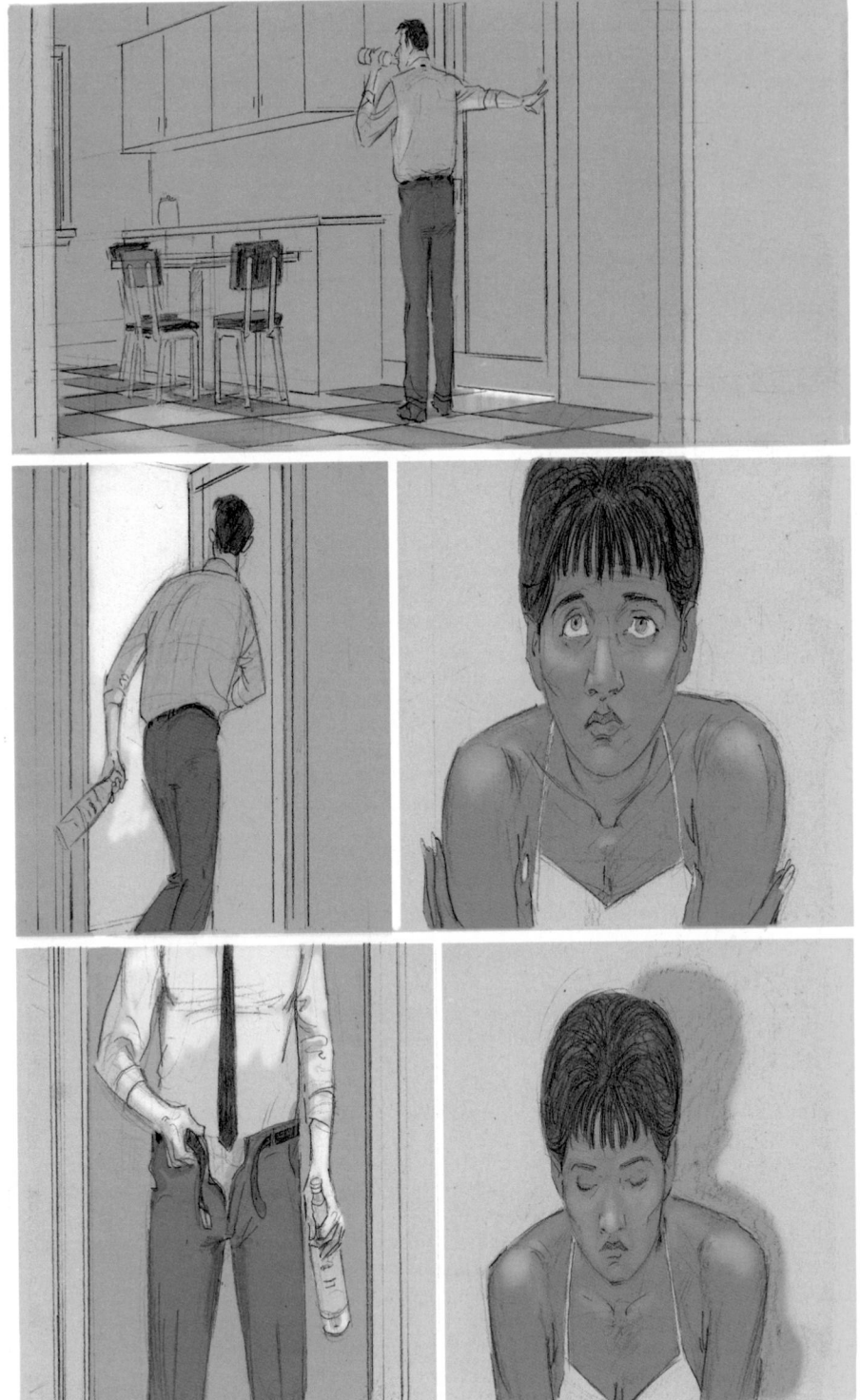

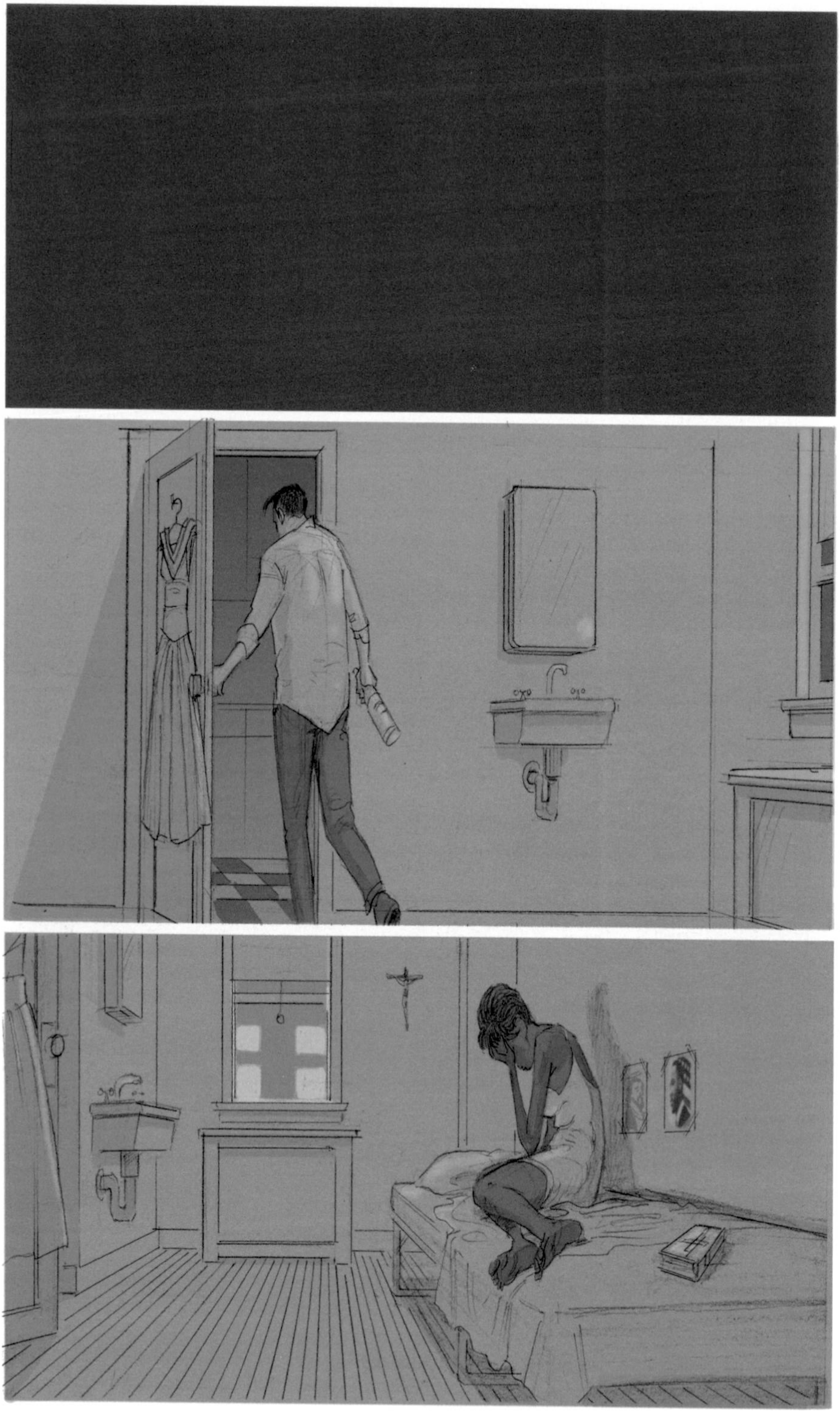

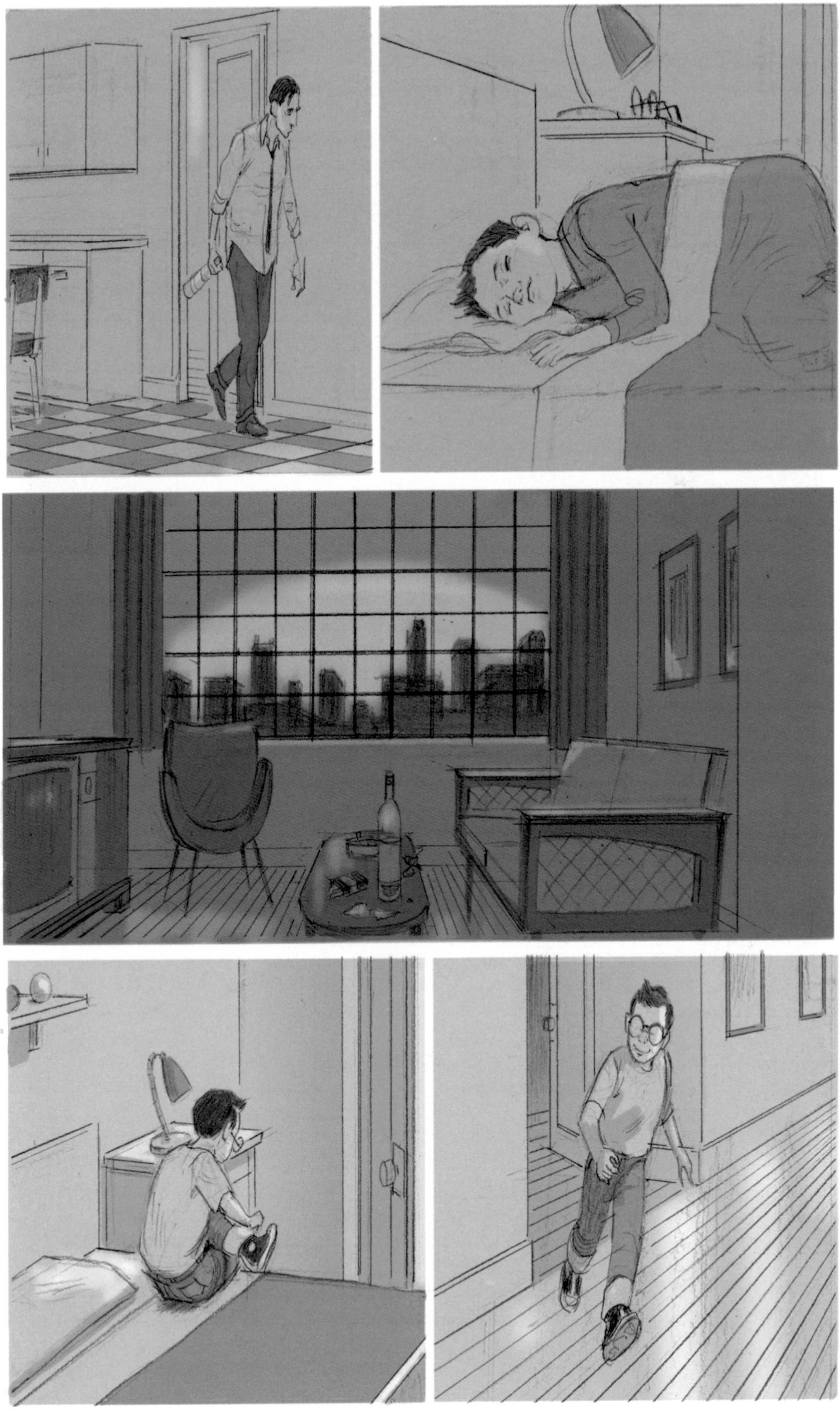

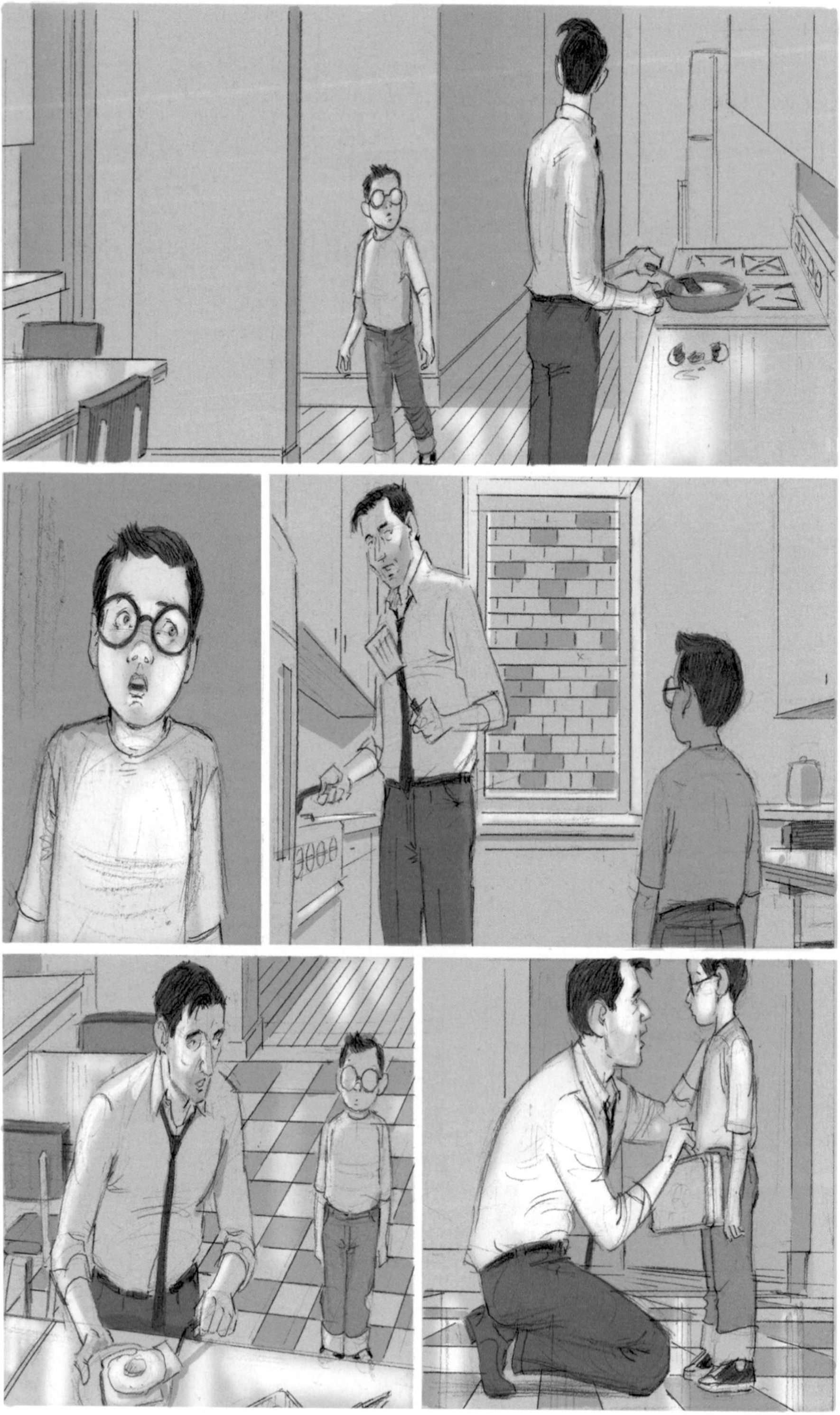

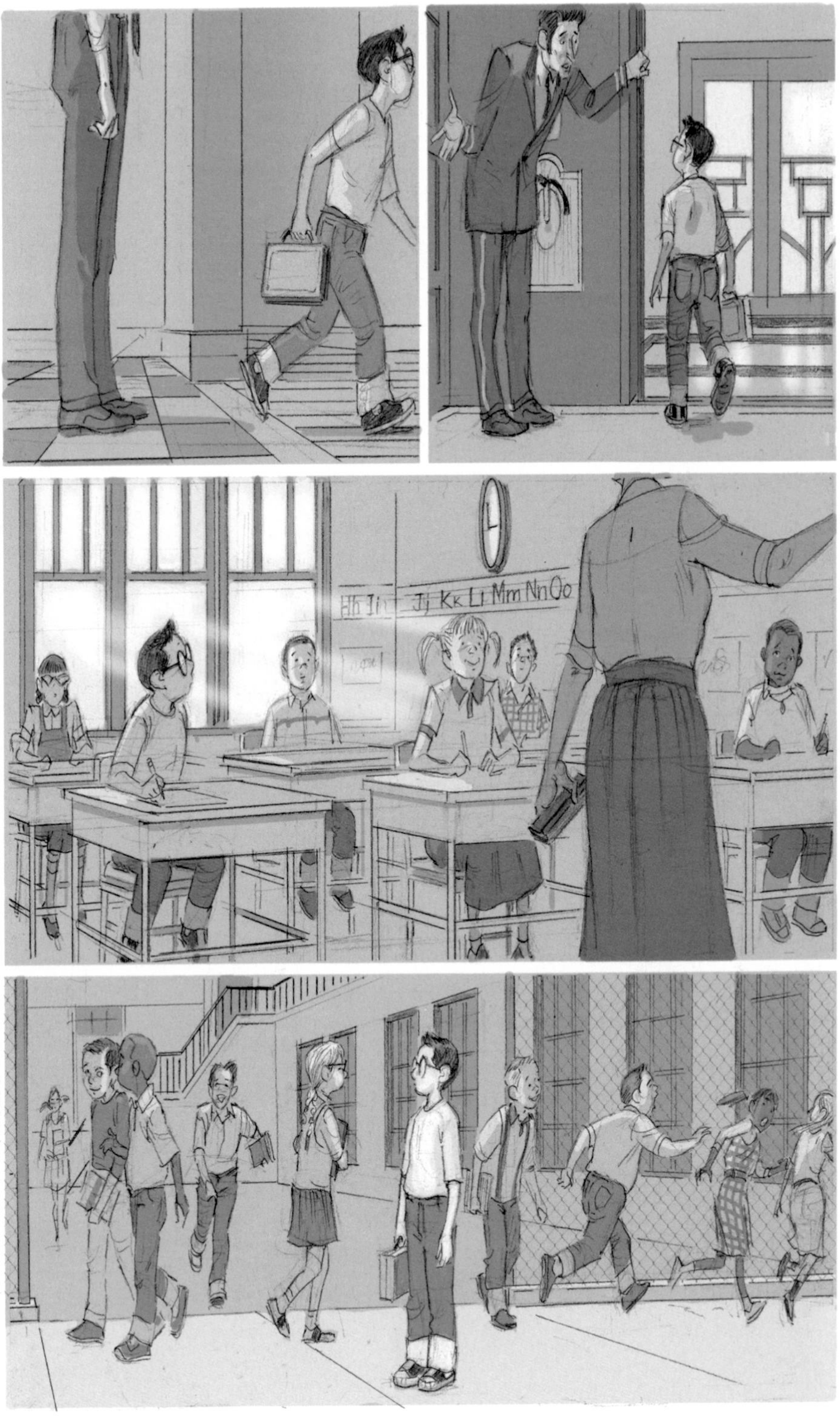
Hh Ii Jj Kk Ll Mm Nn Oo

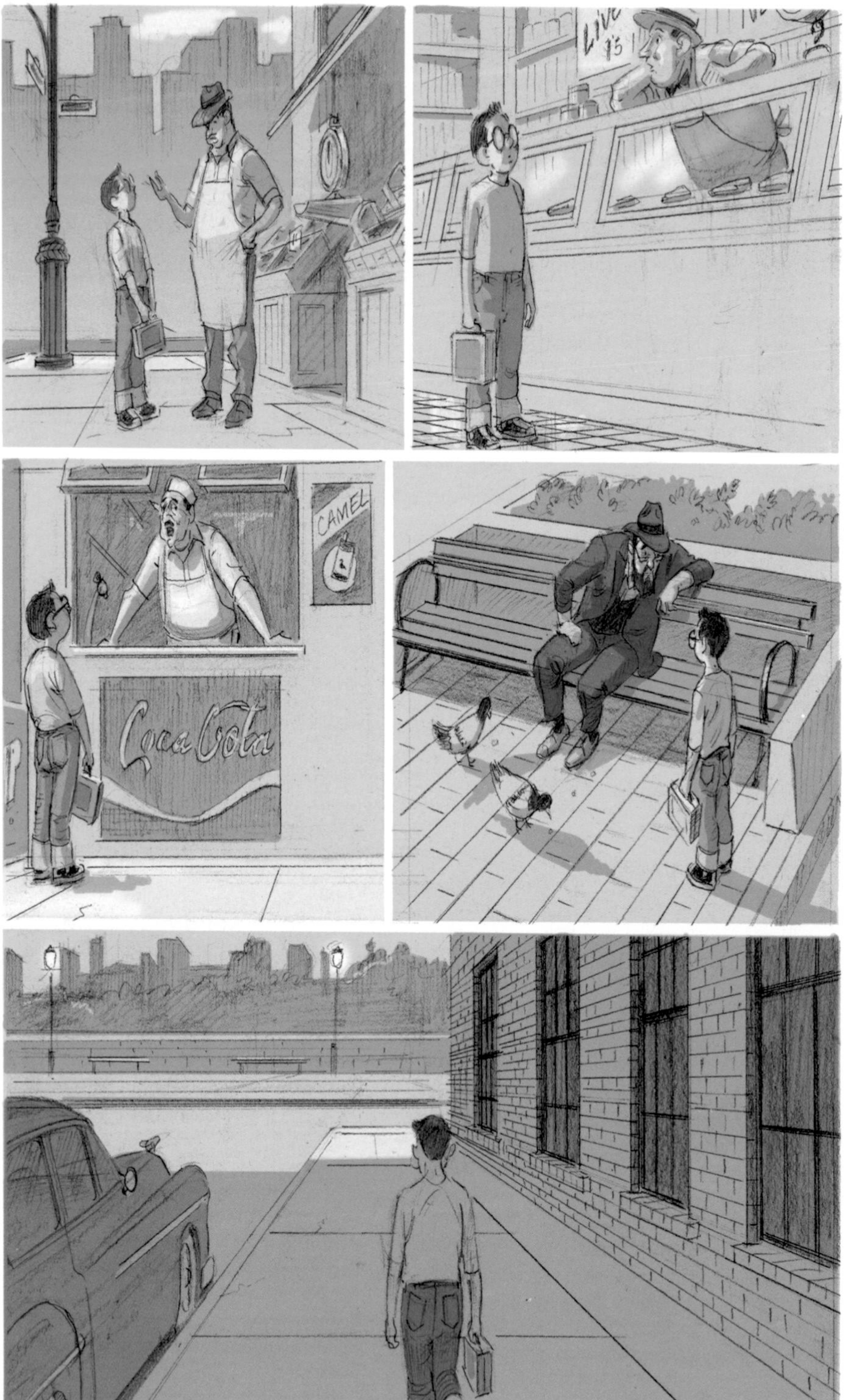
CAMEL
Coca Cola

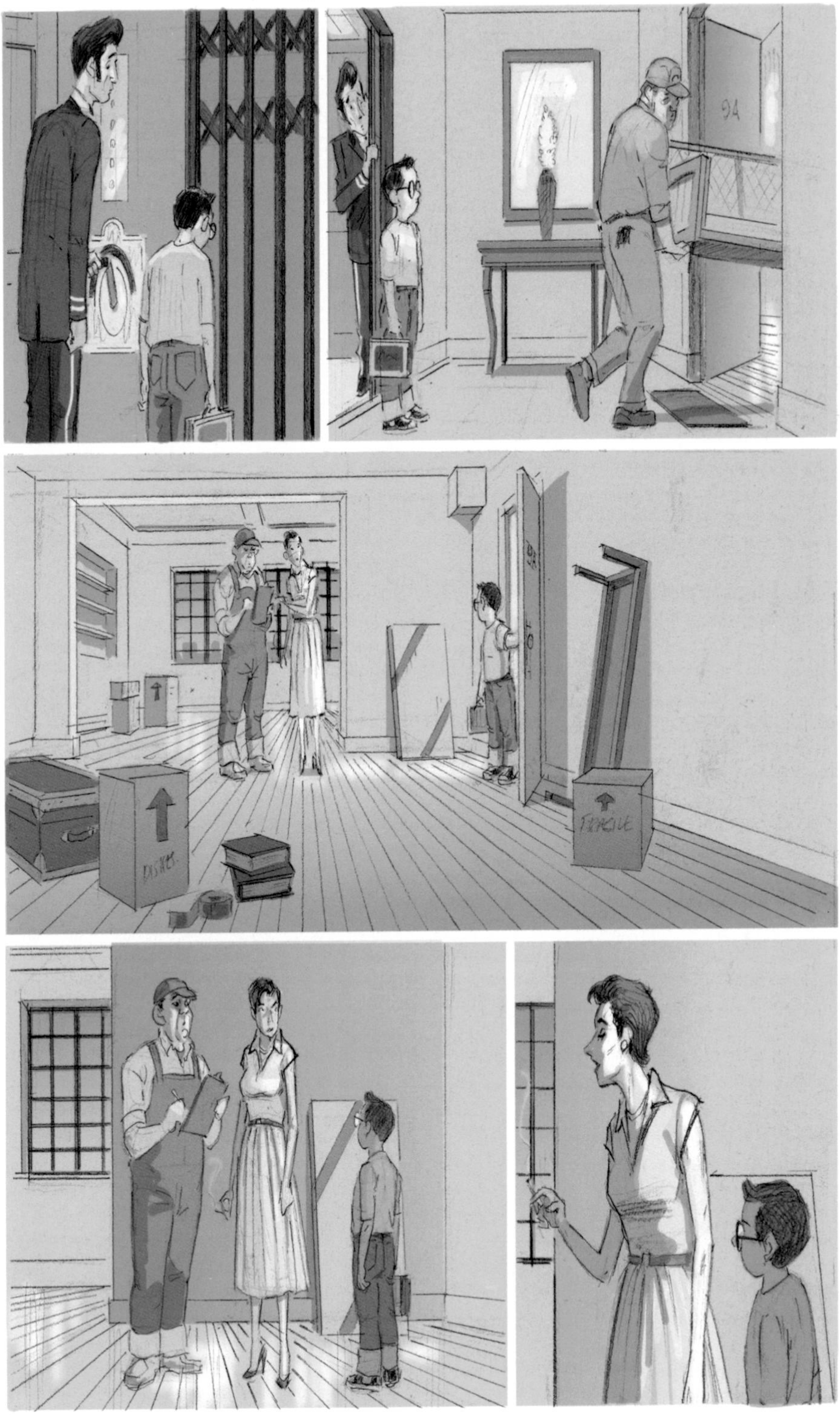
94
DISHES.
FRAGILE

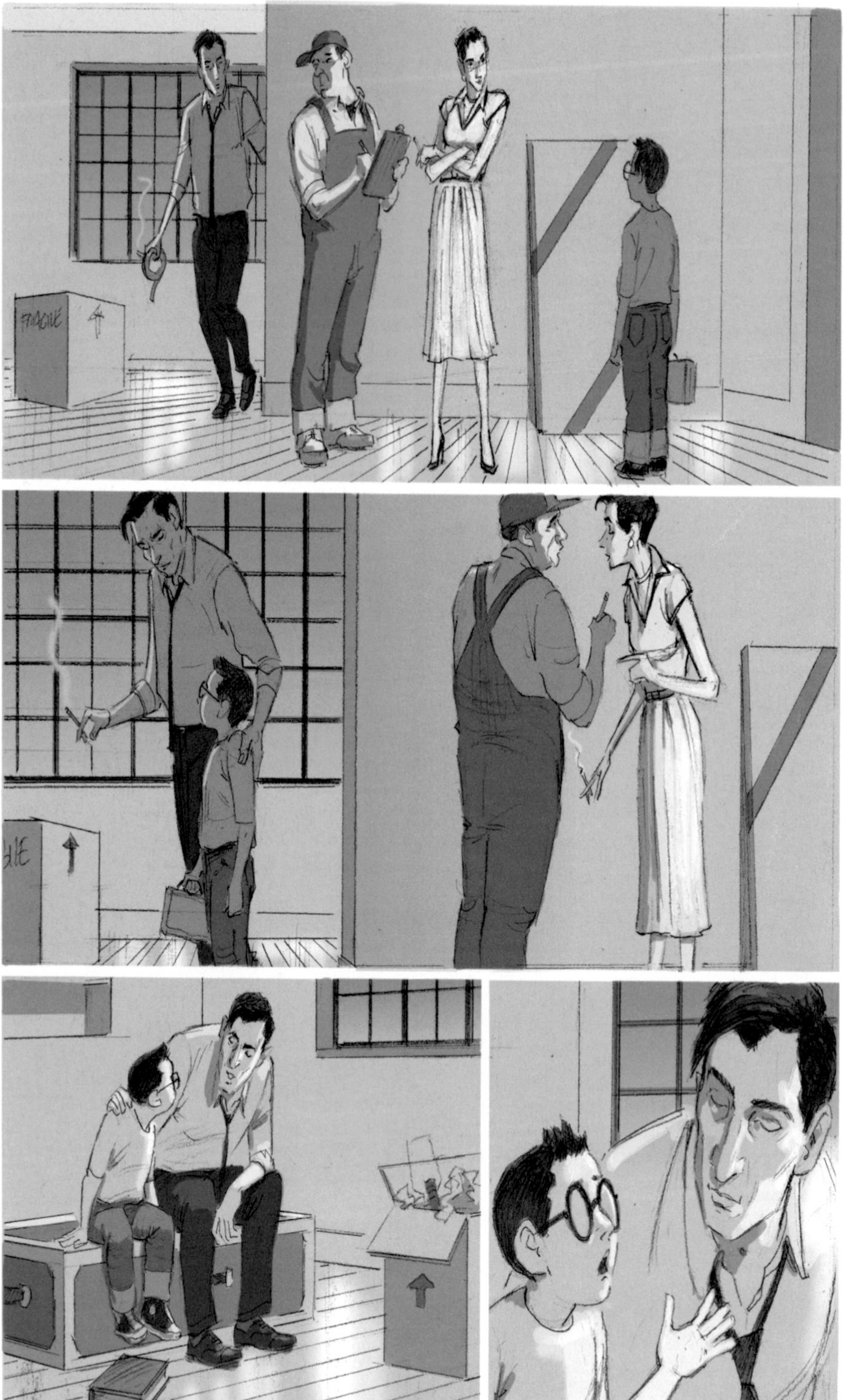
FRAGILE

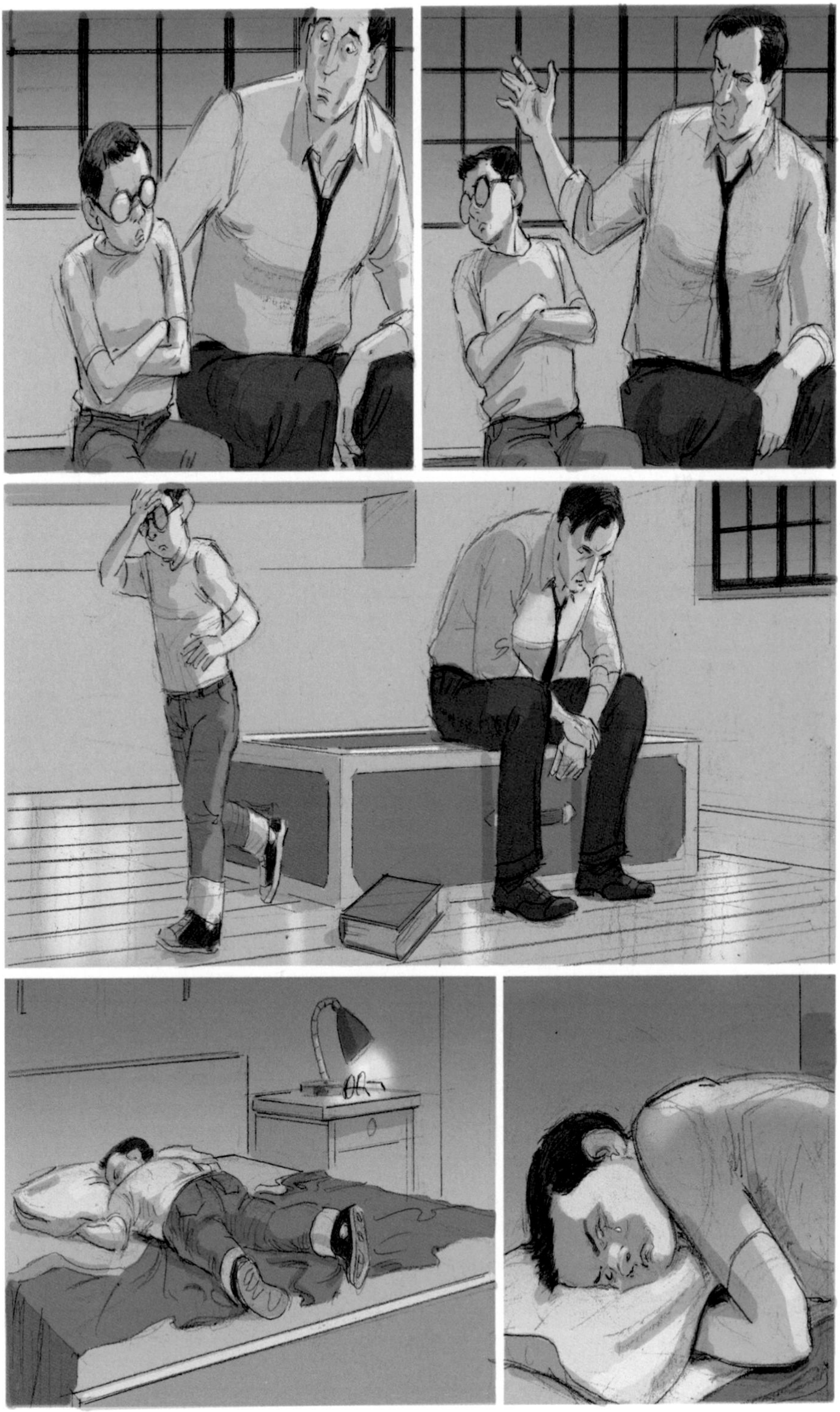

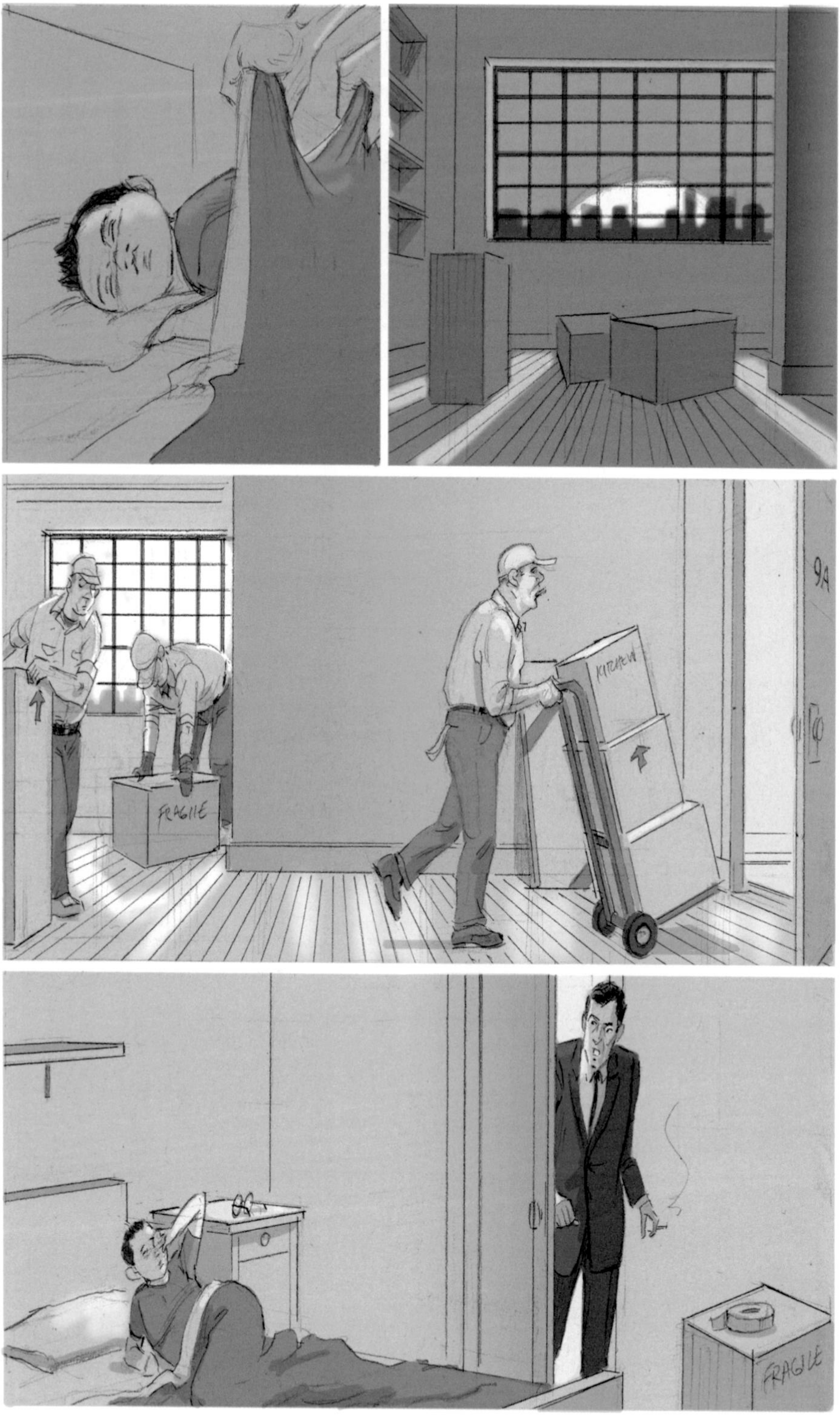
9A
FRAGILE
KITCHEN
FRAGILE

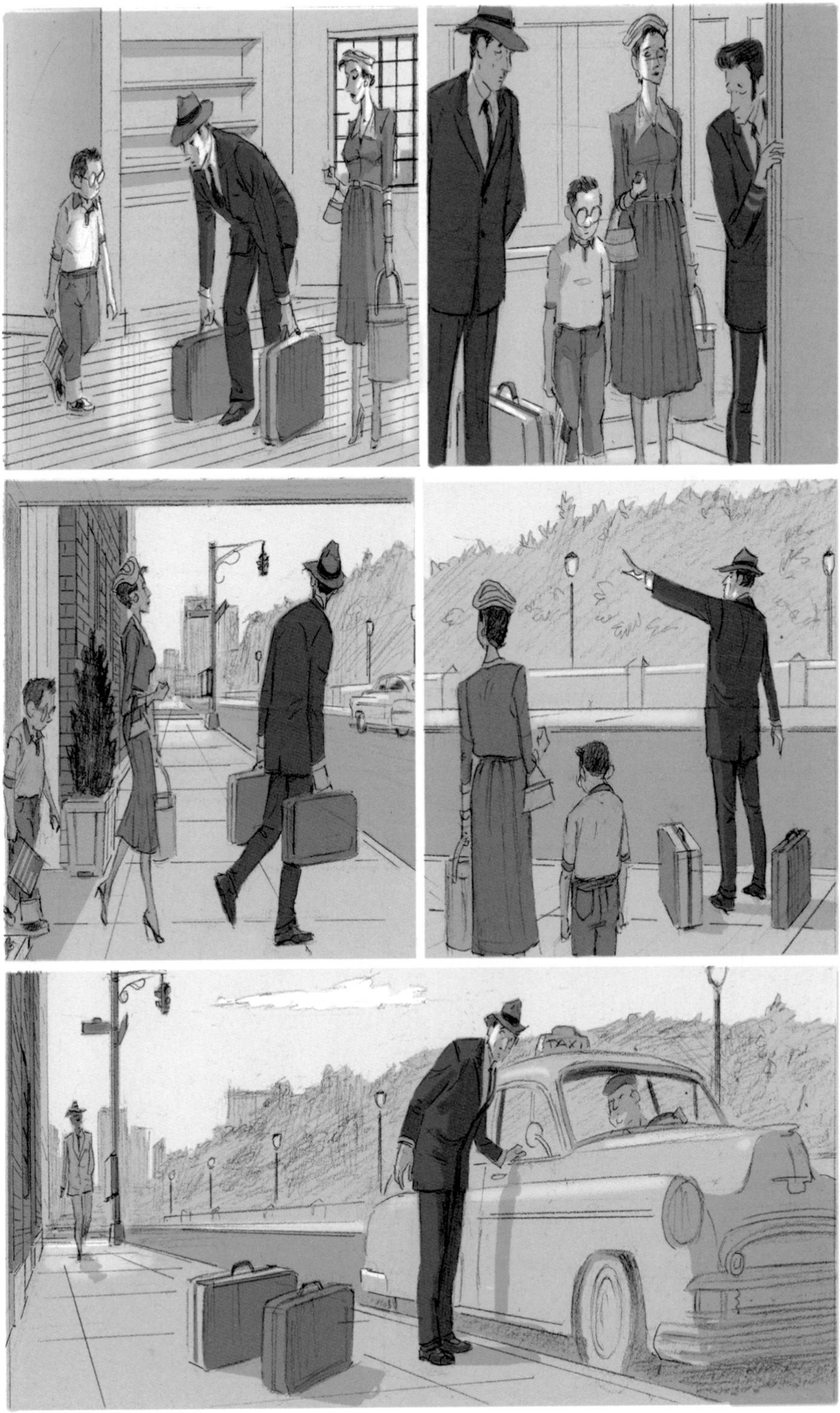
TAXI

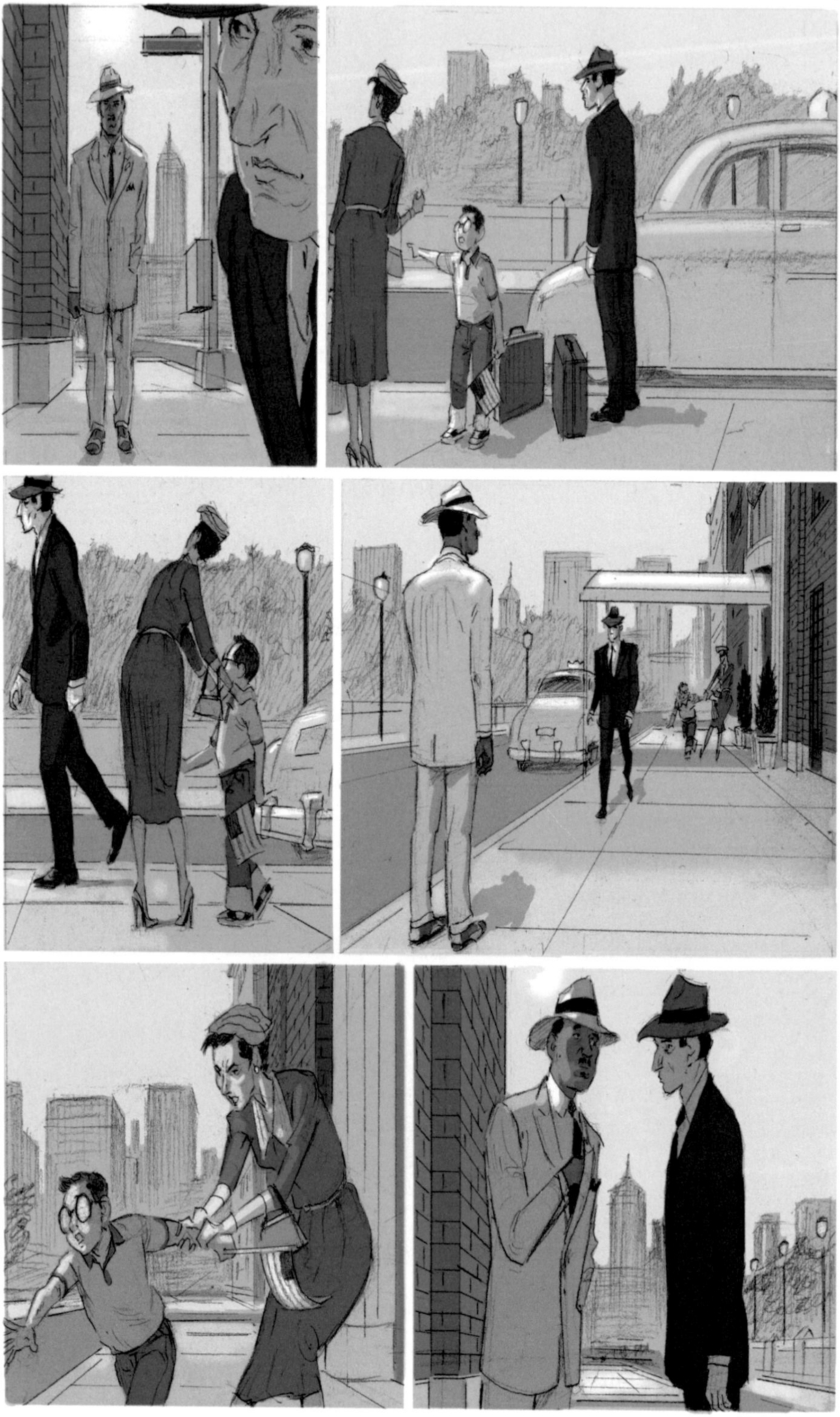

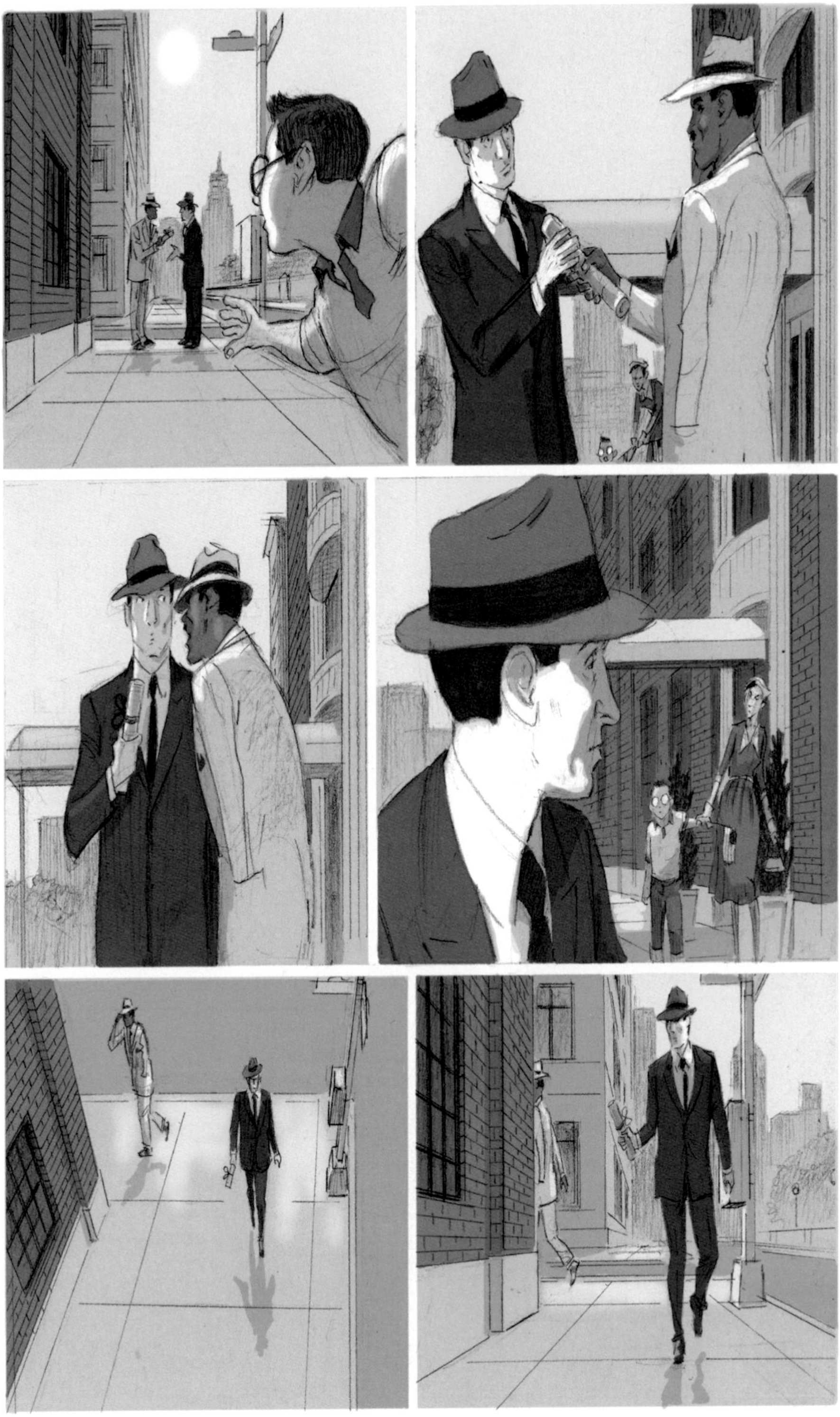

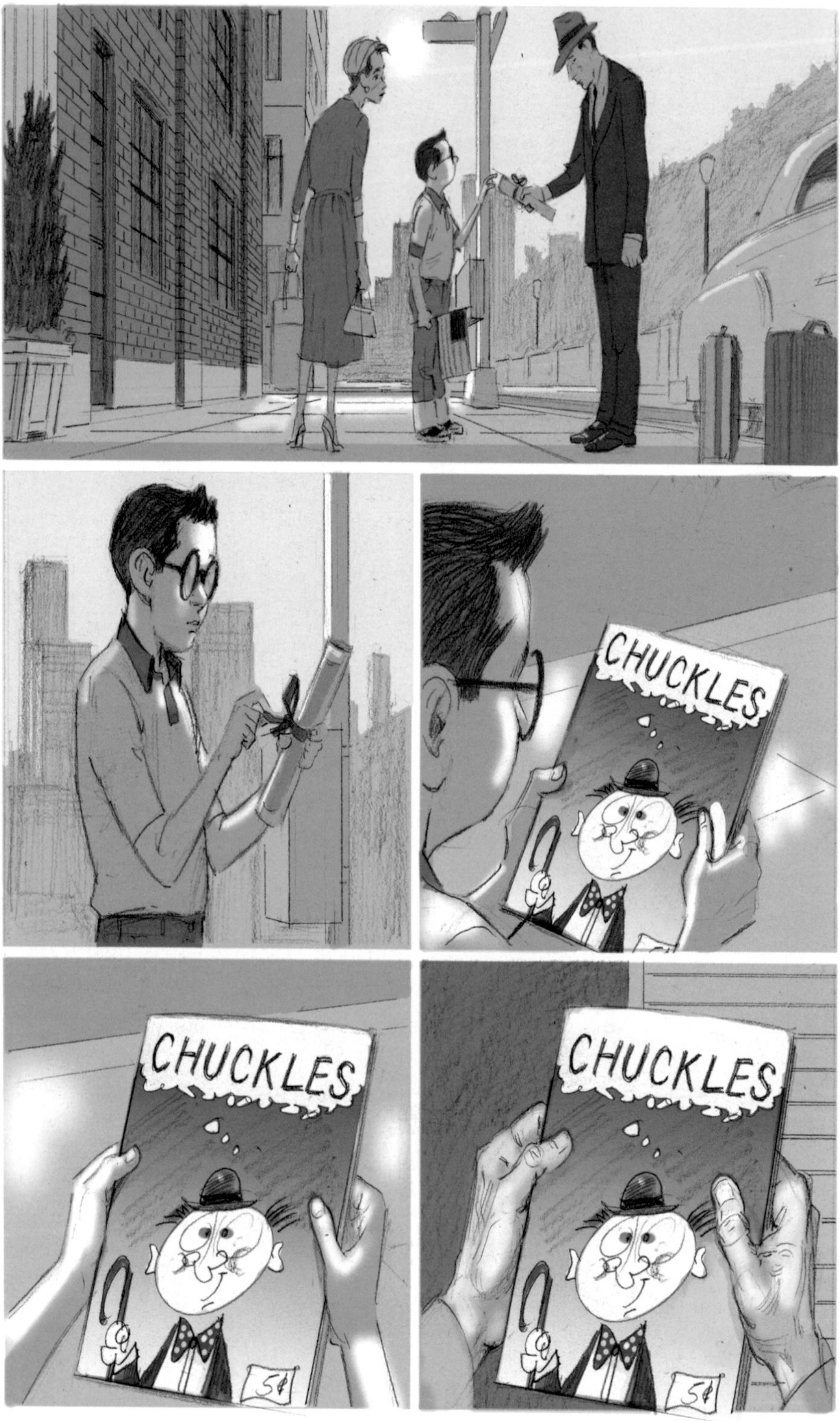
CHUCKLES
CHUCKLES
5¢
CHUCKLES
5¢

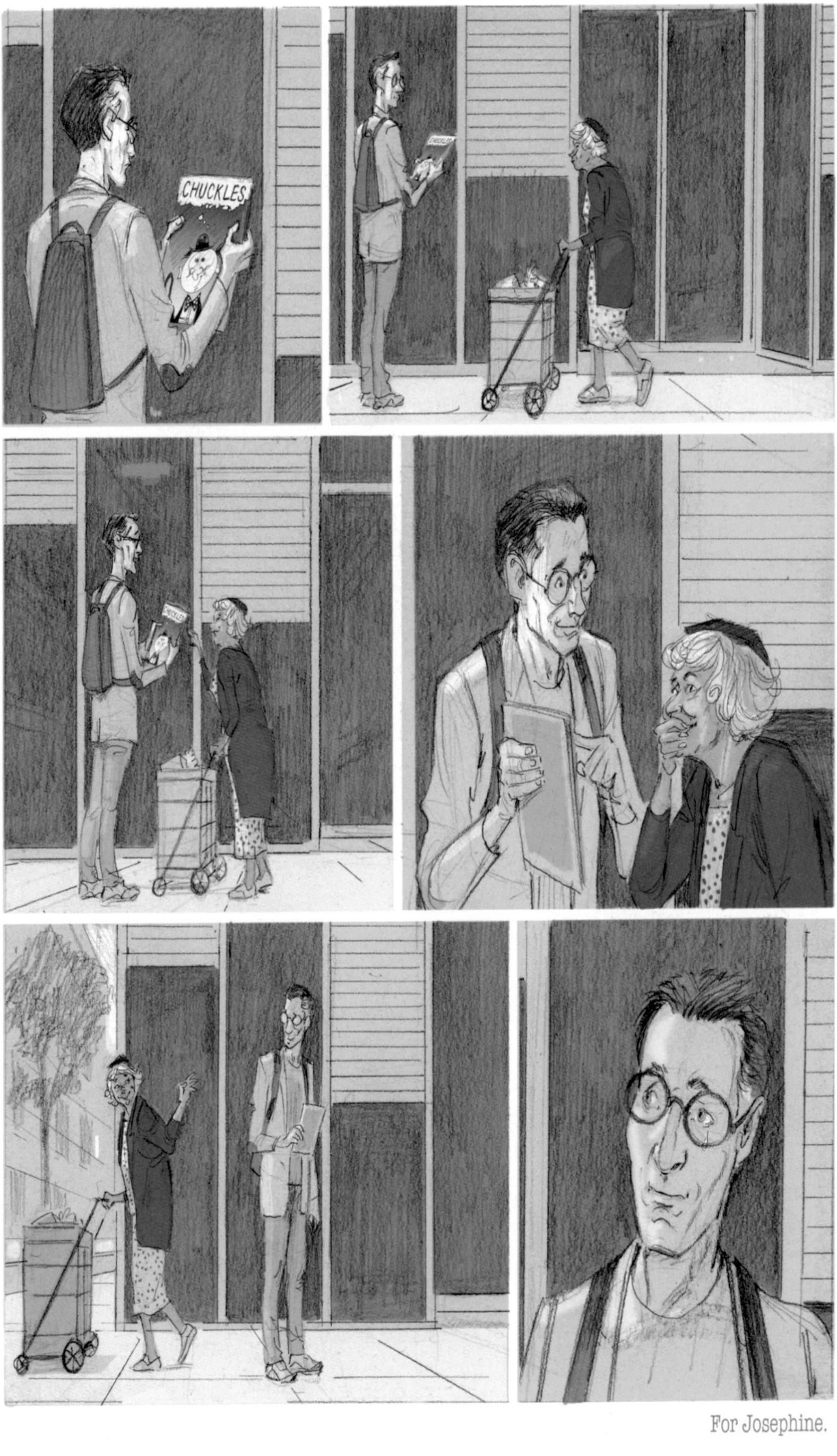
CHUCKLES

For Josephine.

AFTERWORD

I grew up on New York's Upper West Side in the 1950s and 60s. Returning to live there 40 years later, I spent my first days in the neighborhood walking for hours, relishing each block, as if I were becoming reacquainted with an old and valued friend. As I walked, memories of my childhood came flooding back.

Punctuating all of the memories of my early youth were the faces of my caretakers... Leonora, Cleo, Mildred, Louise and Josephine. I knew them by their first names only, but knew well their touch, their smell, and the sound of their voices when they would call my name.

The character of Josephine is a composite of all of these women—whose humanity, strength, and generosity helped to shape my vision of the world, both then and now.

Josephine's storyline is not entirely based on my life, but is rooted in my visual and sensory memories of the times. I only hope that, in this case, a picture is really worth a thousand words.

Kevin Sacco

-30-